Praise for William Rosen's *The Third Horseman*

"...en should be commended for his book. In less than three hundred ... furnishes us with a detailed account of an epochal historical period that covers all the bases with engaging biopics and spirited ...ation."   —*Los Angeles Review of Books*

"...sen takes no stand on the issue of climate change today, which ...s his work all the more chilling. This book is required reading for ...e concerned about rising sea levels, drought, and increasingly ...e weather in an era where humankind has made the stakes so ... higher."   —*Toronto Star*

"...en . . . delights in the minutiae of history, down to the most fasci-...g footnotes. Here, the author delivers engrossing disquisitions on ...te patterns and dynastic entanglements between England and ...land (among others), and he posits that the decisive advent of cooler, ...er weather in the early fourteenth century signaled the beginning ...e end of the medieval good times."   —*Kirkus Reviews*

"...illiam Rosen is a good enough writer to hold interest and maintain ... fraught relations between nature and politics as a running theme. ...ends *The Third Horseman* with a stark observation: in some ways, ...bal ecology is more precarious nowadays than it was in the 1300s."
                    —*Milwaukee Express*

"...e interactions Rosen describes have been studied but are seldom ...orporated into popular history, and the author never overreaches in ... conclusions, providing a well-grounded chronicle. This book will ...peal foremost to history lovers, but it should also interest anyone who enjoys a well-documented story."   —*Library Journal*

PENGUIN BOOKS

THE THIRD HORSEMAN

William Rosen, a former editor and publisher at Macmillan, Simon &
Schuster, and The Free Press, is the author of *Justinian's Flea* and *The
Most Powerful Idea in the World*. He lives in New Jersey.

THE
THIRD HORSEMAN

*A Story of Weather, War, and
the Famine History Forgot*

WILLIAM ROSEN

PENGUIN BOOKS

PENGUIN BOOKS
Published by the Penguin Group
Penguin Group (USA) LLC
375 Hudson Street
New York, New York 10014

USA | Canada | UK | Ireland | Australia | New Zealand | India | South Africa | China
penguin.com
A Penguin Random House Company

First published in the United States of America by Viking Penguin,
a member of Penguin Group (USA) LLC, 2014
Published in Penguin Books 2015

THE LIBRARY OF CONGRESS HAS CATALOGED THE HARDCOVER EDITION AS FOLLOWS:
Rosen, William, 1955–
The third horseman : climate change and the Great Famine of the 14th century / William Rosen.
pages cm
Includes bibliographical references and index.
ISBN 978-0-670-02589-3 (hc.)
ISBN 978-0-14-312714-7 (pbk.)
1. Famines—Europe—History—To 1500.   2. Climatic changes—Social aspects—
Europe—History—To 1500.   3. Climate and civilization—Europe—History—To 1500.
4. Harvesting—Europe—History—To 1500.   5. War and society—Europe—History—
To 1500.   6. Epidemics—Europe—History—To 1500.   7. Europe—History—476–1492.
8. Europe—Social conditions—To 1492.   9. Europe—History, Military.   I. Title.
D202.8.R67 2014
940.1'92—dc23
2013047842

Printed in the United States of America
1   3   5   7   9   10   8   6   4   2

Designed by Carla Bolte
Maps by David Lindroth

For Jeanine

All ways of dying are hateful to us poor mortals
true; but to die of hunger—starve to death
that's the worst of all.

The Odyssey, Book XII (Fagles translation)

When the Lamb opened the third seal, I heard the third living creature say, "Come and see!" I looked, and there before me was a black
horse! Its rider was holding a pair of scales in his hand. Then I heard
what sounded like a voice among the four living creatures, saying, "A
quart of wheat for a day's wages, and three quarts of barley for a day's
wages, and do not damage the oil and the wine!"

Revelation 6:5

CONTENTS

❧

LIST OF MAPS

THE
THIRD HORSEMAN

Eight Crowns in Boulogne

1308

In the fourth week of January in the year 1308, the city of Boulogne-sur-Mer played host to the very top tier of European society. Camped in canvas tents around the city square were dozens of princes, barons, counts, earls, and dukes, and seven kings and queens, including Philip IV, the king of France; King Louis of Navarre; Marie of Brabant, the dowager queen of France; Albert of Habsburg and Elizabeth of Tyrol, the king and queen of the Romans (the confusing name given to the rulers of Germany while they awaited confirmation in the office of Holy Roman Emperor); Charles II, the king of Sicily; and Marguerite, the dowager queen of England. They had arrived to celebrate the marriage of the eighth monarch, twenty-three-year-old Edward II of England, to his twelve-year-old bride, Isabella, the daughter of the French king, thus concluding a treaty and betrothal made five years earlier.

The most notable sovereign missing from the ceremony was the new king of Scotland, Robert the Bruce, whose absence was explained by the fact that he was, at that time, engaged in what would be a three-decade-long war to secure Scottish independence from England . . . and while Edward was pledging himself to Isabella, Bruce was managing a campaign that would, in a matter of months, leave him in control of a fifth of his enemy's country.

Over the course of the next twenty years, the lives of virtually everyone in northern Europe would be powerfully influenced by a dizzying game of war, succession, diplomacy, and rebellion played out in Scotland, England, France, Flanders, and Germany by the monarchs in attendance at the wedding. The French would invade Flanders, and recognize Bruce's sovereignty in Scotland. The death of the king of the Romans would lead to an eight-year-long struggle for his throne. Eventually Edward's child bride would leave her new realm for her native land, later to return at the head of an invading army that would force her husband to abdicate in favor of her son.

None of this, of course, was much in evidence at the royal wedding. The most notable thing about the ceremony, in fact, was the unseasonable weather. As the thirteenth century turned into the fourteenth, daytime January temperatures in Boulogne had averaged about 50 degrees Fahrenheit, and perhaps 10 degrees colder at night, and had been doing so for centuries. At Edward and Isabella's wedding, the barons and earls sleeping in those hundreds of tents shivered to nighttime temperatures well below freezing. The freeze they were enduring was covering virtually all of Europe; ports along the Baltic were frozen in for the second time in the preceding five years.

The weather was changing. More than that, the *climate* was changing, and changing in a way that would affect the lives of millions, often enough by bringing those lives to an untimely end.

The great conceit of history is that humanity's worst disasters occur within some identifiable and discrete time frame. Whether describing the arrival of a pandemic plague fifteen hundred years ago, or the world wars of the last century, conventional narratives offer a clear beginning and a decisive conclusion. The reality is more like a bridge collapsing: A minutes-long climax of forces that have been years— sometimes centuries or even millennia—in formation.

So it was with the events that transfixed northern Europe during the first decades of the fourteenth century. Less than a decade after the wedding ceremony at Boulogne, the most widespread and destructive famine in European history brought privation and starvation to millions. Its proximate cause was a series of what seemed, to its victims, to be isolated and unpredictable weather events: summer storms and freezing winters. Its true origins were an almost incomprehensibly complicated mixture of climate, commerce, and conflict, four centuries in gestation, that put tens of millions of men, women, and children in the path of apocalyptic disaster. Those elements can no more be understood in isolation than one of the great medieval tapestries can be appreciated by listing each of the threads that compose it.

When such a tapestry is viewed from an appropriate distance, however, the picture comes into focus. From Europe's ninth century onward, the great theme at center stage was the most basic of all: How should a society feed itself? What political and cultural system can allocate, protect, sow, and reap the land that was the ultimate source of food? For Europe, during the four centuries before Edward and Isabella stood before a priest on that cold day in 1308, the answer was a pact—a contract sanctioned by law, and sanctified by religion—that bound the laborer to the land, and the landlord to the laborer.

A dozen institutions and doctrines depended on that pact. Some of the most significant:

• Manorialism, the system of land tenure that dominated the agriculture of Europe from the early ninth century and the reign of Charlemagne. It granted rights and duties to the peasants who worked the land, to the sovereign who granted rights of ownership to the land, and to the nobility and gentry who stood in between.

• Feudalism, the medieval system for legitimizing the use of armed force, again through grants of rights and duties up and down the line, from Europe's lowliest peasants to its most powerful monarchs.

• The proto-nations under whose protection feudalism and manorialism survived, themselves struggling for legitimacy in medieval Europe—some of them still sovereign into the twenty-first century, like France; some subsumed into larger (or luckier) opponents, like Flanders.

• The transnational and hierarchical Catholic Church, with a rescript from God to lead a "United States of Europe," and the Bishop of Rome, with the sole authority to sanctify feudal titles, manorial ownership, and the rights of the sovereign.

By the beginning of the fourteenth century, these institutions—manorialism, feudalism, nationalism, and papism—were collectively responsible for feeding a European population that, enabled by four centuries of anomalously mild weather, had grown from ten to forty million. Their aggregate success, however, had the seeds of failure built into it. By the time of the wedding of Isabella to Edward, the objectives of each was irrepressibly in conflict with the prerogatives of another. A crisis had been reached.

The crisis would play out in every region of northern Europe. When the mild weather vanished, seemingly for good, it struck at the heart of Europe's food production, everywhere from the Atlantic to the Urals. It decimated Flanders, destroyed dozens of German-speaking towns, and starved villages from Brittany to Poland. For seven disastrous years, the homelands of the wedding guests would be visited by a series of curses unseen since the third book of Exodus: floods, ice, failures of crops and cattle, and epidemics not just of disease but of pike, sword, and spear. Riding alongside the third horseman of the Apocalypse, astride the black horse of famine, came the second, who *"was given power to take peace from the earth and to make men slay each other."* War.

Both horsemen were to be found throughout northern Europe, but nowhere more dramatically than on the borders separating Scotland from England. It wasn't merely that those unlucky lands were subjected to all of the climate-caused disasters of those calamitous decades: their harvests lost to rain; their herds to disease; and their homes, churches, bridges, roads, and ports destroyed by one terrifying weather event after another, virtually every year between 1314 and 1321. The borderlands were a battleground for every kind of conflict of the era: rebellions of feudal nobles against their kings, wars between nations, and wars of national independence. The confrontations between Scotland and England—between Robert Bruce and William Wallace on one side, and the first three English kings named Edward on the other, with French kings, Italian bankers, and three different popes as interested parties—became, in addition, a laboratory for a new set of battlefield tactics, in which the laboring classes of Europe, organized into disciplined infantry, proved more than the equal of the mounted nobility that had dominated warfare since the time of Charlemagne. The wars between Scotland and England even created victims for a new kind of warfare itself: nationalist guerrilla warfare that targeted farms as fiercely as it did opposing armies; bad enough in normal times, but disastrous during the greatest famine in European history.

In *Haroun and the Sea of Stories,* the novelist Salman Rushdie tells us that all the world's stories are found on the Earth's second moon, reachable only by what he describes as a P2C2E—a "process too complicated to explain." At first glance any attempt to tell the story of the disasters of the first decades of the fourteenth century seems a classic P2C2E. On its own, climate is almost irreducibly complicated, a system involving the most intricate processes of the Earth's atmosphere, so sensitive to a change in initial conditions that, as the cliché description of chaotic systems reminds us, a butterfly flapping its wings in Ecuador can cause a tornado to touch down in Kansas. Combine that with the convoluted evolution of feudalism, manorialism, and the emergence of nationalism; with the strategies of diplomacy and warfare; with the incredible amalgam of molecules that comprises a few inches of soil that produces the world's food (and the sciences that study it: agronomy, soil science, and plant biology) with digestive physiology and gastronomic history, and you have chaos squared.

Long before they ever hear of chaos theory, however, introductory physics students study the more mundane phenomenon known as *resonance*: the tendency of a system, like a pendulum, to oscillate in larger and larger swings when pushed at a specific frequency. Resonance is why a chain of tiny pushes can send a child's swing fifteen feet into the air, and why a series of wind gusts can twist a concrete bridge into a pretzel.

It took centuries for the key resonant forces—rain, cold, disease, and warfare—to accumulate enough energy that they could destroy one life in ten from the Atlantic to the Urals. They began to do so some seventeen hundred miles northwest of, and four hundred years before, the wedding of Edward and Isabella.

CHAPTER ONE

"The Fury of the Northmen"

793–1066

There are many ways to get from the west coast of Greenland to L'Anse aux Meadows, none of them easy. You can fly from Kangerlussuaq to Reykjavik in a little less than five hours, and from there to New York in just under six; from New York to St. John's, on the southeast side of the island of Newfoundland, will take about three more. From there, you either drive or fly four hundred miles west—perhaps ten hours by road; an hour and fifteen minutes by twin-engine turboprop—to Deer Lake. Then, another three hundred miles by car on Canada's picturesque Route 480, along the Newfoundland coast, until you run out of road, and walk the last bit to a peat farm, a reconstructed forge, and half a dozen sod-roofed houses.

All of the available options are far easier than the direct route, first taken a thousand years ago: nine hundred stomach-heaving miles across the North Atlantic in a sixty-foot-long square-rigged wooden ship. But that ship, and others like it, are the reason L'Anse aux Meadows is a UNESCO World Heritage Site: the first European settlement in the New World, and probably the most famous place ever colonized by the merchants and traders we know as the Vikings.

It's nowhere near the largest. A Viking settlement on the banks of the Dnieper River, near Smolensk, has more than three thousand funeral mounds scattered across its forty acres. For centuries, the people who built them controlled the trade that moved along Europe's rivers all the way from the Baltic to Constantinople, and even as far as ninth-century Baghdad, when it was Islam's—and probably the world's—richest and most sophisticated city. Along the Dnieper and Volga, the traders were generally known as Varangians or "rowers" and formed the personal guard of the Byzantine Emperor; sometimes as Rus, from which modern Russia takes its name. Closer to home, in Ireland, they were often known as Finngaills, or "fair foreigners." The earliest occupants of Britain called them Danes—in the story of *Beowulf*, "east-Danes" or "spear-Danes." Most frequently, they were known as Northmen, or Norsemen; after 793, when they raided the monastery at Lindisfarne, on the east coast of England, with "rapine and slaughter," it was said that all over Europe, people prayed, *"A furore normannorum libera nos, Domine"*: From the fury of the Northmen, deliver us, Lord.*

The Norse—the word "Viking" comes from an Old Norse word meaning "voyaging," later refined to mean "raiding," rather than "trading"—were merchants, warriors, farmers, and artisans. Despite a well-earned reputation for fearsomeness in battle, they appeared less savage to their contemporaries than to their modern mythmakers; in 1220, the chronicler John of Wallingford described them as, in thirteenth-century terms, a bit dandified:

> They were—according to their country's customs—in the habit of combing their hair every day, to bathe every Saturday, to change their clothes frequently and to draw attention to themselves by means of many such frivolous whims. In this way, they besieged the married women's virtue and persuaded the daughters of even noble men to become their mistresses.

But first, last, and always, they were sailors. Their only real competition for the title of the greatest sailing culture in history came from the eleventh- and twelfth-century Polynesians who colonized Hawaii and Easter Island, and their greatest accomplishments are best understood in the same context: travel across vast distances with neither magnetic compasses nor maps, navigating by their knowledge of currents, swells, and the migrations of birds and fish.

---

*Though the prayer is apocryphal—that is, no document containing it has ever been found—the sentiment is not.

The fish weren't just an aid to sailors but the most important reason they went to sea in the first place. Long before they were trading gold and amber along the shores of the Caspian, Black, and Mediterranean seas, Norse sailors honed their maritime skills in the most basic of human activities: gathering food, especially cod from the North Atlantic, which was, and is, the world's greatest fishery.

By the beginning of the ninth century, they were ready to expand to the west, east, and especially south. Historians have been puzzling over the impetus for centuries; Edward Gibbon, in the forty-ninth book of his *Decline and Fall of the Roman Empire*,* argued that the brutal conquest of the Saxons by Charlemagne in 804 not only opened the door to invasion of Europe from Scandinavia, but provoked it:

> The subjugation of Germany withdrew the veil which had so long concealed the continent or islands of Scandinavia from the knowledge of Europe, and awakened the torpid courage of their barbarous natives.

More methodical, though less eloquent, historians have looked, instead, to increased numbers of gravesites in the relatively poor lands of ninth-century Scandinavia and Iceland—areas, by most estimates, able to support no more than one to two people per square kilometer—as a clue to just the sort of population pressure that might have inclined Norsemen to go a-viking. Or, perhaps the Norse were simply reacting to a later invasion by Europe's Christian sovereigns, who were forcibly converting the pagan peoples on the continent's periphery by the beginning of the tenth century.

There is, though, a more powerful and plausible cause for the explosive spread of the Norse. The great achievements of the Viking Age were almost entirely enabled by the impersonal workings of climate.

This shouldn't come as a surprise. All human civilizations are hostage to weather, but none more so than sailors, who must confront

---

*Gibbon's great work begins with the death of Marcus Aurelius in 180, and ends, more or less, with the papal schism of the fourteenth century (about which more later). Something as big as Rome takes a very long time to fall.

both the violent nature of the ocean's surface and the capricious atmosphere that imparts motion to their wind-powered vessels. When those mariners are surrounded by seas that produce icebergs and pack ice for up to six months of the year, even a few more weeks of warmer weather a year were literally life-changing.*

Fluid dynamics is the branch of physics that studies liquids and gases in motion—among other things, weather, which gets its dynamism from the heat energy of the sun. That energy is received by every object in the solar system, but if the object in question lacks a fluid atmosphere, it has no weather, which is why a barren rock like Mercury, the closest planet to the sun, has none, and Jupiter, which receives a tiny fraction of the solar energy that hits Mercury, has hurricanes twenty-five thousand miles in diameter that last hundreds of years.

Earth's weather lacks Jupiter's violence, but has its own complexities. Not because the source of heat—the sun—is so variable, but rather because the amount of heat energy absorbed by the Earth during its annual orbits is distributed unevenly. The consequences of that variability are such things as the ice ages—there have been at least four in the last billion years—when glaciers left huge chunks of the northern hemisphere covered with ice sometimes hundreds of feet thick, as well as eras when temperatures were 4 to 5 degrees warmer than today, causing sea levels to be at least twenty-five feet higher.

Weather and climate remain the product of complex interactions between ocean and atmosphere, a dance set to almost unimaginably complicated rhythms, made even more complicated because one partner—the atmosphere—is enormously quicker to respond to change than the other.

The boundary between atmosphere and water is where the dance

---

*Which is not to say that the Norse were just lucky. Once climate permitted travel past the Arctic pack ice, they were ingenious enough to equip their longships with a so-called sun-compass—a circular sundial with an adjustable gnomon that would hit a particular spot on the circle at noon, indicating the ship's latitude, and so allowing dead reckoning. And latitude-accurate dead reckoning was sufficient not only to get from Norway to Scotland, but to Iceland, Greenland, and even North America.

partners meet, but their rhythms are created elsewhere: in the ocean's depths, a three-dimensional maze of conveyor belts, powered by heat and salt. The top layer is warmed by the sun, whose rays penetrate a good forty meters, and not only contains most of the ocean's marine life (and CO_2) but stores more than ten times as much energy as the entire Earth's atmosphere. The reason is specific heat: the amount of energy, measured in calories, needed to raise the temperature of a given mass of a particular substance by one degree Celsius. When the given mass is a gram, the specific heat is measured in small c calories; when it's a kilogram, the measure is kilocalories.* Whether measured in grams or kilos, the specific heat for water is higher than for virtually any other common substance. It takes one calorie to heat a gram of water by a single degree, which is nearly twice as much as alcohol, five times as much as aluminum, and—most important—more than four times as much as air. And that's just the top forty meters; because the total mass of the oceans is four hundred times that of the atmosphere, the amount of heat energy stored in the Earth's oceans is some sixteen hundred times that of the atmosphere.

The result of this enormous oceanic engine, dependent as it is on tiny changes in the proportions of heat and salt, is that a tiny blip in oceanic temperature can alter atmospheric temperatures for a thousand years.† Which is what happened, sometime around the ninth century, when a few of those oceanic conveyor belts fell into a state of equilibrium for a moment infinitesimally short in geologic time, but a significant fraction of human history. The Medieval Warm Period—sometimes, more cheerfully, called the Medieval Climate Optimum (or, more honestly, the Medieval Climate Anomaly)—lasted only from the end of the ninth century to the beginning of the fourteenth;

---

*Just to confuse matters, the "calorie" used to measure the amount of energy in food is actually a kilocalorie.

†So, indeed, can sunspots, which cause an even slighter change in the radiation emitted by the sun. Or volcanoes, which can shoot enough dirt into the atmosphere to change the Earth's albedo—the amount of radiation it reflects back into space—and the amount of heat reaching the surface. In April 1815, the top four thousand feet of Mount Tambora, on the Indonesian island of Sumbawa, erupted into an aerosol dust that gave the world a famous "year without summer" months later.

four centuries when the Northern Hemisphere experienced its warmest temperatures of the last eight thousand years.

The causes of the Medieval Warm Period are the subject of so many competing theories that it seems certain that they are going to remain murky for a while; but its existence is pretty much inarguable. The geological footprint left by moraines—the rocky debris carried by glaciers as they advance and recede—includes plant material that can not only be dated pretty precisely but carries evidence of small changes in annual temperature. Dendrochronologists—biologists who derive all sorts of information from the width and composition of tree rings—have spent decades studying dozens of different species of trees that add a ring each year, and long ago learned that, in temperate climates, the rings differ in width depending on the year's climate. With a tree of a known date—a tree with a hundred rings was a hundred years old when cut down, and used, for example, in a building that is known to have been built, for example, in the year 1000—the temperature of any particular year can be calculated with a high degree of accuracy.

It's more than just the ring's width: the amount of the radioactive isotope Carbon-14 in tree rings measures the amount of solar activity in any particular year. The reasons are, like everything having to do with climate history, intricate: Carbon-14 is formed by cosmic-ray interactions with the nitrogen and oxygen in the Earth's upper atmosphere, so, when there's less solar activity, the amount produced by cosmic rays is relatively greater. Lower solar activity, more Carbon-14. And, sure enough, what are known as "cosmogenic anomalies" match up with what the chronicles report as warm eras in western Europe, not just during the MWP, but the early Iron Age from about 200 BCE.

There's more. There's ice. For more than forty years, geologists have been drilling out cylinders of ice in places like Greenland and Antarctica—places where the ice sheets haven't melted in hundreds of thousands of years. Since the ice accumulates every year at a regular rate, a core—usually between about two and three inches in diameter, but up to two miles long—forms a calendar that records the composition, and the temperature, of the atmosphere over time. And, once again, the ice cores show an unmistakable warming period between the ninth and thirteenth centuries.

Its geographic extent is a little more problematic. Hubert Lamb, the English climatologist who first posited (and named) the Medieval Warm Period, was working from a limited data set; most of his historical sources—estate records, monastery documents, and the like—were European, and insufficient to demonstrate the global phenomenon he believed he had discovered. One result is that the Medieval Warm Period is regularly used as evidence for those who want to challenge the reality of man-made climate change—"during the Middle Ages, temperatures were even *warmer* than they are today."

In reality, though, it turns out to be far easier to measure the temperature locally, whether in Scandinavia or China, than to solve the notoriously tricky puzzle of worldwide climate. Hubert Lamb was right, but the era he discovered and named was a Northern Hemisphere phenomenon, and particularly one that affected the civilizations along the north Atlantic between about 800 and 1200. The best estimates are that temperatures of northern Europe averaged a healthy 2°C higher than they do today; climate-change skeptics notwithstanding, there is still little evidence that *worldwide* temperatures were, on average, warmer than today.

Why the MWP's effects were confined to the Northern Hemisphere—and especially to Europe—can be explained by a climatic seesaw known as the North Atlantic Oscillation, the prime determinant for the weather of northern and western Europe. The first end of the oscillation is a persistent zone of relatively low atmospheric pressure over Iceland; the second, a high-pressure zone over the Azores.* The weather fronts that bring rain to Europe follow a track determined by the pressure gradient between the two. Thus, when the Azores High is, relatively high, and the Iceland Low relatively low, heat from the Atlantic is conveyed to Europe, making for warm summers and mild winters. As a result, the gradient

---

*Lower pressure can have many causes, including wind direction. Persistent "thermal lows" are caused, in general, by warmer air in the upper atmosphere; warmer air is less dense and therefore has less mass for its volume than colder air.

during the MWP generally favored warmer weather in Europe, though not the entire world.

That the North Atlantic Oscillation affected "only" a portion of the world's climate doesn't make it a trivial instrument of change. Its effects were as serious as it got for Europeans living in the era that began with the Viking expansion, and that ended just about the time that Edward II and Isabella of France were celebrating their marriage vows. To the eight out of ten people who farmed the land, sun and rain were what turned land into food. Sun and rain, in the proper proportions, were what supported human life. And there was a lot more of human life at risk in 1308 than had been the case in the year 800.

It's not that European weather during the four centuries of the MWP was uniformly good. Both modern anthropology and historical documents testify to a depressingly long list of droughts, storms, freezes, and lost harvests during the four centuries of the MWP, possibly because of the very human habit of spending more time recording disasters than prosperity. But the weather between the ninth and fourteenth centuries was nonetheless markedly *better*—a little bit warmer, and a little bit more predictable—than any recorded period since the birth of civilization. An increase in temperature and reduction in variability doesn't have to be enormous to initiate a very long, and very consequential, series of events.

The first, and most significant, effect of such predictably good weather was a huge expansion in the kind of land that could be made to produce food. During the MWP, cereals were harvested in European farms at altitudes of more than a thousand feet above sea level—unthinkable today—and vineyards started appearing in northern England. Throughout northwest Europe, land that hadn't produced respectable amounts of food in millennia became productive. Including the lands of the Norsemen.

Erik Thorvaldsson, better known to history as Erik the Red, wasn't the first Norseman to discover the eight hundred thousand square miles of tundra and permafrost located between the Atlantic and Arctic, but he was the first to settle there. Sometime before 950, Erik's father left the family home in Norway, one step ahead of the family of

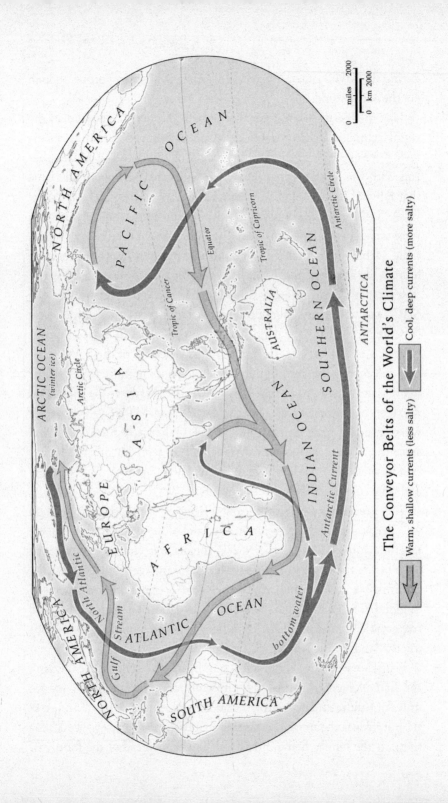

The Conveyor Belts of the World's Climate

Warm, shallow currents (less salty) →

Cool, deep currents (more salty) →

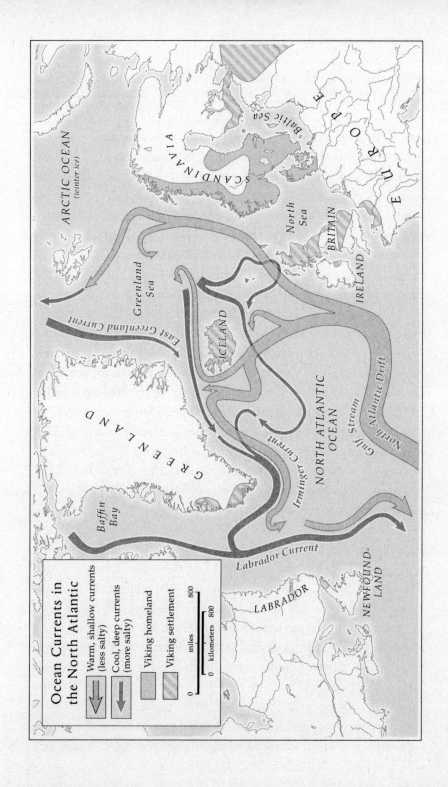

Ocean Currents in the North Atlantic

Warm, shallow currents (less salty)

Cool, deep currents (more salty)

Viking homeland

Viking settlement

miles 0 800

kilometers 0 800

ARCTIC OCEAN (winter ice)

SCANDINAVIA

Baltic Sea

Greenland Sea

East Greenland Current

North Sea

BRITAIN

IRELAND

EUROPE

ICELAND

GREENLAND

Baffin Bay

Irminger Current

NORTH ATLANTIC OCEAN

Gulf Stream

North Atlantic Drift

Labrador Current

LABRADOR

NEWFOUND-LAND

the man he had killed in a violent brawl, to settle in Iceland, which the Medieval Warm Period had turned into a warm enough place for decent if not great farming. Norse colonists established themselves in Iceland by 900, and were able to produce barley (at least until the twelfth century) and hay for dairy cattle. In around 982, Erik, as prone to violence as his father, was sentenced to a three-year exile for his own series of murders—the sons of one man and "a few other men"— and he took his banishment as an opportunity for one of history's best-known real estate promotions. He established, during his three-year exile, a relatively prosperous camp along what was, as a result of the warming trend, an ice-free coastline. By the 870s, not only had the amount of pack ice in the North Atlantic fallen dramatically, but the soil of the islands of the far north was composed of less permafrost than virtually any time in the last one hundred twenty-five thousand years. When Erik returned to Iceland, he was able to promote his new settlement, which he named Greenland partly because of the enormous grassy meadows that he found there but mostly because his "people would be attracted to go there if it had a favorable name."

It was singularly appropriate that the Greenland colony—which would last until the fifteenth century, with upward of four thousand permanent residents, who built, among other things, a cathedral and two monasteries—was such a well-remembered beneficiary of the climatic change, since most of the weather of northern Europe, including the four centuries of the MWP, is determined by an exceedingly complicated set of ocean currents around Greenland and Iceland. The Irminger Current (also known as the East Greenland Current, which is a part of North Atlantic Current, and a subsidiary of the Gulf Stream) runs just south of Iceland, and carries very cold water from the Arctic south, and out of the northern sea lanes. When it is flowing along the path it took during the Medieval Warm Period, the cold water is pushed down an underwater cliff on the floor of the Denmark Strait—a very high cliff, more than four times higher than Niagara Falls, and with more than four *hundred* times the volume. Submerging this quantity of water several hundred meters below the surface keeps pack ice, which forms between January and April, at least one hundred kilometers away from Iceland, and the coast of Greenland, which is where it was kept during both the Medieval Warm and today.

The disappearance of that ice not only drew Erik the Red to Greenland (and his son, Leif, to North America, and—probably—L'Anse aux Meadows) but, as a consequence of the MWP, led most of Europe into its first sustained population increase since the fall of the Roman Empire. And, eventually, to the wedding of Edward and Isabella in Boulogne in 1308.

The connections between four centuries of historically good weather, and four days of historically luxurious celebration, are primarily economic. For virtually all human civilizations before the Industrial Revolution the largest contributor to national wealth was arable land: land on which crops could be grown and livestock fed. Every aspect of life depended on land, and the rural population who worked it. Agriculture didn't just feed the guests at the royal wedding; it paid for the cathedral where the vows were exchanged, and even the clothes on the bride's back.

The agricultural laborers who collectively supported Europe's armies, roads, cities, and most of its commerce were, in turn, dependent on the continent's supply of sunny days. The addition, on average, of even ten or twenty days of sun each growing season—which is what a frost-free May two years out of three would produce, courtesy of the Medieval Warm Period—meant more food: enough food to allow a few more children to survive infancy, and a few more adults to survive for more productive years. Like compound interest, this meant dramatic change over time: a population explosion. Records are scanty before the year 1000, but for the next two centuries, Europe became home to a great many more Europeans: England's population grew from 1.5 million to more than 5 million; France from fewer than 6 million to between 17 and 21 million; and Italy, whose population had declined by more than a third after the fall of Rome, rebounded to nearly double, from 5 million to more than 9 million. Farther east, the phenomenon was even more dramatic: the population of that portion of Europe that makes up modern Germany and Poland nearly tripled.

More food increases fertility. Increased fertility means more mouths;

and more mouths demand more food. The longer growing seasons of the Medieval Warm Period improved agricultural productivity, but not so much that it could keep up with the resulting population explosion. Only new land could do that. The Viking response was to colonize previously undesirable—and unpopulated—places like Greenland, but this was no sort of option for either continental Europe or islands like Britain or Ireland. There, unfortunately, the land that wasn't under cultivation usually wasn't for a very good reason: it was covered with trees.

Western and central Europe, at the time the Roman Empire began its retreat, around the end of the fifth century, was 80 percent forest; by 1300, it was less than 30 percent, which means that, over seven centuries, at least 100 *million* acres were deforested. France's forests alone were reduced from 74 million acres to 32 million. Not all of them were turned into farmland, or even pasture; Europe's trees were valuable on their own, for building, heat, and—as armor manufacture became more and more established—fuel for smelting iron.*

Agriculture and armor manufacture weren't the only reasons for forest-clearing material improvement. Peasants climbed a hundred feet in the air to carve the branches from oaks and aspens, were crippled by deadfalls that refused to topple as predicted, and died in the fires they set to destroy the remaining stumps, as much to reclaim the tree-rich sanctuaries of pagan worship for a more Christian world as to claim them for the plow. Wild landscapes were in a state of sin; cultivated land was literally saved by the "prayer book and the ax."

The process was well along by the seventh century, as abandoned-and-reclaimed properties were established in the zones between existing settlements just in time for the great population explosion that began around 800. The resulting change in the topography of Europe was huge: The northern European plain, and England, from the Midlands to the Channel, were transformed into open stretches of field broken up by the occasional village. All that was left of the great forests was an occasional stand of trees, most notably in the west and southeast of

---

*Until the discovery of a method for purifying coal into coke in the seventeenth century, *all* iron manufacture depended on charcoal, because it had so few of the impurities that make iron brittle.

England, Brittany, and Normandy. The eastern Franks called the new areas *brabants,* from which the formerly heavily forested portion of what is today Belgium got its name. (The forest itself was known as the Silva Carbonnaria, or charcoal-burners forest.)

Converting millions of acres of forest into farmland, especially the sort used to grow cereals like wheat, rye, barley, and oats, actually produced a temporary increase in fertility: when you burn trees (the term of art is *assarting:* a collective endeavor in which trees are cut by a group, who then divide the "new" land like-as-like) in order to plant wheat, the ash left behind actually increases the productivity of the soil. Throughout Europe, sermonizers could, and did, cite Psalm 65: "The grasslands of the wilderness overflow; the hills are clothed with gladness." Over the long term, however, it meant impoverishment, as more and more marginal land was producing a larger and larger percentage of the continent's food.

The result of this centuries-long agricultural expansion was, to a modern agronomist, predictable: yields—the difference between the number of seeds, or bushels, planted, and those available for consumption after reserving seed for the next crop—that dropped precipitously. After centuries of weather that made even poor soil productive, the typical French or English farmer was harvesting no more than ten grains of wheat for every one he planted, and frequently as few as three; in places like Scotland (and places like Erik the Red's homeland, to say nothing of his Arctic colony) the ratio was sometimes barely two to one.*

This is agricultural balance on the edge of a Malthusian knife. When previously unattractive land becomes—at least temporarily— fertile, and population continues to grow, one option is expanding the land under cultivation, but another is extracting the value of the land using a sword instead of a plow. Frontiers become battlegrounds. Warlike cultures invade peaceful ones.

And Norse traders become Viking raiders. Even before they established themselves in Iceland and Greenland, they were raiding as far afield as Majorca, Provence, and even Tuscany. Norwegians occupied

---

*Modern yields are closer to 300 to 1.

the Orkneys, Shetlands, and Hebrides. In 851 Danes invaded and—by 866—essentially conquered England.* Most relevant of all, for those in attendance at Edward and Isabella's nuptials, in 820, a Norse expedition, comprising thirteen ships, arrived at the mouth of the Seine.

They came to raid, but stayed to conquer. In 841, they burned and captured Rouen; within a decade they had built a permanent camp on the now-disappeared (and possibly imagined) island of Jeuvosse in the middle of the Seine, as a convenient jumping-off place for, among other things, raiding Paris, which they did in 857, burning and sacking Chartres for good measure. Every few months, a party of Vikings would sail (or row) up the Seine, and either take everything of value they could, or accept a bribe to go away. By 910, the bishops of Noyon, Beauvais, Bayeux, and Avranches had each been killed in Viking raids. Finally, in the fall of 911, a desperate Charles III, a descendant of Charlemagne, and king of the Western Franks, or Francia (*roi des Francs;* the nation of France was not yet a going concern) signed the Treaty of Saint-Clair-sur-Epte with a Viking chieftain named variously Robert, Rolf, Rosso, or, most frequently, Rollo. The document doesn't survive, and most of its terms, which probably included Rollo's baptism and marriage to one of the king's daughters, remain speculative. The core of the treaty, however, couldn't be clearer: a grant of territory in return for a promise to stop raiding Frankish land.

The land in question was named for its new Norse rulers: Normandy.

The impact of the Norman colony wasn't immediate. Though the colonizers were Danes and Norwegians, and secondhand Norse families from the Orkneys, Ireland, and England, they quickly embraced the customs of their new home. By the time of Rollo's death in 931, he had been baptized into the Christian church; by the time his grandson Richard I succeeded to the rule of the territory, he had not only become a loyal vassal of the soon-to-be kings of France, but gave himself, in the Frankish fashion, a new title, the first duke of Normandy—a territory

---

*Cnut the Great, a king with a complicated ancestry—part Polish, part Danish—ruled Denmark, Norway, England, and most of Sweden from 1016 to 1035.

that had grown from its original grant to include, by 933, the Cotentin Peninsula and the Avranches in Brittany.

The onetime Viking raiders were quick to exchange their old titles, names, languages, and feudal obligations for new ones. What they retained was a powerful tradition of military conquest. As the tenth century turned into the eleventh, Norman knights had campaigned successfully everywhere from Armenia to Byzantine Greece, and even, under Roger I, the descendant of one of Rollo's soldiers, established the Norman kingdom of Sicily, which ruled both the island and the boot of Italy as far north as Naples until the end of the twelfth century.

But when historians speak of "the" Norman Conquest, they aren't talking about Armenia or Sicily. The most significant bit of military adventuring in European history—and the reason that the groom in Boulogne in 1308 spoke a dialect known as Norman French—was the work of one of Rollo's direct descendants, Duke William II of Normandy.

The year that changed Europe, and particularly Britain, forever, began with the death, on January 4, 1066, of England's king, Edward the Confessor. Saint Edward—in 1161, he became England's first and only king to be canonized—had spent his reign in a series of fairly inconsequential attempts to keep one step ahead of both Viking invaders and his own nobility when he died, childless and, most inconveniently, without a named successor.

The realm itself was something of a shaky edifice anyway, a onetime Roman colony that had been invaded, successively, by Saxons, Norwegians, and Danes, one of whom, Cnut the Great, had been Edward's immediate predecessor as England's king. In fact, given the numerous ways in which the Medieval Warm Period unleashed the Viking Age upon European history, it isn't actually so surprising that the three contenders for Edward's throne were each, in one way or another, Norsemen.*

---

*When the Anglo-Saxon Saint Edward took the throne himself, in 1042, he interrupted a fairly long string of Vikings who had worn the English crown; his mother had married Cnut the Great, king of not only England but Denmark and Norway, and when Cnut's son and successor, Harthacnut, died, the throne went to Edward, his half-brother.

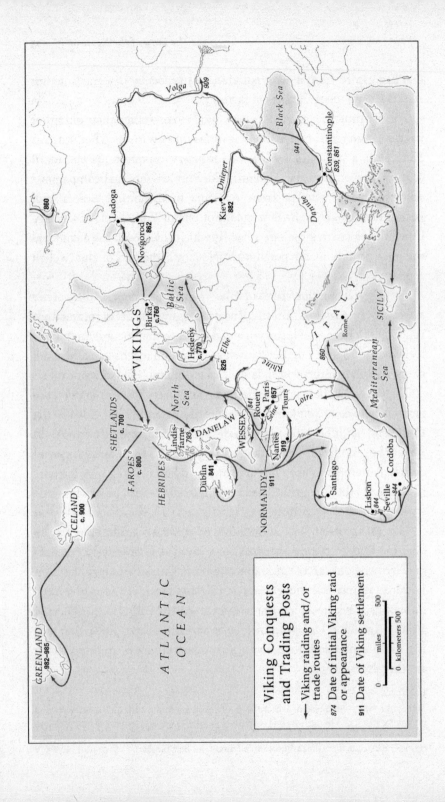

Viking Conquests
and Trading Posts

→ Viking raiding and/or
trade routes

874 Date of initial Viking raid
or appearance

911 Date of Viking settlement

The first, Harold Godwinson, the earl of Wessex, selected as Edward's successor by the *witenagemot*—the assembly of leading nobles that functioned as a sort of privy council to the Anglo-Saxon kings of England—was half-Norse, the son of a Danish princess. The second, a Dane named Harald Hardrada, claimed the English throne by way of a conveniently lost agreement with Cnut's son, Harthacnut, supposedly promising to recombine the Danish and English thrones. And, last, there was Duke William, whose claim rested on an equally convenient—and equally lost—agreement with Edward the Confessor. William's position was not only that Edward had promised *him* the throne during a time when the future saint was living in Normandy but that Harald Hardrada had sworn support when the duke rescued the Norwegian king, who had been shipwrecked on the coast of Brittany.

Conflict was inevitable. Mobilizing took some time, but by fall, both Harald Hardrada and William had assembled armies, and departed for England . . . though they did so in very different ways, and with even more significant consequences. In September 1066, King Harald landed near York, and Duke William in Sussex, each with an army of perhaps ten thousand men, though, as always with medieval orders of battle, solid numbers are hard to come by.

The two battles that followed were each, in their way, decisive.

Though the town of Stamford Bridge occupies the site today, it was nothing but a river crossing over the River Derwent when Hardrada's forces arrived around September 16, 1066. They were led by Harald himself, and by the earl of Northumbria, Tostig Godwinson, the violently estranged brother of Harold, England's newly crowned king. His troops were mostly Norwegians, but included a fair number of Scots, Danes, and mercenaries from northern Europe. They were well armed and experienced, but not especially ready for combat, secure in the news that King Harold was arrayed in the south, preparing a welcome for Duke William and his army. However, in an impressive bit of soldiering, Harold, once apprised of the arrival of the army to his north, led a truly remarkable forced march—185 miles in four days, if the chronicles are to be believed—and, on September 25, surprised his enemy in the worst of all possible situations.* A few thousand troops of Hardrada's army were on the west side of the bridge, with the remainder on the east. All of them had left their armor aboard ship.

Though exhausted from marching, Godwinson's army immediately closed on their opponents and destroyed Hardrada's heavily outnumbered forces on the west side of the Derwent, and prepared to cross the bridge to deal with the remainder. No one knows precisely what delayed them, but *The Anglo-Saxon Chronicle* records the Homeric story of a giant Dane who kept King Harold's forces from crossing the bridge, killing forty Englishmen before he was finally overcome. The heroic effort bought enough time for the Hardrada forces to line up behind their shields in a strong defensive position, some thirty meters above the riverbed. It did not, however, give them the time required to get their armor; not even time to get mail coats on either King Harald or Earl Tostig, both of whom were killed as the battle turned into a slaughter. The best estimate is that the Norwegians landed with three hundred ships, and returned home with fewer than twenty.

Unfortunately, Stamford Bridge was only a battle. Winning the war meant defeating William's Normans as well. Which is why, three weeks later, King Harold's army, battered and exhausted, arrived at Caldbec Hill, on October 13. The following morning, they deployed across the only road from the enemy's camp at Hastings, which was blocked to the west and the east by inlets that have long since been drained.

The two forces that faced each other at Hastings that day were similar in size, but in no other way. Harold's Englishmen were almost entirely infantry: at the center, the king's housecarls, the professional soldiers who formed the core of the English army, armored with helmets and mail hauberks, and mostly armed with three-foot-long, thirty-pound Danish axes. On either wing were less experienced freemen, similarly armed and armored, and stiffened with Anglo-Saxon

---

*The chronicles probably aren't to be believed. The "quick march" of a modern infantry platoon is 120 strides per minute, at thirty inches a stride, or 3.4 miles per hour. At that pace, they would have to have been marching for nearly fourteen hours each day.

nobles: thegns, or thanes. Tactically, they were well trained and equipped to defend, and so they established themselves in a powerful defensive position: at the top of Senlac Hill, in a long but shallow ridge, behind a phalanx of locked shields. William's army, on the other hand, was a combined arms force—perhaps fifteen hundred archers, carrying longbows and crossbows, as well as three thousand to four thousand infantry—but the core of the army, its shock troops, valuable only in attack and pursuit, were two thousand or so heavy cavalry—mailed, helmeted, and armed with lance and sword.

Predictably, therefore, it was the Norman force—really a northern European force, with Bretons on the left and Flemings on the right—that began the attack, with a salvo of arrows that did little against the interlocked shields of the English. William then sent his left division in a probing attack that likewise failed to break the integrity of the English line, though it did succeed, in a manner of speaking, by pulling some of Harold's troops out of the shield wall as it pursued them down Senlac Hill.

And so it went, for hour after indecisive hour: a Norman attack, or feint, that failed to decide anything except the fates of a few dozen soldiers who fell at each one. Eventually, however, William calculated how to turn the attacks into a winning tactic: Every quarter hour or so, he charged a portion of his cavalry at the English line, turning at the last minute in order to provoke a pursuit. Once having pulled a few dozen English housecarls out of the shield wall, the Norman cavalry would turn and cut it to pieces. This they did over and over again, while William's archers were given the order to fire at a high enough trajectory to have their missiles drop down on Harold's forces from above, further weakening the obdurate English shield wall. In legend, at least, it was one of those high-arching arrows that fell on the unprotected head of King Harold himself, killing him instantly.

At that moment, the English army, though still formidable, had lost. It is impossible to overstate the importance of personal leadership in combat, and in the mess that was a medieval battle, there were no noncommissioned officers or company commanders. In the battle's early hours, an English counterattack seemed to have struck down

Duke William, and, in an army no bigger than a modern regiment, the loss of the only real leader would have been disastrous, which is why the duke of Normandy knew enough to climb back onto his horse, remove his helmet, and display his well-known face to his troops by riding along the entire front line of his army, restoring their morale. It was not an option available to the English, and they scattered almost as soon as word of Harold's death spread—all except his most loyal housecarls, who fought literally to the death as their bodies formed a wall around their fallen king. The field had been won, decisively, by the duke of Normandy, and with it the crown of England.

The Battle of Hastings is rightly remembered as one of the signature "battles that changed history," and it certainly deserves to be; it ended five centuries of nearly uninterrupted Anglo-Saxon rule of Britain and inaugurated eight centuries of conflict between the rulers of England and France.

But there's an even more fundamental significance to Hastings, which was not only a battle between two armies but also between two very different ways of life. The military contrast couldn't have been more stark: One force, entirely infantry, with a core of professional soldiers—Harold's housecarls—were paid a wage by the sovereign. The other, William's Normans, was built around heavy cavalry, and such a force was enormously more expensive to maintain. Like every premium form of military technology, the premium came at a premium price. In continental Europe, the only way to finance it—in money and manpower—was a social innovation that, in broad terms, has come down to us as feudalism.

In its simplest meaning, feudalism is a system in which an entire class of men owes military service to the class immediately above them, in return for the right to a specific bit of land. Though the term is widely, and casually, used to describe arrangements everywhere from Mesoamerica to imperial China, its European version was unique: a system that organized society through oaths of fealty—by contract, rather than blood. Its origins are traceable to Charlemagne and his subordinates, but the system owed its endurance to both its flexibility and its unique ability to exploit a new version of a centuries-old military technology: masses of heavy cavalry.

Ever since the sixth century, when the armored cataphracts of the eastern Roman Empire battled against their similarly armed Persian opponents, the use of cavalry as shock troops had been a decisive tactic on European battlefields. But the lancers of late antiquity were armed and armored by imperial treasuries. The heavy cavalry forces of the high medieval era, with lance, mail, and sword for each rider, in addition to a form of armor for at least one of his warhorses, were even more expensive to maintain—among other things, every knight needed multiple mounts, each one bred specifically for combat, and several retainers and grooms to maintain them—and the cost fell squarely on the knights themselves. During the eighth century, a single knight's armor, helmet, sword, lance, shield, and one horse cost fifteen times as much as a cow. By the eleventh, at least ten times as much income was needed to maintain a single knight in the field as a single foot soldier.

To William of Normandy, whose tactics required one mounted soldier for every four afoot, this was not just a logistical problem but a recruiting one. His Anglo-Saxon and Norwegian opponents could field an army with a core of professional ax-wielding infantrymen, personally loyal to the sovereign, who paid them an annual wage. William, unable to do so, assembled an army drawn not just from Normandy but the lands that would subsequently be known as Brittany, Flanders, and Germany. He did so not with the lure of coin but the promise of lands and titles in the island of Britain. Gibbon, in the *Decline and Fall*, describes Charlemagne fearing "the destructive progress of the Normans," but in truth William's victory at Hastings was Charlemagne's as well, because it was William's feudal army—a heritage from the Carolingian emperor—that destroyed the Saxon host. And it was William who, in the manner of Charlemagne, appointed himself as the de facto landlord of all England, and redeemed the promises made to his knights (not merely the great nobles but nearly everyone who carried a lance at Hastings). The victor at

Hastings dispossessed the Anglo-Saxon owners of virtually every acre in England and transferred them to newly made lords, earls, and barons, who held them as his vassals.

At the time of Hastings, the decisive elements of Northern Europe's next few centuries were already largely in place. Enabled by what would eventually be four centuries of warm summers and moderate winters, population and land cultivation both continued to grow, one barely keeping up with the other. For three centuries after William's victory, feudal levies would shape the course of European conflict, and manorial land tenure the nature of European agriculture and trade. The combination of population growth and feudal land expansion—the seeds for a future disaster—were already planted in Europe before the Norman army sailed across the channel in 1066.

Without Hastings, though, there's no obvious reason the same system would have taken root in Britain. As, indeed, it did.

CHAPTER TWO

"Henceforth Be Earls"

1066–1298

The Tragedy of Macbeth ends with Malcolm telling his thanes that they would "henceforth be earls, the first that ever Scotland in such an honour named." Shakespeare's dramatic device had a real historical antecedent. Duke William's accession to the English throne after his victory at Hastings transformed political power in the British Isles, and what the playwright got wrong in detail—Shakespeare's Malcolm, properly Malcolm III Canmore, an eleventh-century king of Scotland, wasn't the one to adopt Norman ways, but his son, David I —was nonetheless accurate in broad. The transplanted Vikings known as Normans had brought a new political structure to England, and shortly thereafter, Wales and Scotland: no more Thane of Cawdor; henceforth Earl of Moray. A dozen new cities—*burghs*, like Edinburgh and Roxburgh—were built. The relatively simple national bureaucracy in the lands north of the river Forth was replaced with the same European model William had brought with him from Normandy: constables, chancellors, stewards, sheriffs, and the like.

But the most fundamental change in Scotland was a profoundly different way of sharing the kingdom itself—that is, its land. Every society establishes rules for such an allocation, since land is desirable, and therefore valuable, for many reasons: houses are built on it, minerals mined from it, wood harvested from it. But land matters most because it produces food.

As a practical matter, *Homo sapiens* must convert the energy of the sun into fuel for operating the body's machinery. And, like every species that hasn't mastered the trick of photosynthesis, they must do so indirectly, by consuming either plants or animals. For hunter-gatherer societies, this is fairly straightforward: killing or scavenging other animals, and eating the edible portions of naturally occurring plants, such as roots and berries. Roughly a hundred centuries ago, some of our more forward-looking ancestors hit on the idea of cultivating those plants: combining seeds, soil, sun, and water in the cycles that can produce a crop for harvesting.*

The key was finding an efficient way to combine sun, water, land, and labor. Fifty years ago, a German American historian named Karl Wittfogel documented his so-called hydraulic hypothesis in a book with the provocative title *Oriental Despotism*, in which he argued that the nature of such riverine societies demanded autocracy; large-scale civil engineering was required to turn the natural flow of a river into the artificial channels needed for irrigation, aqueducts, and reservoirs. The result was the despotism of Wittfogel's title, where pharaohs, kings, and emperors sat at the top of highly organized, bureaucratic, and religiously sanctioned autocracies.

Wittfogel's thesis was controversial when he published it, and is even more so today. But his hydraulic civilizations were unambiguous success stories: the regions where grain first started feeding humanity achieved levels of productivity that weren't surpassed until the nineteenth century. However, as human civilization expanded outside the great river valleys—which possessed, almost by definition, the most fertile soils on the planet—the calculus of sun and water changed, and with it the social organization needed to combine the two productively. Rome could build great aqueducts to bring water to cities and towns but grew its food on plantations that relied on rain more than rivers for their fresh water. The price was lower productivity per acre—acceptable as long as Roman armies were regularly turning conquered territory into the estates of Roman aristocrats, the villas that date to the earliest days of the Roman Republic. And for a

---

*One reason that civilization first appeared in the great river valleys—the Nile, the Tigris/Euphrates, the Yellow, and the Indus—is that they were where sun and water were most abundantly reliable, and agriculture therefore most productive.

thousand years the villa system, granting legal rights over both land and the labor to work it, endured.

By the time Duke William took his domesticated Norsemen across the English Channel, the villa system inherited by the Romans had evolved into the system known as manorialism, the legal doctrine that ascribes primary ownership of all the land in the realm to the sovereign. This sort of ownership—the technical term is *alodial*—was unencumbered by any obligations or duties to anyone. Any of that land transferred by the king to a loyal subject was *feudal:* a fief, in the form of a lease or grant made in return for an oath of fealty, which, in practical terms, meant an obligation to provide a specified number of mounted knights—and occasionally, in addition, foot soldiers—in time of war. Only the grandest nobles received their fiefs directly from the sovereign; most of them turned around and instituted the same system among lesser nobles, who continued the process by subdividing their territories into still smaller estates. At the bottom were the farmers who provided the agricultural produce on which the whole structure relied.

The upshot of this unsteady pyramid of interlocking obligations was that manorial land fell into one of three categories. The first was the demesne (pronounced not as domain but d'main), which was land devoted entirely and specifically to the support of the lord of the manor. Second were the dependencies, or dependent land, which was acreage owned by the lord but worked by tenants, who were allowed the product of the land in return for sharing a portion with the lord and providing a feudal duty to the lord, either in the form of labor or—when needed—soldiering. Third, and finally, was free peasant land, which was usually subject to a rent obligation, though not a feudal one. For all three sorts of land the lord's will was law. A manorial grant included the right to hold a court for the resolution of disputes—the term of art was "sac, and tol, and team"—as well as the unpronounceable rights of both infangthief and outfangthief, which granted the lord the fines or ransom for thieves caught for crimes committed in the manor, whether they were captured "in" the manor or "out."

Manorialism had emerged more or less organically in continental Europe under the Carolingians as a method of allocating land through feudal obligations. Like so much else, it owed its origins to the four centuries of the Medieval Warm Period that both permitted and required the cultivation of more and more land to feed more and more mouths. However, what happened over the course of centuries in Normandy took place in a matter of years in Britain, as a direct consequence of Duke William's offer of feudal grants as an inducement to the knights he recruited and who won the day for him at Hastings. A case in point: After Hastings, Pope Alexander II ordered 120 days of penance for every Saxon soldier killed . . . without specifying who would be required to perform the penance. William's response was to plant dozens of monasteries in the middle of the most worthless land in England—"in a desert surrounded by swampy valleys and by forests out of which only a few homesteads had yet to be carved"— simultaneously increasing his virtue and his new country's arable land. The lordships William granted ranged from the most modest— one village, perhaps, with the lord in residence: a few dozen tenants on a few hundred acres, producing 10 to 15 pounds in cash rents,* plus produce and harvest services—to the grandest. Some of William the Conqueror's original tenants-in-chief evolved from senior officers in an army of occupation into de facto owners of the land itself: the greatest lords of the land might rule fifty or more villages, exercising political power comparable to, and frequently in opposition to, the king himself.

A manorial grant was, in essence, a bargain: productive acreage in return for rents and military service, quid pro quo. After 1066, the *quid,* in the form of acreage, was clear enough; less so the *quo,* or what it was producing. In 1085, nearly twenty years after the invasion, William met with his council and directed them to perform a survey of

---

*The pound, as a currency measure, is even older than the Norman Conquest. From the ninth century forward, rulers of England denominated it as 240 silver pennies. This was supposedly equal to a pound of silver, copying the *libra* used in Charlemagne's empire; hence the £ symbol. In order to confuse both popular historians and their readers, however, a "pound" of precious metal weighs considerably less than a pound of anything else: about 350 grams, or three-quarters of a "real" pound.

his new kingdom: "how it was occupied, and by what sort of men." Then he sent his men over all England into each shire, commissioning them to find out "how many hundreds of hides were in the shire, what land the king himself had, and what stock upon the land; or, what dues he ought to have by the year from the shire." Because William maintained the comforting fiction that he had the land by right of inheritance from Edward the Confessor, he was determined to guarantee that he would receive the rents and taxes that his predecessors had enjoyed, even though he had completely upended the system that guaranteed them.

The Domesday Book—really two books—was completed the following year, and was a brave attempt to put a value on everything of property in the kingdom: every piece of land, livestock, coin, and—not at all incidentally—people. In addition to every other bit of census data, William's great survey included a four-part taxonomy for the rural population.

The first category was the *Liberi homines*, or "freemen." Freemen were subject to the lord's justice but able to own land free and clear. Among other things, they were able to buy, sell, and bequeath it.

Just underneath them, in the agonizingly precise hierarchy of the day, were villeins, or serfs, who were permitted to own land but weren't completely free to move from it. They were legally tied to their lord's lands, though, by long tradition, villeins or serfs who managed to spend a year away from the manor were considered free of their obligations. They were just a bit higher on the social scale than cottagers (sometimes "cottars"; also Bordars), who were permitted ownership of land under more restrictions than villeins. Even they had a class at which they could sneer: the true slaves, who were forbidden not just ownership of land but of their own bodies. Depending on the local traditions, true slaves could be bought and sold without reference to the land they were bound to; though, unlike slaves in the antebellum American South, they weren't necessarily born as property of their lords.*

---

*A rough estimate from several sources suggests that about 12 percent of the non-noble population of eleventh-century England were freemen; a bit more than a third serfs; a bit less than

All of this—the manorial arrangement that distributed the realm's arable land; the feudal military structure that domesticated, somewhat, the professional practitioners of violence who would otherwise fight over that land; and the finely nuanced system of vassalage that tied to the land the labor needed to transform it into food—began at the same time, and the same place, as did the Medieval Warm Period. As the population affected by the MWP was able to grow more food—remember: a few additional weeks of reliable sunshine, over a four-century period, produces a *lot* more food—it expanded. It takes about three to four acres to feed every additional person, so as the European population grew from 12 million to 40 million, 100 million more acres needed to be captured, from forests, marshes, and bogs. No great civil engineering projects were needed to irrigate those acres, not as long as the sun remained steady, the rains reliable, and the growing season even a little longer. What *was* needed was some way to manage the giant increase in arable land, to keep the crops coming as the population kept growing (which, often enough, meant keeping famines—which were a regular feature of rural life—localized).

Manors and knights didn't, of course, solve the food-and-land problem. Nor did they diminish the era's violence, or simplify its politics. Quite the contrary.

By the thirteenth century, feudal manorialism was doing a respectable job of land management, at least in allocating the constantly increasing inventory of arable land in Europe. To be sure, it didn't do much to increase per-acre productivity, but that wasn't really its purpose. It provided a formal structure for the inevitable disputes over sale, inheritance, and the "metes and bounds" of a particular plot of land.

Ignoring, for a moment, the tyranny the system imposed on the rural peasantry, feudal manorialism did far better at resolving disputes nonviolently at the lower reaches of the social hierarchy than the upper. The system did a fair job keeping the lower nobility from killing one another over a piece of land; a poor job at preventing

---

a third cottagers; and the remainder, perhaps one in ten, true slaves. By the fourteenth century, however, true slavery had virtually disappeared.

violent disputes between a realm's dukes and earls; and nothing at all to prevent wars over national boundaries, or the right to sit on thrones. In fact, by enlarging a class of professional soldiers who owed military service in payment for land, it enabled it.

Predictably, then, the centuries following the Norman Conquest were violent ones; and the violence wasn't confined to Britain. The notably bloody civil wars between two of William's fractious grandchildren—an era known as "The Anarchy" or "The Unlaw"—ended with his great-grandson on the throne as England's first Plantagenet king, Henry II. The end of the Anarchy, however, wasn't order, but more war, since the feudal mess that was twelfth-century Europe granted Henry lordly authority over the county of Anjou (the hereditary fiefdom of his father), the duchy of Normandy (which his father had conquered from King Stephen during the Anarchy), and the huge duchy of Aquitaine, stretching from Gascony and the Pyrenees to Poitiers in the north and Clermont in the east, which Henry had acquired with his marriage to Eleanor of Aquitaine in 1154. With all that, plus the kingdom of England (and, when the gods of conquest smiled on him, occasionally Ireland and Wales), Henry ruled the largest empire since Charlemagne, and more of France than the French king, which would be a casus belli until the fifteenth century.

To secure his northern border while fighting battles in France (and insurrections in England, often enough led by his wife and sons) Henry negotiated a series of feudal grants in Scotland to more than a dozen Anglo-Norman nobles: barons with family names like Moreville, Soulise, Comyn, Balliol and Le Brus—or, as the latter became known, the Bruces. Simultaneously, they were given royal charters as vassals to the English throne, which meant that Scotland was essentially ruled by men with one foot in England, and vice versa.

Given the nature of feudal vassalage, Scottish sovereignty was a huge tangle. In 1174, the king of Scotland signed a treaty accepting Henry II as his overlord. When Henry died in 1189, *his* successor, Richard Lionheart, sold the overlordship back to Scotland for 10,000 silver marks, when he decided he preferred attacking Jerusalem to ruling Scotland (so eager was Richard to go on Crusade that he reportedly said he would sell London itself if he could find a rich enough buyer).*

And so it went for the next century, the thrones of Scotland and England closely enough related that Henry II had received his knighthood at the hands of David I of Scotland, while Henry's youngest son, John, returned the favor to David's grandson, Alexander II. The royal families, both Norman in ancestry and language, regularly intermarried.

However, the relative size of the two nations made for a distinctly asymmetric relationship. England counted eight times the population and wealth of its northern neighbor, which made the heads wearing the Scottish crown even more uneasy than usual. In 1251, when King Alexander III of Scotland performed the feudal obligation of making homage—a ceremony in which he acknowledged formally and publicly his vassalage—to the king of England for his English lands, he felt obliged to point out that "homage to my Kingdom of Scotland, no one has any right but God alone, nor do I hold it of any but God."

It's with the death of Alexander III that the uneasiness grew into fear, and then into open war. Though Alexander had fathered three children by his first wife, by 1283, all were dead. Recognizing that the first responsibility of a dynast was to continue his dynasty, Alexander felt the need for an heir keenly, a need that led him, in November 1285, to marry again: to Yolande of Dreux, a French princess twenty-four years his junior.

Alexander's story is a reminder that not all of history's significant turns are caused by grand ideas like feudalism, or anonymous forces like climate change. Scotland's king apparently felt that his kingly duty demanded not just a legitimate heir but the widest possible

---

*The mark—a German word—was widely used throughout medieval Europe, though not especially consistently. In the eastern part of the old Carolingian empire, it was a coin made of about eight ounces of silver (the western part, which was in process of becoming France, used the livre, which, whenever it wasn't being devalued, was nominally equal to a pound of silver). In post-Conquest England, however, the mark was exclusively used as a unit of account, equal to 160 pence, or two-thirds of a pound sterling.

Just to further complicate matters, the ubiquity of Italian bankers—city-states like Florence were the first places in Europe to mint gold coins since the fall of Rome—made the use of florins or ducats (each about 3.5 ounces of gold), yet another standard.

distribution of the royal genetic patrimony, whenever and wherever possible. *The Chronicle of Lanercost*—a history begun in the thirteenth century at the priory of Lanercost, probably by a monk named Thomas of Otterbourne—describes Alexander as a man who "never used to forbear on account of season or storm, nor for perils of flood or rocky cliffs, but would visit, not too creditably, [both] matrons and nuns, virgins and widows, by day or by night as the fancy seized him, sometimes in disguise, often accompanied by a single follower."

This was conscious foreshadowing by the Lanercost authors. On March 19, 1286, the king was celebrating the conclusion of a meeting of his royal council at Edinburgh when he decided that nothing would complete the festivities more happily than a connubial visit to his wife of four months, then staying at the town of Kingorn in Fife. Undeterred by either the raging storm, the advice of his nobles, or even the ferryman who carried him across the Firth of Forth to Inverkeithing, he raced for the coast road that led to his bride.

He never made it; in 1886, the local burghers erected a monument to the place where, presumably, having lost his footing in the winds and rain off the North Sea, Alexander fell to his death. On the statue is the inscription:

> *Ouen Alysandyr Oure King wes dede*
> *That Scotland led in luive and le*
> *Away wes sonce of ale and brede*
> *Of wyne and wax, of gamyn and gle*
> *Our gold wes changed into lede*

> When Alexander, Our King, was dead
> That Scotland led, in love, and [probably] peace
> Gone was the source of ale and bread
> Of wine and wax; of gaming and glee
> Our gold was changed into lead

The result of exposing the king's intemperance to poor roads and poorer weather was that the three-year-old daughter of King Erik II of

Norway, who had survived the death in childbirth of Alexander's daughter Margaret, was the heir to the Scottish throne.

The complications weren't just that Scotland's sovereign was still cutting her milk teeth on the opposite side of the North Sea. The girl—named, like her mother, Margaret—was the last of her line. Until she could marry, and bear a child, the only protection Scotland had against civil war was the health of a toddler now known as the Maid of Norway. That's why, a month after the death of King Alexander, a group of the leading nobles of Scotland met at Scone and nominated six men as *custodes* (usually translated as "Guardians") to govern the kingdom during Margaret's minority.

The selection of the Guardians reflected, as it must, Scotland's political structure, which had been remade, ever since the time of Malcolm III ("Henceforth be earls") on the English model, which was itself a result of the specific circumstances of the Norman Conquest. William had assembled his army with the promise of titles and lands in England, under the feudal doctrine that the French-speaking Normans would have known as *nulle terre sans seigneur* ("no land without a lord"). This meant, in practice, that all the productive land in England was to be divided into manors, each with a lord. To those lords who held their land directly from the king, and therefore owed him military service in return, William granted the title of "baron"— by extension, those vassals entitled and obligated to sit in council with the king.* However, since they were also permitted to grant parts of their fiefs to other lords—to *subinfeudiate* them—the relatively simple map of the eleventh century was anything but simple two hundred years later.

One result was that the border between England and Scotland became an accidental experiment in testing the limits of feudalism. England's earldoms, because of the all-at-once grants that followed the Conquest, were typically granted (and taken away) without any reference to geographic sense: the earl of Surrey might have no lands at all in Surrey, but lots in Yorkshire or Sussex. In Scotland, on the other

---

*This is the origin of the House of Lords.

hand, the system had grown organically over centuries, and was, by comparison, considerably more sensible: thirteen earls, holding the territories of their titles as fiefs; the earl of Atholl was a feudal lord in Atholl.

The first six Guardians—Alexander Comyn, earl of Buchan; Duncan, earl of Fife; Bishops William Fraser of St. Andrews and Robert Wishart of Glasgow; and two "barons," John Comyn of Badenoch and James Stewart—worked together reasonably well as Scotland's rulers for the next four years until tragedy struck. In the fall of 1290, a ship carrying seven-year-old Margaret to Scotland from Norway landed on Orkney. The princess had acquired a fever; and, on September 26, she died.

With her death, the succession was again thrown into chaos. At least fourteen men—most, though not all, Scots; after centuries of intermarriage among the noble families of Europe, plausible candidates could be found in Flanders, Denmark, and even Spain—put their clerks to work describing their own claims. Most of them were almost laughably tenuous, but two were not: Both Robert le Brus, fifth lord of Annandale, and John Balliol of Galloway were descended from David I, and neither was the least bit shy about announcing it. The eighty-year-old le Brus, or Bruce, was known as "the Competitor," and it wasn't a reference to his love of knightly games. So competitive was he that he assembled his own armed force, including both the knights who held land in fief to him, and others who were essentially freelance (the term is telling) and led it to Perth, where the Scottish barons were in council.

Balliol's own supporters armed themselves in response. Civil war loomed. One of the Guardians—no one knows who first proposed it, and, given the consequences, no one subsequently claimed the idea—thought to ask for an outside mediator to settle the competing claims: the king of England, Edward I.

Edward was then fifty-one years old. He had held England's throne since 1272, and his relationship with his northern neighbor had, to this point, been more than amicable. He was a close friend to Alexander III, despite some moderate tension about the homage the Scottish king owed for his own English manors. He was also physically imposing—known as "Longshanks" for his great height—a superb soldier and gifted administrator, "one of the most able and ably advised" of all England's monarchs. He had dominated his own barons, conquered Wales, and built roads and castles almost beyond numbering to consolidate his kingdom. In the fourteenth-century chronicle *The Song of Lewes,* he is described as

> Valiant as a lion, quick to attack the strongest and fearing the onslaught of none. But if a lion in pride and fierceness, he is a panther in fickleness and inconstancy . . . The treachery or falsehood by which he is advanced he calls prudence and the path by which he attains his ends, however crooked, he calls straight, and whatever he likes he says is lawful.

And the end he had in sight, lawfully or not, was Scotland. He'd been looking northward for years before the Guardians called him in; within days of Alexander's death, Edward I had made a personal loan (of £2,000) to the Maid's father, King Erik of Norway, out of concern for his northern border, which he knew his French opponents were already eyeing.

From the eleventh century to the nineteenth, France was always the primary strategic concern of any British ruler. England, by the end of the thirteenth century, had lost most of the French territories that, a century earlier, had rivaled those of the Capetian king. France had three times the population of England and Wales combined, so Edward's desire to expand his own realm is partly understood by the need to counter France. Not that Scotland would help much in that regard; it had fewer than five hundred thousand inhabitants; mostly ethnic Celts, but also including Norsemen, Anglo-Saxons, and—in coastal enclaves that were virtually extraterritorial colonies— Germans, Scandinavians, Frenchmen, and especially Flemings, who were so dominant in the wool trade that they virtually ruled both Aberdeen and Berwick.

For Edward, Aberdeen and Berwick were the real prize. Along with

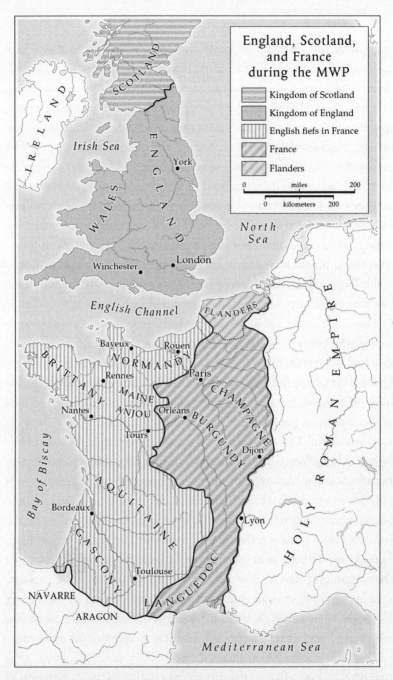

By the end of the Medieval Warm Period, English monarchs ruled more territory in France than their once-and-future sovereigns, the kings of France. Shown are the English territories on the Continent at the time of the death of Henry II in 1189; the boundaries of the Kingdom of Scotland are as of the death of Alexander III in 1286.

Perth, Inverness, Roxburgh, and Edinburgh, they formed the core of Scotland's economy: Not the country's poor farmland, but its well-situated seaports.* Berwick was so wealthy that the *Chronicle of Lanercost* described it as "a city so populous and of such trade that it might justly be called another Alexandria, whose riches were the sea, and the water its walls."

However, Scotland's wealth was more a rationalization than a rationale. Edward's desire to extend his sovereignty northward was just another example (and not an especially notable one) of a phenomenon occurring everywhere in Europe by the end of the thirteenth century. Nations were coalescing into what would become their modern forms from the Urals to the Atlantic, from Scandinavia, to France, and even to the Iberian Peninsula, where Christian kingdoms—Galicia, Asturias, and especially Aragon and Castile—were well embarked on the *Reconquista* that would drive out the Muslims who had ruled it since the eighth century. At the beginning of the fourteenth century, Europe had more than five thousand independent quasi-states: baronies, duchies, kingdoms, and principalities. Three centuries later, five hundred. By the beginning of the nineteenth century, two hundred, and only a few dozen today.

In any event, Edward wanted Scotland. In November 1289, he had negotiated the Treaty of Salisbury that provided, among other things, that the Maid of Norway would not enter into any marriage contract without his consent and then, within weeks, betrothed his own son to her, as a first step to unifying the two kingdoms. In July 1290, the Scottish nobles pushed for another agreement, the Treaty of Birgham, that set out a long list of provisions intended to prevent unification: They demanded that no homage be given for Scottish lands to anyone outside Scotland; that all offices of state must be held by Scotsmen; that there be no taxation of Scots for anything but Scottish purposes; and that no Scotsman would ever be subject to any legal proceeding held outside the kingdom. Edward, "however crooked," agreed, after inserting a clause after all the provisions reading "saving the rights of

---

*Though Scotland did produce, then as now, high-quality wool, which was the most valuable agricultural product in Britain. See chapter 9.

the King of England." Immediately thereafter, he occupied the Isle of Man.*

Despite this, the Guardians invited their southern neighbor to arbitrate Scotland's destiny. One supposes that their inexplicable trust in the good intentions of the king of England was shaken when, on May 30, 1291, Edward assembled the lords of Scotland, and asserted his sovereign authority over the nation's yet-to-be-named king. He did so in a manner typical of the king, who, in the words of a modern historian, combined courteous legality with an undertone of menace, as he asked, "Can you produce any evidence to show that I am *not* the rightful Suzerain?"

The question was rhetorical; Edward had an army, and the Scots didn't. Making the best of a bad situation, the Scots replied that they were unable to accept Edward's generous offer of overlordship, since it would bind a king who was not yet named. Nonetheless, in the name of the "community of Scotland," they offered provisional agreement: they would accept an English overlord, if Edward agreed in turn to return the sovereignty within two months to the new king of Scotland, once he was named. The Guardians then resigned their offices, upon which Edward reappointed them.

Which left a decision to be made: Edward Longshanks was going to be the overlord (or "suzerain"), but who would be Scotland's king? Edward convened a great court—"great" for its size, if nothing else: 104 auditors, 24 appointed by Edward and 40 each by the two great-great-grandsons of King David I: John Balliol and Robert Bruce, the Competitor—to hear arguments, and choose Scotland's next king.

Of the ornate, quasilegal briefs about who had the better claim— one closer in blood, another from the "senior" branch, and so on, with citations going back to the Book of Exodus—the lesser said the better.†
Primogeniture was not yet decisive in such matters, which was a good

---

*Edward's gravestone, with apparently unintentional irony, includes the motto *pactum servo*: "I Keep My Word."

†Zelopehad, one of the Israelites on the exodus out of Egypt, died leaving five daughters and no sons. When they appealed to Moses to grant them their father's inheritance, God supported them . . . and, presumably, therefore, Robert Bruce's claim to the throne of Scotland through Isobel of Huntington, a descendant of King David I.

thing for Bruce, since Balliol was definitely the senior descendant of David I. However, this just made the decision a purely political one: four earls declared for Balliol, six for Bruce; two bishops for Bruce, six for Balliol; the south for Bruce, the north for Balliol, and so on. To the surprise of no one, the forty auditors selected by Bruce voted for him; the forty picked by Balliol proved just as loyal. This, of course, gave Edward's twenty-four auditors the deciding vote, and if anyone was cynical enough to observe that this was probably his plan all along, no record of it survives.

The criteria of Edward's auditors were slightly different from those of the other eighty: to the English king, the best choice was the man easiest to bully, and despite the age of the Competitor, he was not what anyone would call biddable. Neither was he slow to recognize a trap; once he realized that Balliol would be Edward's choice, he delegated his claim to his son, the earl of Carrick, upon which the earl delegated the claim to *his* son. The Competitor's tactic was a delaying one: his son would retain the earldom of Carrick as a fief from Edward, he himself would keep Annandale, and his grandson—a seventeen-year-old named, like his father, grandfather, and half a dozen ancestors, Robert Bruce—would still be able, when the political winds shifted, to claim the throne of Scotland.

The court selected Balliol as Scotland's new king on November 17, 1292. Less than six weeks later, King Edward I of England ended any doubt as to his plans for Scotland: He had already, in June 1291, asserted that "the realms of England and Scotland are joined together." In January 1293, he forced Balliol to free him from all the earlier promises he had made to Scotland's Guardians, most especially the Treaty of Birgham. Scotland was to be an English fief, forever.

However important Scotland was to King Edward's ambitions, it was neither as rich nor as populous as his traditional holdings in France. Though diminished since Henry II's reign a century earlier, he was still the lord of large holdings in the Aquitaine, particularly its most southerly region, Gascony. Or, he was until May 1294, when King

Philip IV of France seized them. Edward immediately renounced his obligation to give homage as the province's duke (he was also still count of Ponthieu, though Normandy had been ceded to the French king by Henry III) and started alliance-building. By 1295, he had recruited the king of Aragon, a number of German principalities, and various parts of the Low Countries, particularly the count of Flanders. Only after he had surrounded Philip of France with potential belligerents did he begin mobilizing his own army. He summoned the knights who owed him military service in payment for their fiefs—the feudal host—and, for the first time, included levies from Wales and Scotland, both of whom responded with a distinct lack of enthusiasm. In the fall, Wales rebelled, and the Scots elected a ruling council—four bishops, four earls, and four barons—to negotiate directly with Philip IV, and sent an embassy on their behalf to sign a treaty of alliance, which they did on October 23.

The treaty called for mutual defense and aggression: As long as France and England were at war, Scotland would wage war on England as well; if Scotland were invaded, Philip IV would send assistance; if Edward left England, Scotland was obliged to invade south. King John Balliol's son would wed a French princess to seal the deal, which was ratified by Balliol and the twelve-man ruling council on February 23, 1296.

Edward's reaction was predictable, and swift. Before the embassy had even returned from France, he seized all the land in England held by Scottish lords, and on March 1, summoned both his army and his fleet to invade Scotland. In April, Edward ordered every Scot in England arrested as a potential enemy combatant, and Balliol, as directed by the council, called the Scottish lords to provide *their* feudal levies. Virtually all of them answered; all of them, that is, except the Bruce family.

The plan, hatched even before the election of Balliol, to have a Bruce on the winning side in any possible conflict between Scotland and England, was still very much in play. The death of Robert the Competitor the preceding year had simply changed the players: The Competitor's son became lord of Annandale and a vassal of Edward I; his son, the youngest Robert Bruce, became earl of Carrick, simultaneously a vassal to the Scottish king and an aspirant to the throne of Scotland.*

It surprised no one that the Bruces, who had never even acknowledged Balliol's kingship, also failed to provide him with armed men to resist the king they *had* acknowledged. There was, however, a cost. When the Bruces refused the feudal levy of 1296, they forfeited their properties in Scotland, which Balliol granted to his brother-in-law, John Comyn, the earl of Buchan.† Partly to retrieve them, and partly to renew his family's claim on the Scottish throne, the newly made earl of Carrick, the twenty-two-year-old Robert Bruce, marched north with the English host.

The army that Edward led into Scotland in the spring of 1296 was far larger and more experienced than the one the Conqueror had led at Hastings two centuries before. For twenty years, the English king had applied great administrative skill to his naturally warlike temperament—he had put down baronial rebellions in the 1260s, gone on Crusade in the 1270s, and conquered Wales in the 1280s—in the creation of an army that couldn't yet be called national but wasn't entirely feudal, either. England's improved administration and increased wealth—among other things, the expulsion of England's Jews in 1290 produced a huge windfall, as Edward expropriated all their property—permitted him to pay a significant number of troops directly, rather than by relying on feudal obligations. Moreover, new taxes, and duties on imports and exports, gave the king a regular supply of cash. With the cash came creditworthiness, and loans from his Italian bankers, the Riccardi and the Frescobaldi. The cash paid not just for Edward's household contingents but for a strong supply system (one that was designed to use sea transport to reinforce armies in the field—a clear advantage in combat everywhere, but especially against the Scots, with their enormous coastline).

As a result, Edward commanded military resources larger than

---

*Though Carrick was an earldom, Annandale was actually a far richer fief.

†Readers who think that three characters named Robert Bruce is excessive will probably be less than delighted to learn that there were two John Comyns: the earl of Buchan and his cousin, the lord of Badenoch.

anyone in Europe; only Constantinople, and the Islamic caliphates, could put larger armies into the field. And, just as army pay was evolving from the typical feudal arrangements, in which vassals were responsible for their own arms, armor, and food, so too was the army itself. Its shock troops were the royal household knights, paid out of the royal wardrobe, and typically providing a third of the cavalry in an expedition; the other two-thirds were more traditionally organized, and led by knights banneret, a rank somewhere between knight bachelor and the true nobles such as barons and earls.*

The army of 1296 wasn't completely dependent on its five thousand heavy cavalry. More than ten thousand foot soldiers, recruited by levies throughout England's counties, and at least five thousand archers accompanied the king north.

The Scots had nothing that could stand in Edward's way. By the end of March, the English had advanced to Berwick, on the River Tweed—the "other Alexandria." Led by the warlike bishop of Durham, Antony Bek, and Robert de Clifford, the English demanded the surrender of the castle's garrison. One source states that the crews of some English supply ships, having run aground, were slaughtered by the Scots, but it seems likely that this is a retrospective excuse for the events that followed. Though Edward permitted honorable surrender by the garrison's commander, Sir William Douglas, and the knights occupying the city's castle, feudal honor did nothing to protect noncombatants. As many as ten thousand of the city's residents—tradesmen and artisans, women and children—were massacred; thirty Flemish merchants, who were obliged to support the king of Scotland by treaty, fought so ferociously that all died at their posts. Thousands of bodies were hung by the city's walls and left to rot for weeks as an object lesson to other rebels.

---

*The knight banneret was one of Edward's innovations, a way of undermining—or at least evolving—the hierarchy of a feudal levy. Typically, a banneret was a commoner, raised to knighthood (in theory, at least, on the field of battle) and granted the right and obligation to lead other knights and soldiers in battle under his banner—a square or rectangular flag, distinguished from the triangular pennons of other knights. In battle, knights banneret were indistinguishable from England's lower gentry, leading "banners" of troops, usually a hundred or more men. However, unlike the barons, they had no independent source of income, as they were paid, like the household knights, from the king's treasury.

If it was intended to intimidate Balliol, it failed. The Scottish king had little value as a military leader; he avoided combat himself and had neither the stature nor the talent to direct a strategy to be conducted by subordinates. But he was enormously important as a symbol, being the only man who could agree to terms with Edward. So when Balliol sent word that he refused to come to Edward in order to pay fealty, the English king reportedly said, "If he won't come to us, we'll go to him," and did. A column of English cavalry under John de Warenne, the earl of Surrey, was sent north, and met, near Dunbar, an undisciplined and overmatched Scots army commanded by John Comyn of Badenoch, where Warenne easily wiped out what was left of Scottish resistance.

Balliol's rebellion, such as it was, was effectively over. On July 10, the Scottish king surrendered at Montrose, where he suffered the latest in a long line of humiliations inflicted by his English overlord: the king's escutcheon—the shield exhibiting his coat of arms—was publicly torn from his uniform, earning him the name by which seven centuries' worth of Scottish schoolchildren know him: Toom Tabard, or "empty tunic." Scotland's Stone of Destiny (sometimes the Stone of Scone, for its traditional location), which had been used in the coronation of every Scottish king for centuries, was taken to Westminster Abbey, and her king to the Tower of London.*

But first, Edward had some more spleen to vent against his Scottish subjects. Robert Bruce, lord of Annandale, who lacked the determination if not the self-regard of both his father, the Competitor, and his son, thought he was to be named Scotland's new king, and said so to Edward, whom he had loyally followed into Scotland that spring. The king's reply, reportedly, was, "Have we nothing to do but win kingdoms for you?" Instead, he named Warenne, the earl of Surrey, as

---

*The Stone, which was eventually placed under the Coronation Chair at Westminster Abbey, and used for subsequent English (and British) ceremonies, became the subject of several centuries' worth of rumors about its authenticity, the idea evidently being that at various moments in history, Scottish nationalists somehow substituted a fake for the real thing. In 1950, four Scottish students stole it (breaking it in the process), and it was a year before it was returned, along with still more rumors about another substitution. In 1996, it was finally, and formally returned to Scotland, and there it can be seen, in Edinburgh Castle's Crown Room. Or, at least, something can be seen. . . .

viceroy of Scotland. (Like the king, Warenne liked Scotland better at some distance, and as a result, soon returned to his Yorkshire home, leaving Hugh de Cressingham as the real ruler of the new "province.") Other Englishmen were appointed to the various royal offices of treasurer, chancellor, and the like. A month after the humiliation and abdication of Balliol, Edward presided over an even more provocative event: the Berwick parliament, which commenced business on August 2, 1296. Every noble in Scotland was commanded to attend, and to offer an oath of fealty, known subsequently as the "Ragman Roll." Significantly, the oaths were given to Edward personally, since he was unwilling to admit even the existence of a Scottish kingdom. He was restoring a rebellious province to his rule, not conquering a foreign nation.

Or so he thought. To be fair, the flame of Scottish national independence had never burned very brightly. A fractious nobility, as much Norman as Scottish, was part of the reason; so was the fact that the very idea of a Scottish nation was still evolving. But neither had Edward extinguished it. It continued to smolder, awaiting the proper moment. It was not long in coming. In May 1297, William Wallace entered the story.

Of Wallace's life prior to 1297 little can be said with any precision. He was of a landowning family, probably vassals of James Stewart, the hereditary steward of Scotland. His father may have been named Alan, or possibly Malcolm. He might have been born in Ayrshire, or somewhere else. He probably had brothers.

He was a huge man, at least six and a half feet tall (you can find chroniclers who claim seven) with a huge beard, enormous charisma, and absolutely no fear in battle. When he appeared in the forest of Selkirk in 1297, after the disastrous sack of Berwick and the defeat of Comyn the preceding year, he must have seemed to have been sent by God.*

---

*The forest of Selkirk, better known today as Ettrick Forest, was the greatest survivor in Britain of the deforestation described in chapter 1. It covered more than one hundred fifty thousand acres (by way of comparison, Sherwood Forest, in England, less than five thousand) and was therefore very nearly perfect for irregular warfare.

Certainly his appeal was enhanced by the fact that Edward's 1296 invasion failed to convince the Scots of the hopelessness of their position. Perversely, Scotland's lack of a real national army meant that it couldn't give the English much of a fight, but also meant that it couldn't suffer a decisive defeat. And that meant that Edward's strategic objective—an obedient subject people—could be achieved only by destroying the morale of the Scots. In that, even before the appearance of Wallace, he failed; despite the humiliation of "Toom Tabard" and the Ragman Roll, the uprising was never completely suppressed by the English, particularly in the north. Balliol may not have commanded an enormous amount of loyalty to his person, but as the king of Scotland, he retained a reservoir of devotion from, among others, Wallace himself. And he was not alone; at almost precisely the same moment Wallace arrived in Selkirk Forest, Andrew, the earl of Moray in Scotland's far northeast, also rebelled against English rule in Balliol's name, attacking and eventually capturing Castle Urquhart on the western shore of Loch Ness, and burning English ships at anchor in the harbor of Aberdeen.

The conventional story of Moray and Wallace is the stuff of muscular legend: the rural peasantry of Scotland fighting harder for their independence than their calculating nobles, since only the former could see further than their own family interests. There's an element of truth in that, but not a very large one. While Wallace was, indeed, able to call soldiers to his flag based on Scottish national pride (apparently because he felt it so strongly himself), Scotland's villeins and freemen took their lead from somewhere else: the Scottish Church.

Under a feudal system, ecclesiastical lords shared the rights of secular ones—they held courts, ran markets, and held farmland as fiefdoms—but without the central feudal obligation of direct military service. Moreover, they were at least nominally subject to supranational authority, through their bishops to the pope.* With the first glimmerings of true nationalism, though, the churches took on more and more of a national character; and the Scottish Church—obsessively,

---

*Still, and for the next decade, in Rome. For more on the Avignon papacy, and another conflict between the loyalty owed king and pope, see chapter 7.

but accurately—feared English dominance over Scottish clergy. It is no accident that in June 1297, only a month after Wallace's first appearance in the historical record, Robert Wishart, bishop of Glasgow, allied with him. Joining them would be Wallace's feudal overlord, James Stewart; Macduff, son of the earl of Fife; and the erstwhile commander of Berwick Castle, Sir William Douglas, who, as a cousin to Moray, served as a bridge between the two insurrections.

Almost immediately upon learning of what he saw as Douglas's treachery Edward commanded the younger Robert Bruce to seize Sir William's castle, Douglasdale, thus presenting the twenty-two-year-old earl of Carrick with an almost ridiculously dramatic choice: Should the young knight—who was not only Norman by heritage and education, but also French-speaking, a lover of tourneys, and lord of substantial estates in England—follow his father's allegiance to Edward? Or pursue his grandfather's ambition for the Scottish throne? The original decision to join Edward had been in opposition to Balliol, but Balliol had become irrelevant. Bruce's family had been exiled from Scotland by the Guardians, and seen their lands restored by the English invasion.

Here was the critical decision of Bruce's life. After a sham assault on Douglasdale Castle, he assembled his followers in south-central Scotland and gave a speech:*

> No man holds his flesh and blood in hatred, and I am no exception. I must join my own people and the nation in which I was born. Choose then whether you go with me, or return to your homes.

Edward commanded more obedience from his other vassals. John de Warenne, earl of Surrey and viceroy of Scotland, was ordered to march his own knights northeast from Yorkshire to Berwick, there to link up with the city's garrison. Two others, Henry Percy and Robert de Clifford, were sent north along the western route and by the end of June had arrived at Irvine, as had, from a different direction, Bruce and a few hundred of his followers. There they found the Scots'

---

*While this seems like the work of a centuries-later hagiographer, it was recorded by Walter of Guisborough, an Augustinian monk in fourteenth-century Yorkshire.

coalition already fraying. Wallace and Moray, it turned out, were fighting on behalf of the absent (and abdicated) Balliol. Stewart and others supported Bruce. Douglas refused to commit to either.

So the forces began to parley. Percy and de Clifford were under orders to avoid risking their troops, since not only was Edward facing a possible rebellion of his own back in England, but he was still in Flanders, trying to shore up his coalition against the French. The English force at Irvine was, outside of the garrison at Berwick, Edward's only organized body of troops in the north. Similarly, the Scots were in a weak situation that could only be improved by negotiating. Which they did, for more than a month, ending with the Scottish surrender that became known as the Capitulation of Irvine.

The capitulation wasn't especially sincere: neither Bruce nor Douglas agreed to provide hostages as demanded, though both lost the lands they held in fief from Edward. Based on subsequent events, it looks a lot more like a *ruse de guerre* than a surrender . . . and while Bruce and Douglas were keeping the forces of Percy and de Clifford at Irvine, the real rebellion simply moved on. Moray and Wallace had slipped away from Irvine, and between August and October 1297 raided Glasgow, Forfar, Montrose, Inverness, and Urquhart, which meant that by the fall, virtually all of Scotland north of the Firth of Forth was no longer controlled by the English.

That didn't mean it was held by Wallace. One of the lessons of insurgency is that it's easier to deny territory to your opponent than to control it yourself, particularly when your opponent occupies every important fortification in the disputed region. Neither Wallace nor Moray had the siege engines—the catapults and trebuchets—needed to batter down the walls of English-held castles, the sappers to undermine them, or the patience to blockade them.

Unable to dislodge the English garrisons from Scotland's castles, Moray and Wallace, along with James Stewart and two thousand foot soldiers, marched south to the town of Stirling. The town, on the Firth of Forth, and the gateway to Scotland's north, was a key objective for Surrey's army, now marching north from Berwick, and whoever arrived first would be able to choose the ground where they wished to fight. Wallace's forces won the race, and deployed their army—the aforementioned two thousand foot soldiers—in a line on the Abbey Crag, a rocky ridge on the north side of the Forth, with the bridge over the river in front and solid ground behind, securing an orderly retreat if needed. On September 10, they faced Surrey's forces as he assembled them on the opposite side of the Forth: at least two thousand heavy cavalry, and more than eight thousand infantry, including a thousand or more archers. James Stewart, understandably anxious about the mismatch of forces, counseled negotiation, but was overruled by Wallace, who declared, "We are not here to make peace but to do battle to defend ourselves and liberate our kingdom."

It's not a criticism of Wallace's heroism or skill to note that he was fortunate in his adversary that day. Hugh de Cressingham, Edward's de facto viceroy in Scotland, wanted a quick victory, and rejected a plan to use the English cavalry to attack the flank of the Scottish line by crossing the river at a downstream ford; the initial sally over the bridge by the English foot had to be repeated when Surrey overslept, and called them back. When, in the late morning of September 11, the English finally began crossing again, this time in earnest, they had to do so over boggy ground, and across a bridge that could accommodate only two horses abreast. The Scots waited patiently until half the English army—five thousand infantry and a few hundred horse, led by Cressingham—had crossed, at which time a few dozen men, hidden at the crossing, cut away the causeway's supports. With the English split in two, Wallace and Moray led a charge down the crag and attacked Cressingham's force before they could form any kind of defense. Though the English foot still outnumbered their opponents, the Scots had what tacticians call local superiority: strung out, with the Forth at their backs, and unable to offer protection to one another's flanks, each pocket of a few dozen English soldiers could be isolated and cut to pieces by a hundred or more of Wallace's spearmen. Surrey, watching the massacre from the south side of the river, panicked, and ordered a retreat of the remaining English forces back to Berwick. Cressingham was killed, his body flayed, and pieces of his skin were sent throughout Scotland as a signal of the rebellion. According to the *Chronicle of*

Lanercost, Wallace used one long strip of Cressingham's skin as a "baldrick for his sword."

The victory at Stirling Bridge was total, and it inspired Scotland's fence-sitting nobility, particularly both John Comyns, one the earl of Buchan and the other the lord of Badenoch. But despite the overwhelming disparity in casualties—the best estimates have Surrey losing upward of five thousand men, while Wallace's losses numbered in the hundreds—the victory had other costs. The English invading force had lived off the land and severely depleted the Scottish crops just prior to harvest; the lowlands between Berwick and the Forth suffered a sharp but local famine through the fall and winter of 1297. The forces remaining at Stirling were rapidly running short of food and forage, and Wallace, in response, took his troops into northern England, confiscating all the Northumbrian grain he could carry and all the cattle he could drive, and carrying both as plunder back to Scotland.

Just as distressing as the lack of food was the loss of the earl of Moray, second only to Wallace as a leader of the rebellion, and certainly the one with the most strategic perspective: the best understanding that a war for Scottish independence was just as much about economic autonomy as military victory. His last official act, before he died from the wounds he received at Stirling Bridge, was the letter he and Wallace sent, on October 11, to the "worthy and beloved friends, the Mayors and citizens of Lübeck and Hamburg" (the key ports on the Baltic), notifying them that Scottish ports were once more open to trade with the Hanseatic cities.*

Also significant: in the letter, Wallace and Moray described themselves as "commanders of the army of the kingdom of Scotland, in the name of the famous prince lord John [Balliol], by God's grace illustrious king of Scotland, by consent of the community of the realm." The conflict was drawing a new portrait of just what that "community of the realm" was all about—whether it denoted the land, which was the traditional basis of feudal manorialism, or the people. In the old

---

*For more about the Hanseatic League, see chapter 10.

version, the people were secondary to the land, and their labor (and military service) followed whoever had the land in fief. The rebellion sundered that connection, since his troops fought for Wallace not as vassals but as Scots, and won their victory at Stirling Bridge not for a feudal lord, but for the community of the realm. Scotland, almost accidentally, had become an incubator for the infant idea of nationalism.

By the spring of 1298, William Wallace, whose family came of the lowest nobility in Scotland, became its de facto ruler. Sometime before March, Scotland's greatest warrior was finally knighted; certainly by an earl—very likely by Robert Bruce—and named "William Wallace, Knight, Guardian of the Kingdom."

The first act of the new Guardian was the formation of a new privy council that included Bruce, members of the Comyn family, and William Lamberton, a Benedictine monk and chancellor of Glasgow Cathedral whom he named bishop of St. Andrews, and so the effective head of the Scottish Church. King John Balliol continued to reign, but he no longer ruled (if, indeed, he ever had). Scotland's new Guardian was now the country's ruler, and, proving that he understood the niceties of Scotland's strategic and diplomatic position, Wallace proposed both a plan for a mutual aid treaty with France (to ensure that Edward would face attack from the south if he invaded Scotland) and charged Lamberton, the new bishop, with enlisting the pope against England when he reached Rome for his consecration.* Given that doing so required traveling past hostile English and—whenever the historic alliance between Scotland and France wasn't at its strongest—French armies, the journeys were the opposite of easy.

Far more ominously, at almost the same moment that Lamberton was named bishop of St. Andrews, and Wallace Guardian of Scotland, Edward I had returned to England from Flanders. After learning of the disaster at Stirling Bridge and Wallace's subsequent raids into Northumbria, he made a quick peace with Philip IV of France and raced home to find that the Scottish threat had, perversely, eased his

---

*From the standpoint of the church, Scotland was, except for some of the islands, a single province, and at the end of the thirteenth century, it was customary for all Scottish bishops to be consecrated by the pope directly.

ability to raise money for a punitive expedition. A year before, in order to pay for both Surrey's Scottish expedition and the alliance against France, the king had, by November 1297, demanded lay subsidies—essentially property taxes on all the moveable goods in the kingdom; that is, everything but real estate—amounting to more than £200,000. As a reminder that Edward's kingly authority wasn't any more absolute in the fourteenth century than King John's had been in the thirteenth when he had been compelled to sign the Magna Carta, the English nobility forced Edward to sign a document known as the "Confirmation of the Charters."* The Confirmation obliged Edward to foreswear taxing without the "will and assent of the Church, the earls, barons, knights, burgesses, and other free men of the kingdom."

After Stirling Bridge and Northumbria, and helped along by propaganda describing Wallace as a savage who flayed prisoners, killed babies, and raped nuns, assent was forthcoming. Edward announced a huge conscription of English troops and hired mercenaries from his feudal lands in Gascony and Wales until his total force numbered nearly fifteen thousand: twenty five hundred cavalry, and at least twelve thousand infantry (including more than two thousand Welsh bowmen). On June 25, 1298, he mustered them at Roxburgh and marched north, intent on earning the title he reputedly wanted inscribed in his tomb: "Hammer of the Scots."

His target was Edinburgh, but Wallace, badly outnumbered, avoided the English forces with constant westward marches. The obvious strategy was to remain out of reach of the superior army until it ran out of supplies and went home. And for a while, it worked. But although they could burn Scottish villages and fortifications (the king reportedly commanded one of his lieutenants, Sir John Fitz Marmaduke, "You are a bloodthirsty man, I have often had to rebuke you for being too cruel. But now be off, use all your cruelty, and instead of rebuking you I shall

---

*The charters in question were the Magna Carta and the Charter of the Forest, the latter forced upon Edward's father, Henry III in 1217, two years after the English barons did the same to his grandfather, King John. It's really a single document, the so-called Great Charter of the Liberties of England, and the Liberties of the Forest—still a live statute in England.

praise you"), they could not feed themselves from the lands they burnt. Edward's army was chronically short of food, despite the king's plan to resupply by sea. The Welsh archers, newly conquered and restive, threatened to desert to the Scots, and after a brawl with the English, were charged by the English cavalry, leaving eighty of them dead.

Why Wallace finally decided to give battle—despite his well-deserved reputation as an irregular fighter—is unclear, but on July 24, 1298, he arrived at Falkirk, thirteen miles west of Edinburgh, and waited.

The following day, Edward and his army arrived to find the Scots deployed into four *schiltroms*: infantry rings with spears facing outward, and front ranks kneeling. Each phalanx was protected by a series of wooden stakes hammered into the ground, and angled so as to disembowel a charging horse. In between each of the *schiltroms*, Wallace placed his bowmen, with his relatively small force of a few hundred cavalry on a hill behind. The Scottish spearmen, many of them veterans of Stirling Bridge, were both disciplined and confident of victory.

Their adversary, however, was no Hugh de Cressingham, or duke of Surrey. Edward of England was one of the most experienced and canny tacticians of his era, a victor in dozens of battles against everything from French castles to Arab light cavalry. The king responded to Wallace's deployment by dividing his own heavy cavalry into four columns and sequentially charging them against the Scottish line. They were unable to break the *schiltroms*, or even get past the stakes protecting them, but that wasn't their purpose. They were sent to scatter Wallace's mobile force and destroy his missile artillery: his archers.

The Scottish archers were overmatched. Their weapons were only about four feet long, and simple physics meant that the six-foot longbows carried by Edward's Welshmen (and the crossbows of his Gascon mercenaries) would easily outrange them. Without Scottish cavalry to worry about, the English king (whose horse had fallen, breaking two of the royal ribs) was able to place his archers in the front line, where they could fire each of the two dozen three-foot-long arrows they carried into battle into the *schiltroms*. And then reload and do it again.

Several hours of devastating volleys later, the *schiltroms* were fully exposed, allowing cavalry to charge through. Thousands of Scots died where they stood, including the earl of Fife. Though defeated, Wallace managed to escape; in legend, at least, with the help of Robert Bruce, who burned the town of Carrick and disappeared into the woods surrounding it.

The battle of Stirling Bridge stands as one of only a handful of times since the height of the Roman Empire that spear-wielding infantry defeated heavy cavalry. In the same vein, Falkirk is remembered because of the dominance of combined arms, particularly infantry-protected archers.

But there's another reason to recall Stirling and Falkirk. During the rebellion of 1296, John Balliol and Scotland's ruling council mobilized their army in the traditional way, calling for both "free service" and "Scottish service." The first was a call for freemen—freeholders, knights, sergeants, and nobility—to appear with arms appropriate to their respective ranks: knights in full armor, on warhorses protected by mail, and sergeants and freemen on horses "armored" in boiled leather. "Scottish service" referred to everyone else: men without horses, serving as infantry and wearing no body armor, wielding a spear or a "Lochaber ax"—a six-foot-long halberd, with a blade on one side and a hook on the other, well-designed for pulling a man from his horse. The troops Wallace led to victory at Stirling Bridge, and to defeat at Falkirk, on the other hand, weren't called to arms by "free service"; most of the knightly class in Scotland were unavailable because of the enforced homage required by the Ragman Roll (and, in any case, Scotland's last king was out of the country, the de facto prisoner of Edward Longshanks). The Scottish army was exclusively called to "Scottish service." The system that had evolved to manage and defend the arable land of Europe during its explosive growth during the Medieval Warm Period—feudal manorialism—was being undermined by a new kind of nationalism, at just the moment in history when four centuries of mild weather was coming to an end.

❧❧

CHAPTER THREE

"Penalty for Their Betters"

1298–1307

In the opening scene of *King Lear*, the title character displays the flaw at the heart of feudalism.

> Know that we have divided
> In three our kingdom: and 'tis our fast intent
> To shake all cares and business from our age;
> Conferring them on younger strengths, while we
> Unburthen'd crawl toward death.

Having offered each of his daughters a third of his kingdom, Lear expects the traditional feudal bargain: the lord grants land; the vassal pays with loyalty and obedience. But the bargain works only as long as the lord remains more powerful than the vassal. When the king is "unburthen'd" to the point that his only claim on his subjects is their love for him (Cordelia: "I love your majesty according to my bond, neither more nor less") the system collapses. Madness, blindness, and death follow.

Shakespeare, writing in 1606, was looking back at a regime that had been dead for at least a century. It had been a long time dying. As the thirteenth century turned into the fourteenth, the structure that had evolved to organize both the productive and destructive resources of European societies—feudal manorialism—wasn't yet in full retreat. But decline it did, for the next two centuries.

The reasons for its decline had little to do with the ones behind its ascent. It's an exaggeration to say that the manorial system was entirely *caused* by the four centuries of long summers and mild winters that marked the Medieval Warm Period. But neither is it a simple correlation. Europe's distinctive system of military obligation and land tenure would have looked very different had the region never experienced the population explosion of the MWP. On the other hand, it is a coincidence that feudal manorialism started to disappear at the same time as the MWP. Feudalism wasn't ended by a change in the climate, but the emergence of nations. England had a head start on that particular development (though France wasn't far behind) because of William of Normandy's transformation of his conquest from a patchwork of clans and petty kingdoms into a hierarchical feudal pyramid with himself at the top: legally the landlord of all England.

The pyramid outlasted its feudal roots; the monarchs at its top recognized that to delegate power to vassals was to risk ending up like Lear. English monarchs mostly managed to avoid that particular mistake, steadily increasing their own authority at the expense of their barons. When Edward Longshanks attempted to expand that authority over all Britain, he was doing so as a national sovereign, against a nation without one. No matter the charismatic leadership of William Wallace, Scotland needed a proper king if it was to survive.

Even before war with England gave a new urgency to the subject, the path to the Scottish throne had been a tangled maze, a game that demanded a mastery of legal forms, both secular and canonical; knowledge of half a dozen different family trees; and a willingness to resolve disputes with edged weapons. Dynastic conflict in fourteenth-century Scotland was as complicated, and as bloody, as anything in *Macbeth*. Small wonder, then, that the route of Robert le Brus was as straightforward as the shell of a nautilus.

The fallout from the Falkirk disaster wasn't long in arriving. By fall of 1298, Wallace resigned as Guardian, and his movements over the next seven years are almost impossible to document. Robert Bruce and John Comyn of Badenoch, were, in his absence, named the new Guardians of Scotland, both of them theoretically guarding the realm on behalf of John Balliol. In Badenoch's case, this was a triumph of hope over experience, as he had not only been soundly defeated by the earl of

Surrey the year before, but in his earlier stint as Guardian had agreed to invite Edward Longshanks to decide the fate of Scotland. Edward, meanwhile, returned to Carlisle, in England, to find his own nobles in passive rebellion, refusing to support a new tax—the term of the day was "subsidy"—needed to reprovision his army for another Scottish invasion.

Even without an English army to fight, Scotland continued the conflict. In July 1299, a raid on the English garrison at Roxburgh failed, revealing not only deficiencies in the nation's military capabilities with Wallace gone, but also severe strains in its political leadership. The insurgents were torn between fighting outside threats or internal rivals, and this time the inside game pitted supporters of Comyn against Bruce loyalists. At a meeting immediately following the failed raid, Comyn and Bruce came to blows—"John Comyn leapt at the Earl of Carrick and seized him by the throat"—and were restrained only by the intervention of James Stewart and the bishop of St. Andrews, William Lamberton.

By summer of 1300, after nearly a year of factional conflict, Bruce resigned as Guardian. A few months later Edward invaded the southwest of Scotland again, and was again met by what had become Scottish strategic doctrine: avoid direct battle, retreat, and destroy all the provisions in the invader's path—a tactic that forced the rural peasantry on both sides of the border to bear the cost of the war. The only real defense of the scorched-earth response was that it worked. In August, having never lost a battle—he barely fought one—but increasingly unable to supply his army and handicapped by the feudal convention that allowed his barons to refuse service for longer than eight weeks, Edward withdrew, offering Scotland a six-months' truce.

The Scottish leadership put the time to practical use. At the end of the year 1300, Comyn had, like Bruce, resigned his Guardianship. To replace them, a new Guardian was appointed: John de Soulis, a compromise candidate, related to the Comyns, son-in-law to the High Steward, a neighbor of the Bruces, and an undoubted patriot (and supporter of Balliol). He was also, unlike his predecessors, more diplomat than soldier, and he immediately opened a new front in the war with England.

De Soulis's strategic objective was to secure political support from Pope Boniface VIII, who remained, at least nominally, the sovereign of what was still widely referred to as Christendom; loosely speaking, the community of European Christians owing allegiance to the bishop of Rome.* The evolution of the papacy, from religious authority over only one of Christianity's important sees—from the fourth century to at least the seventh, the bishops of Alexandria, Antioch, and especially Constantinople frequently regarded themselves as independent of papal authority—was, like the Viking Age, armored knights, and vassalage, an unlikely consequence of the impact of the Medieval Warm Period on Europe.

Europe's only realistic structure for the control of its territories was feudalism; and, with the population explosion of the Medieval Warm Period, the only system for working that land was manorialism. The combination produced Europe's distinctive caste system, with wealthy and powerful nobles and sovereigns at the top; nowhere more than in Rome itself, where a half-dozen families played the feudal game of thrones in microcosm, with the throne of Saint Peter as the prize. By the eleventh century, it was a rich prize indeed, as the popes had more, and richer, feudal vassals than any secular ruler. The Cluniac order—so named for its home monastery in the Burgundian village of Cluny—had more than twelve hundred manors throughout Europe; and despite their notional adherence to the prayer-poverty-and-penance regimen described in the sixth-century Rule of Saint Benedict, their priors were as wealthy as any count or duke in France. The Cistercians, a defiant spinoff from the Cluniacs, administered more than eight hundred of their own monasteries from the Danube to the Derwent, including the most innovative factories and the most productive farms in Europe. Moreover, unlike secular fiefs, ecclesiastical ones never had to worry about the death of a lord, and subsequent squabbling over inheritance.

---

*For more on the medieval papacy, and its stormy relationship with the Holy Roman Empire that dates, more or less, from the coronation of Charlemagne in 800, see chapter 10.

Abbeys, monasteries, and priories were, like the Church itself, immortal, and the wealth produced by their vassals' productive labors, therefore, accumulated like an estate that could pass from generation to generation untaxed and undivided.

The ownership of real estate by legal entities that are theoretically immortal is known, formally, as *mortmain,* a portmanteau Latin word meaning "dead hand." The term suggests, correctly, how the practice was viewed by medieval jurists and kings. Bad enough that huge tracts of productive land were immune from the royal taxes due on the death of their owners; even worse that secular owners frequently bequeathed estates to the Church in order to avoid both tax collectors and feudal levies. Edward I hated the latter practice so much that he enacted two statutes, in 1279 and 1290, forbidding it without royal permission.*

Bequests of land were only one source by which the medieval Church enriched itself. Enormous donations were frequently made by European sinners in fear of the torments of hell. In an age of largely unquestioned faith, only the priests, bishops, and archbishops who were the vassals of the pope could offer or deny the sacraments that meant salvation. And they weren't especially shy about using their particular power. In 1095, Pope Urban II had mobilized the armies of Europe to retake the holy places of Jerusalem, in what became the first of the Crusades. Alexander II authorized and blessed the Norman invasion of England. Gregory VII excommunicated the Holy Roman Emperor Henry IV—twice—in a dispute over which of them had the right to nominate and invest bishops.

By its very nature, papal power increased with the expansion of feudal manorialism, because such a large number of feudal lords were bishops, priors, and the like, by custom and canonical law subject to the authority of the pope. And, of course, that's how it declined as well. All things come to an end, whether anomalously good climate,

---

*It's a common trope, in England and elsewhere. Beginning in 1539, Edward's several-times successor, Henry VIII, used his final break with Rome as a justification to confiscate the wealth and income of every monastery, priory, and convent in England and Wales.

feudalism, or papal authority, each of which was on its last legs by the end of the thirteenth century.

It was not a coincidence. As national sovereigns consolidated their own authority, the power and independence of their vassals declined. Kings could raise armies of their own, police their own territory, and—most important—tax their subjects. Popes couldn't, not without the consent of the secular rulers themselves. By the beginning of the fourteenth century, the ability of the bishop of Rome to control events was therefore in irreversible decline, but that didn't mean he was completely powerless. And if Boniface, who became pope in 1294, could no longer dictate to powerful monarchs like Edward I of England or Philip IV of France, he was far from impotent: Boniface's ability to influence events was greatest when two other parties were in conflict.* And so, John de Soulis, Scotland's new Guardian, turned his attention to Boniface early in 1300.

The battle for Boniface's support, fought out in salons and across dinner tables, with weapons like legal precedent and casuistry, lacked the cinematic character—cloth-yard arrows flying through the air; spears disemboweling warhorses—of the battles of Stirling Bridge or Falkirk. But it didn't want for drama. Ever since 1299, William Lamberton, named the new bishop of St. Andrews as one of Wallace's first acts as Guardian, had been Scotland's chief advocate in Rome, and while he had thus far failed to achieve victory, he had at least forestalled any sort of defeat. In 1300, he was joined by an even better-known defender of the cause of Scottish independence: William Wallace himself.

After resigning the Guardianship, Wallace had departed Scotland, leaving his onetime supporters somewhat dismayed that he had evidently given up the fight. They needn't have worried. Wallace's destination was France, where he planned to enlist Philip IV as an ally in his courtship of Rome. In this he succeeded, persuading the French king to provide him, on November 7, 1300, with a letter to Pope Boniface that read, in part:

---

*In 1296, Boniface issued a papal bull entitled *Clericos Laicos,* which forbade any priest or monk from paying any tax to any secular authority. Philip ignored it.

Philip by the grace of God, king of the French, to his beloved and loyal people appointed at the Roman Court, greetings and favour. We command you that you ask the Supreme Pontiff to consider with favour our beloved William le Wallace of Scotland, knight, with regard to those things which concern him that he has to expedite.

The "things" that concerned Wallace boiled down to only one: the pope's right to intervene in the conflict between Scotland and England—a position just as stubbornly denied by Edward's representatives, who presented it as a purely domestic matter, involving the rebellion of duly sworn vassals against their overlord. The Scottish strategy was to ask—over and over and over again—for a trial at papal court; the English response was to block, or at least delay, such a trial.

In early 1301, Lamberton and Wallace finally got their trial. The Scots may well have had the better argument, which was that when Edward accepted even a six-months' truce with an entity speaking in the name of the "community of the realm" of Scotland, he had de facto recognized it. Most likely, they also had the interests of the papacy on their side, since four centuries of papal authority depended on being the final court of appeal for all disputes in Christendom. Either way, in 1301, Boniface ordered Edward "for the love of Mount Zion and Jerusalem," to withdraw from Scotland, which he declared a fief of the Holy See, or face excommunication.

Edward, to the surprise of no one who had been paying attention during the twenty-eight years since he had been crowned, was not so easily intimidated. In July 1301, the gifted and proud English king is reported to have replied, "I will not keep my peace for Mount Zion nor silence for Jerusalem," and, for good measure, he invaded Scotland yet again, and with predictably inconclusive results. The truce that ended his brief incursion, to run until spring of 1303, was brokered not by the pope, but by Philip of France, now host to the French-born titular king of Scotland, John Balliol.

Philip's involvement added substance to the longstanding rumor of Balliol's return to Scotland at the head of a French army. The two people most concerned with such a prospect were Edward I and Robert Bruce, since the Comyns were almost certainly going to prosper in a Balliol-ruled Scotland; the earl of Buchan, after all, was Balliol's brother-in-law. On February 16, 1302, the sixty-three-year-old king of England and the twenty-eight-year-old earl of Carrick decided—for the moment, at least—that each had more interests in common than in conflict. Bruce admitted that he had joined Wallace's rebellion "through evil counsel" and formally submitted to Edward as a direct vassal. The king, in turn, promised that Bruce wouldn't be disinherited in the event of a Balliol return, and guaranteed that Bruce would keep

> life and limb, lands and tenements, and will be free from imprisonment [and] because the kingdom of Scotland may be removed from out of the king's [i.e., Edward's] hands . . . and handed over to Sir John Balliol . . . the king grants to Robert that he may pursue his right and the king will hear him fairly and hold him to justice in the king's court. If, by any chance, it should happen that the right must be adjudicated elsewhere than in the king's court, then in this case the king promises Robert assistance and counsel as before.

It was naked political cynicism. Bruce had, for the second time (if you count the Capitulation of Irvine) betrayed the Wallace rebellion purely for reasons of self-interest. His calculation here, however, was complicated by more than his desire to keep Balliol from the throne. Bruce had fallen in love with the teenage daughter of one of Edward's greatest vassals, the earl of Ulster, and in his case, the title referred to actual lands and estates; Richard de Burgh was the leading Norman noble in Ireland.

No record of the first meeting of Elizabeth de Burgh and Robert Bruce survives; though they were married in 1302, both the precise date and place are unknown. Even Elizabeth's age at the time of her marriage is nothing more than a guess, though she was certainly no more than eighteen. What is known is that she was beautiful, rich, and tremendously well connected (her father possessed huge tracts of land in England and Ireland, and her uncle was none other than James

Stewart, the High Steward of Scotland). Moreover, she and the young earl seem to have genuinely loved each other. Their love would be the marriage's only constant through decades of armed struggle, imprisonment, and enforced separation.

One partnership begun; another about to end. Any reduction in the potential threat France offered to England made Edward, *eo ipso*, more of a threat to Scotland. Thus, anything that distracted Philip of France made Scotland very nervous indeed. And, at the same time Robert Bruce was marrying Elizabeth de Burgh, just such a distraction appeared on France's northeast border.

France's troubled history with Flanders began, like just about everything else during Europe's Medieval Warm Period, with Charlemagne. Or, more accurately, with the division of the Carolingian Empire on the death of his son Louis the Pious in 840.* Four centuries later, the province—much of modern Belgium and northern France, from the Scheldt River to Calais—was nominally ruled by the count of Flanders, though his sovereignty was largely at the pleasure of whoever sat on the French throne.

The limits that a large and aggressive neighbor imposed on the Flemings' independence did nothing to restrain Flemish prosperity. By the end of the thirteenth century, Flanders was, with northern Italy, the wealthiest sector of Europe, with a per capita GDP at least 20 percent greater than France's, and 25 percent more than England's. It was also Europe's most urbanized region, with as much as 40 percent of its population living in towns, especially Bruges and Ypres. That this success story occurred in a county that was characterized by poor soil, a very high water table (the name "Flanders" is from the old Dutch word for "flooded"), and a set of extremely aggressive neighbors with violent tempers seems a mystery. One part of the solution is found in the Flemish climate.

The persistent Azores High, the high-pressure zone that was the likely cause of the warm and dry four centuries of the MWP in

---

*For more about the consequences of the partition of Charlemagne's brief empire, see chapter 10.

Europe, is a huge elliptical anticyclone—that is, an egg-shaped body of air with a clockwise rotation.* In such a formation, the areas of maximum curvature are at the two narrow ends of the ellipse, which is also where the pressure is highest. When the North Atlantic Oscillation carries warmer air from the Atlantic to Europe, as it did so frequently during the MWP, the eastern pressure ridge of the Azores High lies directly over Flanders. The resulting warming and drying of the various estuaries of the Scheldt River created the kinds of potential locations for the small towns that became characteristic of the county. Where towns and farms couldn't be built—on salt marshes, for example—the industrious Flemings built dikes around the reclaimed land, creating the pastures known as *polders*.† While the rest of Europe coped with population growth by converting forests into farmland, the Flemings turned swamps into towns and sheep pastures. The Flemish cloth industry was a direct, and very profitable, consequence.

Another consequence of the climate-driven growth of towns and textiles was that Flanders became the first place in northern Europe where commoners regularly became richer than the nobility; weaving cloth, it turns out, is far more productive than growing wheat. This made the relationship with England—the largest wool producer in Europe—more and more important, and therefore more and more troubling to the county's nominal suzerain, the king of France.

Edward I had been building alliances with Flanders since the 1270s, though, as the Scots could have told the Flemish, England's king wasn't the most constant of friends. In 1297, he made a separate peace with Philip IV, and gave his tacit approval to the French king's decision to not only annex the county, but to imprison Guy de Dampierre, count of Flanders, and his son, the future Robert III.

In the spring of 1302, Philip IV of France sent a force into Flanders

---

*In the Northern Hemisphere, anyway; in the Southern Hemisphere, counterclockwise.

†Their neighbors to the north, in Holland, had an even more dramatic problem; there storm floods made the drained land so vulnerable that it sank more than twenty feet, essentially turning the region into a group of barrier islands until the great dikes of the sixteenth century were finally built to keep the North Sea at bay.

in pursuit of rebels who had been agitating for independence. French troops could occupy the county without—as, again, the Scots could have warned—pacifying it. They didn't catch the rebels, but they did evict thousands of citizens of the prosperous Flemish city of Bruges from their homes. On May 18, the city's burghers returned, and massacred not only the French garrison, probably three hundred in all, but also every Fleming accused of collaborating with the enemy. The so-called Bruges Matin (in France) or Brugse Metten (in Flanders) was followed by a general call for troops throughout the county.

The weavers, carpenters, blacksmiths, and shepherds of the Flemish countryside answered the call. So did the merchants and artisans of the towns. Guy of Namur and Willem van Gulik—both members of Dampierre's family—were named to command, and they led their troops to a small victory at Oudenarde before arriving at the fortress town of Courtrai on the Lys River northeast of the textile city of Lille on June 26, and settling in for a siege. On July 8, a French relief force arrived.

Even more than Stirling Bridge, the Battle of Courtrai occupies the cliché space reserved for history's great turning points, this one in the history of warfare. The opposing sides were almost perfectly asymmetric: the Flemings—perhaps seven thousand of them—were almost all infantry, most of them armored in mail, and carrying either a long spear, known as a *geldon,* or a *goedendag,* essentially a baseball bat with a spear point.* Just as important were their shovels; the Flemings dug hundreds of ditches in anticipation of the arrival of French heavy cavalry, along a narrow canal connecting them to the Lys.

The French didn't disappoint. Robert of Artois led a traditional feudal force including around three thousand heavy cavalry, primarily knights with their squires and men-at-arms; a thousand crossbowmen, and four thousand infantry.

On the morning of July 11, van Gulik flooded the ditches and positioned his troops behind them in solid line, eight files deep, with their backs to the river. Count Robert attempted to break the line, first with

---

Goedendag means "good day" in Dutch, a language with an unappreciated gift for irony.

his crossbowmen, but their slow rate of fire, perhaps two quarrels every minute, evidently made him impatient enough to send his infantry into the attack. Had he better tactical sense, he might have let them continue to bloody the Flemings, but, like most commanders of the era, Robert's entire professional training had been as a mounted knight, and he wasn't about to reward foot soldiers with the glory properly owed to the cavalry. In three lines, the French cavalry charged, and foundered in van Gulik's ditches. As the first line was stopped by a combination of Flemish geldons and muddy ground, the second ran into them, followed by the third. Three thousand knights and squires were stopped dead in a constricted space from which they could neither advance nor retreat; and a cavalryman who can't maneuver is a very easy target indeed. When the Flemings finally advanced, in line, they turned the field into a slaughterhouse.

Some of the French were able to break off combat and attempted to retreat; others tried to surrender and discovered that the same class consciousness that prompted Count Robert to give the honor of the victory to his noblest troops worked just as well in reverse. Though the code of chivalry, sanctified through the centuries, allowed knights to surrender to other knights in the expectation that they would be ransomed, the code didn't consider an army of commoners. The Flemings wanted a victory, not a payday, and took no prisoners. More than half the French cavalry were killed outright, and at least seven hundred sets of spurs taken as trophies. Those trophies were subsequently displayed in the Cathedral of the Virgin in Courtrai, from which the battle takes its even better-known name: the Battle of the Golden Spurs.*

The lessons of Courtrai were profound. The battle dramatically changed the calculus of chivalric warfare. Since it cost ten times more to put a knight in the field than to arm and train a spearman, the total destruction of seven thousand heavy cavalry by three thousand infantry made a powerful case for what a modern strategist would call a reallocation of forces. Also: partly because of the greater population

---

*The spurs were retaken by the French two years later after the battle of Mons-en-Pévèle. However humiliating the defeat at Courtrai, to France, with a population fifteen times larger than Flanders, it was just a battle in what would be a very long war . . . as we shall see.

density of Flemish towns, the urban militias had more opportunity to practice drilling together than did a typical feudal army, which might be made up of units that met one another only on the day of a battle—a persuasive argument for a different sort of training. Moreover, soldiers fighting on their own land, and less entranced by the possibility of either personal glory or ransom, made for a scary force—even scarier when they had no expectation of a comfortable imprisonment while awaiting ransom for themselves. The Flemings had to choose between victory and death.

If it took some time for those lessons to sink in—the French were still learning them at Agincourt, more than a century later—the immediate impact wasn't negligible. In the words of the modern historian Geoffrey W. S. Barrow, "The history of [Scotland's] war of independence has no greater irony than the fact that the great upsurge of proletarian nationalism in Flanders . . . did more to make Scotland an English province than any other single event." The massacre at Courtrai was measured in the lives of thousands of French knights, but it also cost Scotland any possibility of a French ally in their fight against Edward, since until Flanders was pacified, France would be unable to present a credible threat to England. Less than a year later, in May 1303, Edward I and Philip IV signed a mutual defense treaty.

That same month, Edward, the prince of Wales and heir to the English throne, was betrothed to Philip's only daughter, Isabella.

Edward I was a gifted soldier and able administrator, a loving husband and a terror to his vassals and enemies alike, handsome, athletic, and tall. The laws of heredity, however, allowed him to bestow only the last three on his son. The life of the prince who would become King Edward II was memorably disastrous. For centuries, his best-known portrayal was by Christopher Marlowe, in the posthumously produced 1593 play *The Troublesome Reign and Lamentable Death of Edward II, King of England*. For present-day readers, the most vivid depiction is probably the effeminate prince bullied by his father and cuckolded by William Wallace in the movie *Braveheart*. This image of Edward has been remarkably consistent for centuries; as early as 1321, an anonymous poem, entitled *The Simonie, or the Evil Times of Edward II*, enumerated the king's military failures and personal scandals in 480 brutal stanzas.

The future prince of Wales was born at Caernarfon Castle on April 25, 1284, the youngest of (at least) fourteen children of Edward I and Eleanor of Castile.* Two of Edward's three older brothers died before he was born, and the third, Alfonso, only four months after. The loss of the rest of his siblings—his sisters to marriage, or the convent— was more or less completed by the deaths of his mother, in October 1290, and his grandmother, Eleanor of Provence, in June 1291. High mortality among young children and middle-aged adults was a demo- graphic fact of life in the Middle Ages—and in every age before the current one—and though tragic, Edward's early losses were typical of his family, and of his time and class.

Not that Edward's life was typical for anyone except royalty and the highest nobility. A prince lived at the top of a feudal pyramid that put remarkable financial pressure on the pyramid's base. A complaint recorded by the Annals of Dunstable in 1294 read:

> Two hundred dishes a day were not sufficient for [Edward's] kitchen. Whatever he spent on himself or his followers he took without paying for it. His officials carried off all the victuals that came to market, even cheese and eggs . . . they seized bread from the bakers and beer from the ale-wives, or if they had none, forced them to brew and bake.

This, even though the ten-year-old prince's expenses drew some £3,795 annually from the royal household accounts, which is worth somewhere more than £2 million today (by another method of calcu- lation, which measures it against the average wage, it would be more than £35 *million*; that is, the prince's household spent roughly eigh- teen hundred times as much as that of his typical subject).

---

*Despite the legends that Edward I had promised his recently conquered Welsh subjects a "native- born king," the investiture of the young Edward as Prince of Wales didn't occur until 1301.

Odd, therefore, that the most common complaints about the young prince—far more common than his profligacy—were his unkingly hobbies. Edward liked "thatching roofs, trimming hedges, plastering walls, working metal, shoeing horses, driving carts, rowing [and] swimming." For some reason, dozens of his bemused biographers note an enthusiasm for digging ditches, an activity at which he apparently took great joy. He wrote plays; fraternized with fools, actors, and rustics; gambled; caroused; and played, evidently with both enjoyment and skill, the Celtic violin (the *crwth*).

But princes do what princes must, and Edward, though an unlikely soldier, accompanied his father on the brief and inconclusive invasion of Scotland and was drafted again in May 1303. In his first campaign of 1300, the king had led more than nine thousand foot soldiers and eighty-seven bannerets of cavalry, with perhaps another eight thousand armed and horsed troops. The 1303 expedition, assembled as soon as the French-brokered truce of three years before had expired, was at least twice as large, though still not enough for the intimidating victory that the English king wanted; he even sent Robert Bruce, more prisoner than lieutenant, north to raise a Scottish force in Edward's name.

With at least five times as many soldiers as the combined forces marshaled against him, the opportunities for pitched battle were few. Instead, there was ruin. North and south of the Forth, riverbanks were dug up, dikes destroyed, orchards and croplands burned. King Edward, ever the military innovator, had ordered three bridges prefabricated and floated up the North Sea coast in order to cross the river Forth and besiege Stirling Castle from the north.

The invasion of 1303 was the fourth by Edward since the death of Alexander, and his patience—never in large supply—had entirely vanished. The king's ruthlessness toward the Scots, which would only grow over the remaining years of his life, is usually recorded as a personal failing: a streak of cruelty verging on sadism. There's a lot to recommend this perspective. The king delayed accepting an offered surrender from Stirling's defenders for four full days, just so he could continue battering at the walls, and threatening the defenders with disembowelment and hanging. More famously, his rage at William Wallace barely stopped at the edge of insanity.

Wallace had scarcely been heard from militarily (though he had been active diplomatically) since Falkirk, but he was still the symbol of Scottish resistance. And Edward knew it. King Edward was unable, during the 1303 campaign, to sign even a trivial document without a reminder that Wallace still awaited capture. When offering safe conduct to Scottish nobles, he would, for example, swear that he would "watch to see how each of them conducts himself so that he can do most favour to whoever shall capture Wallace." When Stirling fell, in July, it seemed that it would be only a matter of weeks before someone betrayed the rebel leader.

Actually, it took more than two years. After the invasion of 1303, Wallace, a spent force militarily, appeared only during minor skirmishes along the Scottish borderlands. The king, meanwhile, mended fences with his onetime adversaries, feasting some, while bribing others. No doubt it persuaded some Scottish nobility of the wisdom of betraying Wallace to Edward, but it took until the middle of August 1305 before the great symbol of Scottish resistance was captured, betrayed by a onetime follower, Sir John Menteith. Menteith is said to have blamed Wallace for the death of his brother, and—in legend at least—revealed his location to the English by turning a loaf of bread upside down in the tavern where he was taken.

After waiting more than nine years for his revenge, Edward's haste in delivering it appears almost unseemly. Less than two weeks after the capture of the rebel leader, on August 23, Wallace stood trial at Westminster Hall in London. Admitting all of his crimes, save treason—he argued, not without some logic, that he could not have committed treason against the English king for the simple reason that he had never sworn allegiance to him—he was nonetheless convicted of it, which exposed him to the cruelest of punishments of an age that made an art of them. The first documented appearance of the so-called traitor's death in England was its use by Henry III against a failed assassin in 1238. No doubt filial loyalty led to its adoption by Edward I, who sentenced the rebellious Welsh nobleman Dafydd ap Gruffydd to die by drawing and quartering in 1283. Tactics like the traitor's death are used for their shock value, which means that their utility as a deterrent declines with familiarity. By 1305, only the extraordinary would capture England's attention, and Edward's justice was equal to the task. Wallace was dragged alive for miles through the streets of London, then half-strangled by the hangman's noose. After, while still alive, he was castrated and disemboweled, his guts and genitalia burned. Then, and only then, was he beheaded, and his body hacked into four parts, with one quarter each sent to Newcastle, Berwick, Stirling, and Perth. Wallace's head was mounted on London Bridge as a warning to anyone who might be tempted to rebellion.

The king's obsession with the capture and—there is no other word—obliteration of William Wallace seems to be more than garden-variety brutality, even in such an unimaginably bloodthirsty age. Edward had permitted Scottish nobles like Comyn to go free after defeat, and they were far guiltier of betraying a solemn oath than was Wallace, who never gave one, and went to his death saying so. Whether or not Wallace, a knight and vassal of King John Balliol, deserved the title, the king saw him as an outlaw who had somehow become a national hero. Because he was a commoner leading a national (rather than feudal) army, Wallace was a reproach to everything that supported Edward's own kingship. Feudal justice and the codes of chivalry allowed that opponents could be placated, once defeated. Outlaws could only be destroyed, *pour encourager les autres.*

The Scots took the hint. In May, the newly pacified nobles assembled a parliament at Perth, and named a ruling council, to include Robert Bruce; William Lamberton, the bishop of St. Andrews; and John Comyn, Lord of Badenoch. On the surface, Edward, who now insisted that the council ruled "the community of the *land* of Scotland" rather than "the community of the *realm*"—a bit of hairsplitting that nonetheless underlined his legal position—had won, and was prepared to be magnanimous, particularly toward the earl of Carrick and his family. Robert's brother, Edward Bruce, received a much-coveted position in the household of the prince of Wales; another brother, Alexander—an extraordinary scholar; "no one who read arts at Cambridge before or since his time ever made such progress"—was made Dean of Glasgow.

Bruce's actions in support of the various insurrections had been fairly covert, after all. He appears to have sabotaged the transport of some key components of the siege machines that Edward used to hammer Stirling Castle, and was more than dilatory in providing levies when demanded. On April 4, 1304, he had written to the king that he had "no success whatever in his attempts to borrow for the purpose [of procuring horses and armor]." He had been even more circumspect in his relations with Wallace. The most dramatic version of the dynamic between Wallace and Robert Bruce is one in which the former is the supremely honorable hero, whose only goal was the freedom of his nation; and Bruce little more than an opportunist, ambitious for his own family and glory. It works so well as drama because it has a lot of truth to it; Bruce made common cause with Edward I for years both before and after Wallace's capture. But it misses the whole truth; on half a dozen occasions, Bruce was ordered to capture Wallace in Selkirk Forest, but each time, he seemed to have gotten a warning to the target in advance.

Whatever face Bruce presented to King Edward, he kept another one turned to Scotland. A year before the capture of Wallace, on June 11, 1304, Bruce signed a secret pact with Lamberton—ostensibly innocent, actually a conspiracy against the Crown—that called for them "to resist prudently attacks by rivals . . . to provide help and succor to one another at all times and without any deceit. Neither Bruce nor Lamberton will attempt any major enterprise without consulting his colleague, and each will warn the other of any danger and try to obviate it." Insofar as anyone can read the minds of the two conspirators, their plan seems to have been to wait for King Edward—who was, in 1305, already sixty-six years old—to die.

What forced everyone's hand was the position of the lord of Badenoch. The details are a little short on documentation—the primary source is the 1375 epic poem *Le Brus,* written by John Barbour, archdeacon of Aberdeen—but the story is that Bruce and Comyn had, in October 1305, each signed and sealed documents pledging a bargain:

Whoever was to be the next king of Scotland would give up his feudal lands to the other. That is, if Comyn became king, he would grant his Badenoch estates to Bruce; if Bruce were crowned, then Comyn would receive both the earldom of Carrick and Annandale, which Bruce had inherited on the death of his father the previous year. Supposedly, in January 1306, Comyn informed the king of the existence of the letters and promised to deliver his copies, thus sentencing Bruce, then at Edward's court in London, to death.

The story continues: Edward announced his plans to arrest Bruce in the presence of Ralph de Monthermer, the king's son-in-law, and one of Bruce's supporters and friends. When Bruce received a rather poetically coded message from de Monthermer—a silver shilling with Edward's portrait stamped on it, and a pair of spurs—he knew enough to pack up family and retainers, and head for the safer precincts of the north. En route, in one of those dramatic coincidences that are too contrived to be true but too satisfying to remain untold, Bruce and his party encountered a Scotsman riding the way they had come. Bruce's suspicions aroused, the man was searched and found to be carrying the letter that Comyn had promised Edward.

Whether because of the discovery of his betrayal, or some other reason, there's no doubt that Bruce did send a message to Comyn, asking for a meeting in Dumfries, in Scotland's southwest, on February 10. The truth is that no one knows what was said when the two left their men outside Greyfriars Church and met at the church's altar, but the result is clear: Bruce stabbed Comyn with his dagger and left him to die; in Barbour's version, Bruce's follower, Roger Kirkpatrick, informed that Bruce believed he had killed Comyn, replied, "I'll make sure" (*"mak siccar"*) and returned to the church to do just that.

Barbara Tuchman, in *A Distant Mirror*, her chronicle of the fourteenth century, notes that the "childishness noticeable in medieval behavior, with its marked inability to restrain any kind of impulse, may have been simply due to the fact that so large a proportion of active society was actually very young in years." In February 1306, however, Bruce was thirty-two years old, and lacked that particular excuse. He was now a murderer, with every one of Comyn's relatives and friends out for his blood, as well as a public traitor to the most powerful ruler in Europe. Bruce's choice was simple: exile or rebel. He chose rebellion.

The odds weren't favorable. There was, however, one way to improve them. For twenty years, the Scottish Church had been the most consistent and powerful voice behind a free Scotland (and, therefore, a church free of English dominance), and it hadn't lost faith in Bruce as its best guarantee. Bruce confessed Comyn's murder to Andrew Wishart, bishop of Glasgow—along with Lamberton of St. Andrews, and David de Moravia, bishop of Moray, the most important prelate in Scotland—and was given absolution, not just for the murder but the sacrilege of killing him in Greyfriars Church.

With the Church behind him, Bruce moved very fast indeed. In weeks, he gathered a force of loyal men-at-arms, and, using the element of surprise, captured the castles that dominated the western approaches to Scotland, giving himself a strategic buffer against the expected English punitive expedition. He established a route for reinforcements and supplies, both from western Scotland and Ireland.

And he declared himself king.

On March 23, 1306, Robert Bruce, earl of Carrick and lord of Annandale, was crowned in the Abbey of Scone in robes and vestments that had been hidden for more than a decade (though without, of course, the Stone of Destiny, still in Westminster) in a ceremony that was attended by at least five earls and four bishops, including Wishart, who performed the coronation. Tradition called for the crown to be placed on the new king's head by the earl of Fife, who was a ward of the English king and, as cousin to the murdered John Comyn, hostile to Bruce. His sister, however, was another matter. Undeterred by her brother's status as a de facto hostage, Isabel of Fife, countess of Buchan, raced to Scone, arriving two days after the coronation, and, in a repeat ceremony, placed the crown on Robert's head.

Robert Bruce's betrayal might have been easier for King Edward to bear had relations with his son and heir been congenial. In fact, the king of England was as much at war with his own household as with the Scottish rebels, to the point that on June 14, 1305, the prince of Wales was banished from court. The proximate cause seems to be a dispute between young Edward and one of his father's favorites, Walter Langton, bishop of Coventry, over poaching on the bishop's lands. Since a punishment like banishment was grossly disproportionate for such a peccadillo, the true reason must have been something else. The something else was almost certainly a courtier named Piers Gaveston.

Gaveston was, at the time of Edward's banishment, a twenty-one-year-old nobleman, born in the part of Gascony that was still a fief of the king of England; his father, Arnaud de Gaveston, was an old companion of Edward I, who appointed Piers a squire of the royal household, and, in 1298, one of the *pueri in custodia*: official companions of Edward Caernarfon.

One chronicler, in the 1320s, wrote that when "the king's son saw [Gaveston] he fell so much in love that he entered upon an enduring compact with him, and chose and determined to knit an indissoluble bond of affection with him, before all other mortals." The *Vita Edwardi Secundi*, an anonymous history written around 1326, took a more classical tone: "Jonathan cherished David, Achilles loved Patroclus. But we do not read they were immoderate. Our King, however, was incapable of moderate favour, and on account of Piers was said to forget himself, and so Piers was accounted a sorcerer." Thomas Burton, the Cistercian leader of the Abbey of Meaux, describes Edward as "too much given to sodomy."* Robert de Reading, a monk of Westminster and author of the *Flores Historianum*, a well-regarded chronicle of the day, wrote that the king was "overcome with his own wickedness and desire for sinful, forbidden sex."

Even if no one can know the complete truth about what went on in the prince's bedchamber, it was absolutely clear that their contemporaries thought that Edward and Gaveston were lovers, and, for the king, that was enough.

King Edward's distaste for even the possibility of homosexuality

---

*Unsatisfyingly, he doesn't say what amount of sodomy would be less than "too much."

was, perversely enough, evidence of what had been until then a widespread and not especially notorious practice. Through the thirteenth century, ceremonies that can only be called homosexual marriages—so-called spiritual brotherhoods that were sanctified by priests, using the same prayers as "traditional" marriages, including the joining of right hands at the altar, followed by the ceremonial kiss—were being performed in churches throughout the Mediterranean. Alcuin, the most famous of the scholars at the court of Charlemagne, wrote a letter to a bishop that reads

> I think of your love and friendship with such sweet memories, reverend bishop, that I long for that lovely time when I may be able to clutch the neck of your sweetness with the fingers of my desires. Alas, if only it were granted to me, as it was to Habakkuk, to be transported to you, how would I sink into your embraces.

During the fourteenth century, however, what had been tolerated, though not universally applauded, became criminal. A year after young Edward's banishment, in 1306, the Byzantine emperor decreed that sex between men would henceforth be a prohibited activity in the same category as incest and sorcery. The same month that the king of England banished his son, a new pope, Clement V, had been selected, and he made his first order of business the promotion of the royal wedding of Edward and Isabella, even going so far as to request that a proxy marriage between the two be held at his own coronation in November. Hardly anything could make the price of Edward's rumored affections for Gaveston more obvious, and Edward I determined to counteract them by separation. It can't have helped much that one of the prince's regular requests, during the months estranged from his father, was that Gaveston be allowed to join him.

It's too much to say that by spring of 1306 all was forgiven. However, the urgency of the situation in Scotland trumped King Edward's worries about his son's supposed degeneracy, and he once again prepared to teach his northern vassals a lesson. He was clever enough to realize that his English subjects might be wearying of invading

Scotland every year or two, and he set out to promote the latest re-
vival of this particular long-running drama as a crusade, comparable
to the struggle to liberate Jerusalem from the infidels. On May 22, in
a lavish and public ceremony, the king knighted his son and several
dozen other young noblemen, and granted the prince of Wales the
duchy of Aquitaine as his personal fief. In front of three hundred
knights gathered at Westminster Hall, King Edward publicly swore
vengeance for the murder of John Comyn; Edward the prince vowed
never to sleep two nights in the same bed until he reached Scotland,
and almost immediately headed north. The positioning of the prince
of Wales as a newborn Sir Lancelot—a cynical, but understandable,
bit of political theater produced by his father—was successful enough
that Barbour himself, writing his poem about Robert Bruce more than
sixty years later, described young Edward in 1306 as "the strongest
man of any that you could find in any country."

Strong, possibly. Ruthless, certainly. The 1306 campaign was the cruelest yet; the king sent his son north, accompanied by Aymer de Valence, earl of Pembroke (and the murdered John Comyn's brother-in-law)
leading a force of three thousand cavalry. They were directed by the
king to be as calculatedly brutal as possible—to, in the parlance of the
time, "raise the dragon banner": to fight without quarter. The prince
took his charge seriously. He "would spare neither sex nor age. Wherever he went, he set fire to villages and hamlets and laid them waste
without mercy." It was too much even for the king, who rebuked his
son, though less for his brutality than for his choice of targets—bad
strategy to make the rural poor pay "the penalty for their betters, as the
rich had taken to flight." Not for the first time, war was brought to the
borderlands of England and Scotland.

History's true losers aren't vanquished adversaries, but victims: In
fourteenth-century Europe, and especially in the wars between Scotland and England, those who paid the harshest price for both victory
and defeat, in times of dearth and even in the soon-to-disappear times
of plenty, were the villagers.

Versions of villages date from the Bronze Age, and Iron Age

Europe started using some sort of cultivation plan around 600 BCE that was different from simple slash-and-burn agriculture. Slave-manned villas—whence the name—appeared in Roman-occupied Gaul during the first century BCE, and peasant-run plantations, with freemen cultivating their own plots, were a fixture throughout the later Roman empire as legionaries were pensioned off to farms from Spain to the Balkans. But the first multigenerational agricultural enterprises that resemble what we think of as the classic medieval village—an enduring nucleus of dwellings surrounded by cultivated land—didn't make an appearance until the tenth century.

Medieval British villages were therefore widespread long before Duke William defeated King Harold at Hastings; the 1086 Domesday Book named more than thirteen thousand of them, most with fewer than four hundred acres under cultivation. After a few centuries of consistently mild weather, a typical open-field village might cover more than a thousand acres, its barns and sheds concentrated in the center. In northern Europe, unlike the Mediterranean, where topography caused most villages to be built around hilltop castles, the church or manor occupied by the landlord was usually centrally located as well. Pastures, meadows, orchards, and plowed fields surrounded the nucleus. The demesne—the land whose produce was exclusively for the use of the lord—would usually take up a hundred acres or so; the remainder of the land was farmed by free tenants, villeins, and serfs, or given over to pasture and meadow. Almost every village was built near a stream or river partly for irrigation, mostly for the power to operate at least one mill for grinding flour, possibly another for fulling—that is, cleaning and matting wool fibers to strengthen them; "felt" shares an etymological root—probably a church, certainly a well or two. A decent-sized village might have three or four mills, plus a forge and bakery (each one owned by the lord, and leased to the miller, the smith, and the baker), but four out of ten villages were home to fewer than four hundred people, and only one in ten had more than six hundred.

Even so, some 80 percent of Edward's subjects—whether they accepted the name, or, as in Scotland, didn't—lived in such villages.

Their housing was as basic as possible: long halls, perhaps forty feet by fourteen, timber-frame, covered with branches smeared with clay in the construction technique known as "wattle-and-daub." A croft in the back might be home to a small kitchen garden. People lived at one end, animals at the other. Village houses were rebuilt constantly as roads were constructed, rivers changed course, and men with weapons marched by. Some rural villages were relatively prosperous, some impoverished. Some grew more or less of one crop or the other, while others depended—more or less—on livestock. However quaint they seem to the modern imagination, though, their most salient characteristic to medieval eyes was their vulnerability.

Because they were almost inevitably built along roads—they had to be, in order to have any chance of getting their goods to markets, on average more than six miles away—they were just as inevitably in the path of armies marching to war. Only the largest were fortified, and even then any defenses were primarily for the barns, dairies, orchards, kitchens, and residences of the secular or ecclesiastical lord who held the manor in fief.

In any case, fortifications were no defense against the unremitting harshness of agrarian life. The rural population of Europe, even during the gentle years of the thirteenth century, was always only one bad harvest away from starvation. The system on which the entire structure depended was fragile beyond belief: a single bridge destroyed by floods might starve a country for months; an iced-in harbor could halve the calories available to an entire region.

And even when things were good, they were bad. Farming is a hard life. Skeletons exhumed from rural medieval graves reveal that their onetime owners were almost universally afflicted with severe osteoarthritis, bone deformation, and the brittle, ivory-like degeneration known as eburnation. Harvesting using an eighteen-inch sickle (the scythe wasn't widely used in Europe until the sixteenth century) is a repetitive movement, and forced farmers to spend dawn to dusk bent at the waist. A threshing flail weighs more than twenty pounds, and must be brought down on harvested grain twelve times a minute, for hours at a time. The total caloric expenditure was comparable to what one might find in someone training for the Olympic Games. Not, however, the input: except when times were flush, hunger and malnutrition were endemic. In most villages, the value of each additional pair of hands for sowing and harvesting was uneasily balanced by the cost of every additional mouth.

For some villagers, one answer to the difficulties of rural life was to leave it—for the market towns and cities, and, for some, as volunteers to serve in the king's wars. Not many, though; a feudal levy that demanded even ten thousand foot soldiers would offer employment to fewer than one man from each village. For most of the rural population, the only response was stoic endurance, when, as was the case in the 1306 invasion, those levies were commanded to destroy the crops, houses, and barns that must have seemed identical to the ones in which they were born.

During 1306, the villagers on the Scottish borderlands witnessed one indecisive skirmish after another. Bruce won no victories—in fact was ambushed and defeated, more than once—and was on the run from the English when his wife, Elizabeth Bruce; the king's sister, Mary; and Isabel, countess of Buchan were captured. When King Edward had ordered no quarter for rebels, he had also declared that the wives of his enemies were likewise outlaws, which made them subject to rape or murder without consequence. Neither Isabel nor Mary Bruce were raped, but their punishment was nonetheless barbaric: wooden cells—cages, really—were built and attached to the walls of Berwick and Roxburgh castles, where each one was imprisoned. They would spend the next four years as a public warning to other rebels. Only Elizabeth Bruce escaped such a sentence, and only because she remained the daughter of the loyal earl of Ulster. Even so, she would be kept under house arrest for the next eight years.

At that, the women were gently treated compared to the captured men. Dozens, perhaps hundreds, were executed. Simon Fraser, a knight who had fought with Wallace and Moray before joining Bruce, was given the traitor's death of drawing, hanging, quartering, and beheading. So were Bruce's companion Christopher Seton and two of

Bruce's brothers: Neil, and Alexander, the scholarly dean of Glasgow. John of Strathbogie, the earl of Atholl was captured and hanged in London, his body burned and head displayed on a spike on London Bridge. He was the first earl to be executed in England in more than two centuries.

But while King Robert spent the latter half of 1306 on the run, news of him and his band of followers moving from cave to cave, eating roots and berries, and wrapping their feet in animal skins when their shoes wore out, spread across lowlands and highlands, becoming legend. Another fourteenth-century chronicle, John Fordun's *Scotichronicon*, reads:

> [After] mishaps, flights, and dangers; hardships and weariness; hunger and thirst; watchings and fastings; nakedness and cold; snares and banishment; [and] the seizing, imprisoning, slaughter, and downfall of his near ones and—even more—dear ones (for all this he had to undergo, when overcome and routed in the beginning of his war) no one, now living, I think recollects, or is equal to rehearsing, all this. Moreover, with all the ill-luck and numberless straits he went through with a glad and dauntless heart . . . in the art of fighting and in vigour of body, Robert had not his match in his time, in any clime.

By February 1307, accompanied by only a few hundred men, Bruce was ready to return to mainland Scotland; the first reliable sighting of the refugee king was at the start of Lent, which began that year on February 8.

Scotland's strategic objective was the same as before: An independent country, free of English control. Scottish tactics, though, were about to change, since fighting set-piece battles with knights on horseback serving as shock troops was destined to be a losing game against an opponent who could field five or ten times as many heavy cavalry. This was a hard truth for the king of Scotland. Robert Bruce had been, before taking the throne, a tourney knight of enormous reputation; possibly the best in Britain, where tournaments—week-long competitions in which dozens of knights fought one another, either singly in jousts, or in melees with up to forty or more on a side—had been one of the keystones of chivalry since the Norman invasion.

Whatever their actual value as military training (and both Stirling and Courtrai had already revealed the limitations of heavy cavalry), tournaments were unquestionably good at reinforcing a mastery of, and respect for, the shock attack of armed-and-armored knights. The Robert Bruce who had been defeated in 1306 was a product of the tournament world; the one who returned in 1307 was about to transform himself into one of the great guerrilla commanders in history, with notable results for the peasantry of both Scotland and England. The famous verse known as "Good King Robert's Testament" is an explicit guide to his strategy:

> On foot should be all Scottish war
> Let hill and marsh their foes debar
> And woods as walls prove such an arm
> That enemies do them no harm
> In hidden spots keep every store
> And burn the plainlands them before
> So, when they find the land lie waste
> Needs must they pass away in haste
> Harried by cunning raids at night
> And threatening sounds from every height
> Then, as they leave, with great array
> Smite with the sword and chase away,
> This is the counsel and intent
> Of Good King Robert's Testament

"On foot should be all Scottish war." In May 1307, with only six hundred Scots infantry by his side, King Robert defeated a three thousand–man force led by his old adversary Aymer de Valence in a battle at Loudon Hill in Ayrshire, using the same tactics as Wallace used at Stirling Bridge: channeling English knights along a narrow causeway through a bog, restricting their shock value, and permitting

Scottish spearmen to kill both horses and men. It was Bruce's first major victory and another reminder of the vulnerability of mounted knights.

If 1307 was the year that rebellion was reborn in Scotland, it marked a very different transformation in England. On July 7, Edward I died. One of his eulogists, John of London, declaimed, "Once with Alexander, king of Macedon, we defeated the kings of the Medes and the Persians and subdued the provinces of the East. Now, at the end of time, with great King Edward, we have borne a ten-year war [and] invaded Scotland and cut down her tyrants at the point of the sword."

With the death of Edward I, a man of titanic ambition and even greater fury passed from the earth. It was the bad luck of his successor, the second Edward, to live and rule in his shadow, obliged to continue his father's policies without anything like his father's genius for administration, or his force of will. Even worse, he would have to contend, as his father had not, with an able and determined Scottish king, who had mastered a strategy that made English military strength next to useless.

Two and a half centuries before, the future of Britain had been decided by three of the Norsemen—Duke William of Normandy, King Harold Godwinson, and Harald Hardrada—who had spread throughout Europe as a direct result of the four centuries of the Medieval Warm Period. Now two of William's descendants—two more Normans, Edward II and Robert Bruce—would do the same.

Precisely at the moment when the temperate years were about to end.

CHAPTER FOUR

"Douglas's Larder"

1307–1312

In January 1307, six months before his death, Edward Longshanks received an entreaty from his son and heir. Edward the younger had asked his father for permission to give Piers Gaveston a title—not just any title, but one of his own: the county of Ponthieu, which had been part of the dowry of his mother, Eleanor of Castile. King Edward's response was characteristically tender:

> You baseborn whoreson! Do you want to give lands away now, you who never gained any? As the Lord lives, if it were not for fear of breaking up the kingdom, you should never enjoy your inheritance.

As reported by the Augustinian monk Walter of Guisborough, the king proceeded to grab his son by the hair, pulling out as much as he could, and then throw him bodily from the room. He next exiled Gaveston, not to return to England except "at the pleasure of the king," who softened the blow somewhat by providing £66 annually for his living.

Even so, the king's death, on July 7, was a liberating event for his son, who recalled his favorite from exile less than a week later. By the end of the month, he issued his first charter, making Gaveston the new earl of Cornwall.* And by the fall, Edward and Gaveston had re-

---

*Earldoms, in England, remained titles in the gift of the king, who could create them as needed, since they were unconnected with any particular lands; the previous earl of Cornwall, Edmund, had died seven years earlier, and the title had been vacant ever since.

turned to London, in time for the latter's marriage to the new king's fourteen-year-old niece, Margaret de Clare, arranged, according to the *Vita*, to "strengthen Piers, and surround him with friends."

Like so many things involving Edward and Gaveston, the plan backfired: following the wedding, the new king announced a great tournament, at Wallingford, to celebrate the nuptials, which—the *Vita* again—"roused the earls and barons to still greater hatred of Piers." With the earls of Surrey, Arundel, and Hereford taking the field against him, Gaveston summoned the "younger and harder knights of the kingdom" to embarrass the presumably older and softer nobles. As one might expect, this failed to endear the king's favorite to anyone.

One of the most consistent themes of Piers Gaveston's life was his unerring talent for giving offense. Most of this was his own doing, but not all. To England's class-conscious great nobles, his ascent from the minor gentry into the king's circle was the very definition of social climbing. They were insulted by his investiture as an earl in his own name, and his marriage, less than six weeks later, to the daughter of one of the greatest peers in England.

Those objections were, however, drowned out by the preparations for another wedding: the far more important marriage between Edward and Isabella of France, to whom he had been betrothed for four years, and which, now that the princess was closer to marriageable age, had been scheduled for the following January.

The daughter of Philip IV was, in 1308, about twelve years old, though evidence for birthdates as early as 1291 exist. She had been raised in the richest and most cultivated court in Europe, where she had certainly been taught to read and, possibly, to write. She was also widely regarded as the most beautiful princess—possibly the most beautiful woman—in Europe. The French chronicler Godefroy de Paris described her as "the most beautiful woman in the kingdom and the Empire." Walter of Guisborough called her "one of the fairest ladies in the world." She was certainly one of the best dressed. The trousseau assembled for her wedding included dozens of dresses and seventy-two headdresses. Her personal tailor managed a staff of sixty seamstresses alone, and her *Household Book* records that they produced, in a single year, fifteen robes, thirty pairs of stockings, thirty-six pairs of shoes, four cloaks, six hoods, six bodices, and enough tunics and underclothes that they used up thirty pounds of candles working after sunset.

Maintaining such luxury was inevitably going to represent a large and ongoing drain on the royal purse. Isabella's dowry, negotiated at exhausting length over the preceding four years, included all the lands previously held by Eleanor of Castile before her marriage to Edward I, including the disputed lands in Gascony over which the two kingdoms had been battling for a century, which produced £4,500 annually—more than the wages of two thousand laborers. And that wasn't all: her father had provided her with at least 18,000 *livres tournois*, or another £4,500 in gold, jewels, and silverplate—at least £3 million (or $5 million) in modern currency—probably confiscated from the crusading order known as the Knights Templar, two thousand of whom had been arrested in France in November 1307.*

Here was the woman who brought Edward across the narrow channel separating England from France. He had planned to leave before Christmas 1307, but chose instead to spend the holiday with Gaveston. The favorite had been named to serve as Keeper of the Realm during the time the king would be in France, no doubt cementing the affection of the same nobles who had been humiliated by Gaveston's friends in the Wallingford tournament two months before. In any event, Edward departed Dover on January 22, and arrived in Boulogne-sur-Mer three days later, the victim of the winter weather that had frozen ports all along Europe's Baltic coast. In retrospect, it was a bad omen about both the end of the Medieval Warm Period's mild winters, and the beginning of an exceptionally stormy marriage. In front of the extraordinary assemblage of royalty and nobles—seven different serving monarchs, plus Edward himself; and half a dozen future ones, including three of the bride's brothers—the two were married by the city's bishop in his own cathedral church. Eight

---

* For more about the Templars, see chapter 8.

days of celebrations, feasts, and tournaments followed, until the new king and queen of England departed for home, and their respective coronations.

Edward and Isabella entered London on February 19 (they had spent two weeks at Eltham Palace, the home of Antony Bek, the bishop of Durham). The capital city was then home to about fifty thousand people, which made it the largest city in Britain, though still smaller than either Granada or Seville in Spain; Venice or Milan in Italy; and much smaller than the new queen's home in Paris, whose population was at least four times larger. Its most notable structure was still the Tower of London, originally built by William the Conqueror, but much enlarged by Edward I; the first Saint Paul's Cathedral was still being built in 1308, and would not be completed for four more years. It was typical of the city, which was one large construction zone: Westminster Hall was under reconstruction, as was the Palace of Westminster, whose restoration was personally overseen by Edward II in the months after his father's death. The Tower of London was being enlarged to accommodate new and luxurious apartments—including a menagerie for the royal pets—to go along with its treasury (not *the* Treasury, which, with the Exchequer, were in the Palace of Westminster) and arsenal.

On February 25, 1308, Edward and Isabella were crowned king and queen of England in Westminster Abbey. All the important nobles in England, and many from continental Europe, were in attendance. The king's scepter was carried by Humphrey de Bohun, earl of Hereford and Essex; the earl of Lancaster carried the sword *Curtana*, the ceremonial sword of Edward the Confessor. Henry de Lacy, the earl of Lincoln, carried the royal staff, and the king's younger brother, Henry, the rod. But the star was Piers Gaveston, the newly made earl of Cornwall; not surprisingly, since he had been picked by Edward to manage the proceedings, and had given himself all the best parts. Dressed in imperial purple, he redeemed the sword *Curtana*, carried in the crown of Saint Edward, and attached the ceremonial spur to the new sovereign's right boot as he sat on the throne constructed to house Scotland's Stone of Destiny. Gaveston's talent for annoying everyone but the king had reached hitherto unsuspected heights, and this time included both the new queen (who noticed that Gaveston was wearing some of the jewels included in her wedding gifts) and her uncles, the dukes of Evreux and Valois, who were disgusted when the king chose to sit next to Gaveston rather than the queen at the subsequent feast.

The new king's coronation rituals were the same as his father's. His coronation oath was not. It contained a clause additional to the traditional three: a promise "to be held by the just laws and customs that the community of the realm should determine." Given subsequent events, the plain meaning seems to have been this: England's highest nobility intended to assert their control over the new king—control that had been essentially invisible with his father.

At this particular moment in history, the "highest nobility" meant England's earls, since no more exalted title would exist until 1337. When Edward II was crowned, the realm had sixteen earldoms, but only twelve earls, since a number were doubled up due to inheritance, marriage, or good luck. Chief among them was Thomas, earl of Lancaster, Derby, and Leicester (and, upon the 1311 death of Henry de Lacy, earl of Lincoln as well). Lancaster was the wealthiest man in the kingdom, except for the king himself, and possibly not even him, with an annual income exceeding £11,000. Only slightly behind Lancaster in stature were Humphrey de Bohun, earl of Hereford and Essex, and the husband of Elizabeth Plantagenet, the new king's sister; and Guy de Beauchamp, earl of Warwick. Completing the list were Gaveston himself, the newly made earl of Cornwall; John de Warenne, earl of Surrey; Aymer de Valence, earl of Pembroke; Edmund FitzAlan, earl of Arundel; Gilbert de Clare, earl of Hertford and Gloucester (and Gaveston's father-in-law); Richard de Burgh, earl of Ulster (and Robert Bruce's father-in-law); John of Brittany, earl of Richmond; and Robert de Vere, earl of Oxford.*

Before the dishes from the coronation banquet had even been taken

---

*It is an obligation of all popular historians, upon mentioning the de Vere family, to say something about the authorship of the plays of William Shakespeare. Consider it said.

away, England's earls were choosing up sides in what would become the first great conflict of Edward's reign.

Half a dozen of the kingdom's most powerful earls were conspiring against their liege lord in order to accomplish a single goal—the separation of the king and Gaveston. One motive for their sabotage was an understandable discomfort with Gaveston's youth; the author of the *Vita* compared Edward II to King Solomon's successor, Rehoboam, "who rejected the counsel of elders, and followed the advice of the young." And Gaveston wasn't just young; he was obnoxious, with a habit of giving less-than-flattering nicknames to his peers: "Burstbelly" for the earl of Lincoln; "old hog" or "the Fiddler" for the earl of Lancaster; the earl of Warwick was "the Black Dog of Arden"; the earl of Pembroke, "Joseph the Jew"; and the earl of Gloucester, "Whoreson," apparently because his mother had remarried.

Another reason was tactical. England's nobles recognized that the new king was far more compliant than his father, who had spent decades reminding his most powerful nobles that they were *his* vassals, made or broken at his whim. In this, Gaveston was little more than a convenient way to reinforce feudal privileges against the growing power of a relatively weak king. But he was also an inconvenient reminder that the titles on which the increasingly unsteady edifice of feudalism depended conferred only as much status as the last person to receive one. No Roman senator, forced to welcome the emperor Caligula's horse to their company, was more resentful than England's earls at the prospect of Piers Gaveston as earl of Cornwall.

Thus, a newly confident and angry group of earls faced off against the king and his loyalists, at this point still including Lancaster. Within a month, the two sides were arming for war, fortifying the king's castle at Windsor, and breaking bridges across the Thames that might offer lines of attack. In March, the hostile earls—of Warwick, Hereford, Pembroke, and John de Warenne, the last of his family to serve as earl of Surrey—arrived in London, each at the head of a retinue of armed knights. Civil war loomed. In April 1308, the rebellious nobles used the clause that had been added to the king's coronation oath to demand immediate banishment and forfeiture of titles for

Gaveston, whom they termed "a robber of the people and a traitor to his liege lord and his realm." Unable to resist their pressure, the king agreed to exile his favorite as of June 25, though his acquiescence didn't prevent him from granting Gaveston the revenues from the king's lands in Aquitaine, totaling some £4,000 annually, and naming him as lieutenant in Ireland as a going-away present.

By the summer of 1308, Edward and his nobles were at least partly reconciled, the anger against Gaveston reduced to a simmer. When the archbishop of Canterbury promised Gaveston excommunication if he were to return to England, Edward wrote directly to the pope and had the threat removed. It wasn't an especially diplomatic bit of diplomacy, and in April 1309, the new parliament presented the king with eleven articles intended to remind him that the precepts of the so-called Great Charters—the Magna Carta, which had been forced upon King John by his nobles in 1215, and the lesser-known Charter of the Forest, signed two years later, during the minority of his son and successor, King Henry III—were still in force.

The parliaments of the early fourteenth century were, like so many other institutions of that transformative era, about to undergo dramatic change. The so-called Model Parliament that Edward I had called in 1295 not only included the nation's lords, both secular and ecclesiastic, but established the tradition of sending two knights from each rural county, and two burgesses from each self-governing town, or borough. When it met in April 1309 as a sort of prototype House of Commons, they bullied the new king with a half-dozen statutes intended to reduce the power his more formidable father had exercised.* In return, Edward got what looked like a poor bargain: Gaveston's return from his exile.

The nobility of England weren't quite mollified yet. In 1310, they presented another Bill of Articles to Edward that sounded a new and more belligerent tone: "So poor are you and so devoid of all manner of treasure that you have nothing wherewith either to defend your land

---

*Thirty-two years later, in 1341, the county and borough representatives would form England's first true House of Commons when the knights-of-the-shire and the burgesses met for the first time separately from the (equally new) House of Lords.

or keep up your household, except by extortions." Faced with the implicit threat of deposition, the king agreed to the appointment of twenty-one so-called *ordainers*—a group of the realm's highest nobles and bishops, most hostile to the crown's prerogatives. Only Gaveston himself, and Walter Reynolds, the new bishop of Winchester, could be said to be supporters of the king.

Given how heavily the dice were loaded, it wasn't much of a surprise when, on August 2, 1311, the Lords Ordainer produced a list of forty-one ordinances, including restrictions on the king's ability to go to war, to tax, or to borrow—his Italian banker, Amerigo dei Frescobaldi, to whom he owed some £22,000, was banished—or even to leave England without the approval of the ordainers. Even less surprising was Ordinance number 20: Gaveston, who, in an earlier version of the Ordinances, had been described as a "traitor" and "an open enemy of the king" was to be exiled "for all time and without hope of return."

Edward complied—at first. He exiled his favorite yet again, in November 1311, but Gaveston's return by Christmas destroyed the fragile peace between the king and his vassals. Edward then repudiated the Ordinances, claiming that he had agreed to them under duress, restored Gaveston's titles and lands, proclaimed the once-and-future earl of Cornwall's reinstatement at the Guildhall, and sent him to Scarborough Castle, under orders to surrender it to no one except the king himself.

Had the events of the spring of 1312 not hurtled to such a tragic and bloody conclusion, they would resemble an absurdist farce. In March, the archbishop of Canterbury summoned the earls of Lancaster, Pembroke, Hereford, Arundel, and Warwick to witness the long-delayed excommunication of Gaveston, after which they agreed to join together to capture him. The earls and their knights galloped off to Scarborough, only to discover that the king and Gaveston had met and escaped to Newcastle together, and that they had missed them both. Lancaster followed; the fugitives slipped away, to Tynemouth Priory. Lancaster appeared again, but Edward had already gone on to York, Gaveston back to Scarborough in an apparent attempt to throw off pursuit.

He failed. On May 19, Gaveston was cornered at Scarborough, and surrendered to the earls of Pembroke and Surrey under very generous terms: Parliament would try him, and the two earls would guarantee his personal safety. Pembroke and Gaveston traveled south to York, the earl planning to take Gaveston to his own castle at Wallingford, where he had agreed to stay until Parliament decided his fate. On June 9, however, probably more out of carelessness than betrayal, Pembroke left his prisoner unguarded in Deddington, near Oxfordshire. The following day, Gaveston's words came back to haunt him: the earl of Warwick captured him, crying, "I think you know me; I am the Black Dog of Arden. Get up traitor!"

At Warwick Castle, the onetime earl of Cornwall was tried and sentenced by the earls of Warwick, Lancaster, Hereford, and Arundel to be beheaded; and on June 19, Gaveston was taken to Blacklow Hill, on an estate of Lancaster, and executed by two Welsh soldiers. According to one legend, the body lay there until found by four shoemakers. A friar, unable to bury the body, since its owner had died while under sentence of excommunication, "carried away Gaveston's head in his hood and brought it to the king."

The Simonie, the 1321 poetic screed on "the evil times" of King Edward II, indicts the king's reign on three counts: The first was Edward's scandalous relationship with Gaveston; the second, his failure to preserve his father's victories in Scotland. But the *real* attack on Edward in *The Simonie* is something different. The poem's very first lines read:

> *Whii werre and wrake in londe and manslauht is i-come,*
> *Whii hungger and derthe on eorthe the pore hath undernome,*
> *Whii bestes ben thus storve, whii corn hath ben so dere . . .*

> Why war, vengeance, and murder has come to the land;
> Why the poor carry the weight of hunger and famine;
> Why the beasts in the field starve, and grain is so meager . . .

Edward had the extraordinary bad luck to rule England at the moment when an expanding population arrived at the limits set by the land's productivity. A king's reputation can survive a deficiency in military capability or moral stature, but not a lack of bread.

The reason grain was "so meager" took a long time to emerge. More than six centuries after Edward's reign, in 1966, Cambridge University Press published the first volume of its revised *Cambridge Economic History of Europe*, entitled *The Agrarian Life of the Middle Ages*. The volume's article on England was authored by an émigré economic historian named Michael Moissey Postan, who had left tsarist Russia at the time of the October Revolution, and settled in England. It was the first appearance of what came to be known as the "Postan Thesis"—a destructive combination of climate, chemistry, and colonization.

Postan recognized that fourteenth-century Europe was the result of a centuries-long process that he termed "internal colonization": the destruction of the great European forests, reclamation of coastal acreage by the construction of dikes and embankments, and the drainage of marshes. During the same climatic era as this "internal colonization," Europe pushed back against its external frontiers: not merely geographic frontiers, but religious. The knightly orders of Calatrava, Alcántara, and Santiago began the long process of driving Islam out of the Iberian Peninsula, where it had been established since the eighth century; later, the Crusader order known as the Germans of the House of St. Mary in Jerusalem—that is, the Teutonic Knights—conquered pagan Prussia. The two processes worked in parallel: in the words of the modern historian Archibald Lewis, "Behind the moving frontiers of the Reconquista [were the] peasantry who settled much of the newly conquered land in Aragon, Castile, and Portugal . . . east of the Elbe, the lands [the Germans] seized were frequently settled by German peasants from the west."

The period of the Medieval Warm, in fact, is almost perfectly matched to the era of frontier expansion, with all its consequences: increasing trade and the exploitation of such newly found natural resources as Scandinavian timber; the Baltic fisheries; and mines of salt, silver, lead, zinc, and copper. Europe's frontiers pushed east across the Elbe, south across Iberia (as well as the Balearic Islands, Sardinia, and, via the Normans, both the island of Sicily and the southernmost part of the Italian peninsula) and, of course, north into England, Wales, and Scotland. The internal frontiers—the forests, marshes, and swamps—were even more significant. The primeval forests were "hacked down and divided into assarts. Polders rescued maritime Flanders, Holland, and much of Northern Germany and Eastern England from the sea."

The defining characteristic of frontiers, however, is that they come to an end. As the thirteenth century turned into the fourteenth, Europe's internal frontiers had reached their limits. Population growth exceeded the supply of land. Wages decreased, and rents increased, substantially. Overall productivity stagnated, while population continued to grow.

The result, according to Postan, wasn't simply the already well-documented fact that medieval agricultural yields declined. His thesis was that the decline was a direct result of the farming techniques that were forced upon the rural peasantry by an ever-increasing number of mouths to feed. The pressure to produce ever more food discouraged fallowing—allowing a portion of every farm to go unplowed, unsown, and unharvested. It encouraged the production of cereals at the expense of everything else. And it demanded the conversion of pasture to farmland, which both reduced the supply of manure and moved it farther and farther away from the crops that needed it. The problem wasn't merely that they weren't producing enough food for today, but that, every year, they compromised their ability to do so for tomorrow.

Though they didn't know it, they had a nitrogen problem.

Nitrogen is, by far, the most common component of the Earth's atmosphere, comprising more than 70 percent of its volume. It would not, therefore, seem to be the sort of thing that is ever in short supply, which is a good thing, since the element is essential for just about every organic process, including the creation of amino acids and proteins. However, atmospheric nitrogen isn't actually very useful at any stage of either plant or animal metabolism. What plants need are actually *nitrates*—one molecule of nitrogen, combined with three of oxygen, or NO_3—in order to produce the photosensitive molecule known as chlorophyll, every version of which has four nitrogen atoms. Plants get all the NO_3 they need from the soil, where bacteria and fungi have produced it, in a series of steps, from the ammonium and ammonia that comes from decomposed plant matter.

There are a number of ways to disrupt this elegant self-sustaining sequence, and the most significant is agriculture itself: harvesting plants, rather than letting them decompose and return the nitrogen to the soil in the form of fertilizer.

Nitrogen is the first essential element to be used up, which means that the most destructive thing humans can do to soil is not burning the trees and plants that live in it, or building houses and barns over it, or even exterminating the animals that depend on it, but cultivating it with food crops. However, even with intensively cultivated land, there are many ways to replace the nitrogen removed when crops are harvested—a good thing, since the addition of nitrogen to soil generates huge increases in productivity: twenty bushels of wheat for every "nitrified" acre, as opposed to six without.

It's not that medieval farmers weren't aware that soils could be depleted. They even knew some of the solutions. The most obvious was fertilizing cropland with nitrogen-rich manure. Slightly less obvious: replacing the sort of crops that use up nitrogen with those whose roots serve as homes to bacteria that are able to "fix" it in the soil. As early as the first century BCE, Roman farmers knew that turning a wheat field into a pasture nitrifies the soil because clovers are natural nitrogen fixers; planting peas and legumes does the same thing.

Fourteen centuries later, though, European farmers weren't planting nitrogen fixers. Or, more accurately, they weren't planting enough. The reasons are controversial but are almost certainly a consequence of the same mild-weather-enabled population explosion that led to manorialism itself. As more and more pasture and woodland was converted to farmland, the "production" of manure was reduced at the same time that the acreage needing fertilization increased.* Even though fallowing (or planting peas) could increase the *long-term* productivity of an acre of cropland, medieval farmers—both landlords and tenants—were virtually incapable of anything but short-term thinking. The economic historian Gregory Clark makes the point that the defining characteristic of feudal manorialism was the price its participants put on the future. The temperament that led to wars over personal slights (or even murderous rages) is the same as the one that encouraged the unsustainable use of arable land. It was a culture constitutionally inclined to sacrifice the future in order to satisfy the present.

Tenant farmers, by definition, have what's known in economic jargon as a high rate-of-time discount: they don't care about benefits that are earned after the end of their tenancy (especially since improved yields were subject to increased rents). And the landholding barons, earls, and monarchs who should have put a high value on the future—that is, should have had a low rate-of-time discount—didn't have any more interest in deferring gratification than the poorest villein farmer. Despite their obsessive interest in adding to their ancestral lands by marriage or conquest, they did remarkably little to improve them—to increase their agricultural productivity. With no more forests to cut down, or land to reclaim, the only way to preserve the system for another generation of lordlings was by taking land from someone else.

Even if the land was as poor as the lowlands of Scotland.

In 1909, the English journalist and Nobel Peace Prize winner Norman Angell wrote a pamphlet, later republished as a book entitled *The Great Illusion*. In it, he argued that war between modern European countries was inherently futile, since each nation's wealth—a function of what he called "credit and contract"—could not be expropriated

---

*Burning down Europe's forests actually increased—temporarily—the nitrogen content of the soils left behind, by adding wood ash to it. However, assarting itself had been made possible by a revolution in iron making, beginning in approximately 900, which produced huge numbers of axes, saws, and other tools for felling trees. The same revolution led to the diffusion of the heavy plow, which, perversely, was so good at removing weeds that it also depleted the newly assarted land of potential nitrogen replacements.

by a conqueror without destroying it entirely: either the assets of a conquered territory stayed in the hands of its existing population, or it vanished. Thus "conquest in the modern world is a process of multiplying by x, and then obtaining the original figure by dividing by x."

Angell was on to something; the conquest of medieval Scotland was, by any rational economic calculus, a poor bargain for both of England's King Edwards, who together spent more than the entire value of the country in one failed expedition after another.

That particular bit of logic works both ways. Robert Bruce and his followers didn't calculate the monetary costs of resistance any more than England measured the benefits of conquest. Far stronger passions than economic ones were needed, and no one exhibited them more powerfully, or more durably, than the man who would play Little John to Robert Bruce's Robin Hood: Sir James Douglas.

Douglas's father, Sir William, had been the commander of Berwick Castle during the 1296 English invasion, and had joined Wallace (and Bruce) the following year, before surrendering to Edward Longshanks and being imprisoned in the Tower of London, while James, then twelve, was sent to France for his own safety. When Sir William died in 1298, the newly made bishop of St. Andrews, William Lamberton, who was then in Paris negotiating with the French, took the young Douglas into his own household.

There he remained until Bruce's decision to strike for the throne. When Comyn was murdered, Lamberton was at Berwick, apparently working diligently on behalf of the provincial government authorized by King Edward. Once he heard about the events at Greyfriars, he made plans to leave Berwick secretly and headed to Scone for the coronation. At the same time, James, now twenty, either stole, or was "allowed" to steal, one of Lamberton's horses—the chroniclers loved the story so much that they even recorded the horse's name: Ferrand— and rode from Berwick to join Bruce on the road to his coronation. As Barbour told it in his romantic poem, James met Bruce's party on their way to Scone, and immediately fell to his knee, giving Bruce his homage as Scotland's rightful king. "Thus they made their acquaintance that never afterwards by any chance of any kind was broken while they lived. Their friendship increased ever more and more for Douglas served always loyally, and Bruce . . . gladly and well rewarded his service."

For once, Barbour was probably understating the case. Bruce may have earned a reputation for living off the land after his 1306 defeat, but that he lived at all was because of Douglas. While Scotland's "army" (probably fewer than two hundred men) headed west, with Aymer de Valence in hot pursuit, they were trapped on the shores of Loch Lomond, with no way across. And there they would have been captured had Douglas not found a propitiously hidden boat sunk among the reeds that could carry three men at a time across the loch. This became one of the themes of the 1307 refugee campaign: Douglas rising in prominence, tellingly, not as a fighter (yet) but as a forager—or, more precisely, a poacher: for finding venison, pike, and salmons, "there was not one among them there . . . more than James Douglas."

An insurgency must feed itself to survive against an occupying army; to defeat one, however, it must destroy the occupier's morale, and Douglas was born for the job. His own estate had been forfeit when his father was captured in 1298, and he had joined with Bruce at least in part to restore his own fortunes. In March 1307, just after the king and his men had returned to Scotland, he gave Douglas leave to take his barony back, and James left immediately for Douglasdale, in the south-west of Scotland, accompanied by only two companions. In the oft-told, too-good-to-be-true story, upon his arrival, he recruited a band of loyal locals, waited until the English garrison headed to the parish church to celebrate Palm Sunday, and then fell on them with his two soldiers and a few dozen of his father's former vassals. He then proceeded to his "own" castle, where his cook prepared the feast that had been planned for the English garrison. And then, in the legend that became known as "Douglas's larder," the Scots ate the feast prepared, burned the remainder, ransacked the castle's stores, salted the well, and beheaded every one of the English prisoners before leaving, bringing the men of Douglasdale to augment the king's not-quite-army.

That army's prospects had, at just that moment, started to brighten. After Longshanks's death, and Edward II's brief march through Scotland, Bruce finally had the opportunity to establish his authority as king, and the campaigns of 1307–08 really mark the turning point of Bruce's fortunes. After defeating Aymer de Valence at Loudon Hill in May 1307, he returned to Carrick, of which he was still nominally the earl, recaptured the castle, and defeated the garrison. He sent Douglas to establish control of Ettrick Forest, as a base for raids on English strongholds, and took Inverness Castle in a surprise attack, killing the garrison and razing the castle to the ground. In December, he agreed to a truce with the earl of Buchan—the "other" John Comyn, cousin to Bruce's victim at Greyfriars—and then spent the spring undermining him: Instead of attacking Comyn directly, he raided the rural peasants who supplied the Comyns with food and rents, offering them the choice of being burned out or shifting their tribute to Bruce. He offered temporary truces to enemies like the earl of Ross and John of Lorne. And, in May 1308, he defeated Comyn himself at Inverurie despite being so sick that he couldn't sit upright on a horse without two men holding him up.

After Inverurie, with the earl of Buchan in full flight, Bruce proved that he was just as brutally effective against his Scottish enemies as against the English. The "harrying of Buchan"—sometimes called the rape of Buchan, which included summary executions of every Comyn supporter, the burning of every Comyn manor, and the destruction of every Comyn farm—was so complete that it would be nearly a century before the lands would even be claimed as a fief, and never again by a Comyn.

Even outside of Buchan, the Comyn cause was shattered; the earl of Buchan was nothing like the soldier that his cousin of Badenoch had been, and was unable to meet Bruce on anything like successful terms. Neither were his allies immune: Bruce defeated the Macdowalls of Galloway and the Macdougalls of Lorne before any English support could return in force, which brought Buchan, Ross, Argyll, and Galloway, the four areas most loyal to Comyn—and, through him, to John Balliol—under his control.

By March 1309, Bruce had consolidated his authority throughout Scotland, persuading the Scottish clergy—including Lamberton, the bishop of St. Andrews, who had just been paroled by Edward II and sent north as a peace offering, though not Bishop Wishart of Glasgow, who was in the custody of the pope—and earls to declare that the original coronation of John Balliol had been wrongly decided, and that Robert Bruce the Competitor (the current king's grandfather) should have been king after all. Balliol was an illegitimate ruler, entirely the creation of the English; and that Robert Bruce was the true and nearest heir to Alexander III. However satisfying this may have been to Bruce and his supporters, it made Edward II's attempts at conciliation moot. He wasn't about to accept an independent Scottish king, and Bruce wasn't about to accept anything else.

More consequentially, Bruce had entered into correspondence with his nation's favorite fair-weather friend, Philip IV of France, who proposed a truce between Scotland and England, which meant recognizing Bruce's claim as Scotland's king. Literally: the documents Philip sent to Edward referred to Robert Bruce only as the earl of Carrick, while those he sent to Bruce addressed him as King of Scots.

When the letters came to light, their implicit message did not, needless to say, sit especially well with Edward II, who rebuked his father-in-law about his acceptance of Bruce's kingship. Philip, instead of apologizing, demanded that Edward do fealty to him in Paris for his French holdings, but Edward, fearful for Gaveston's safety—correctly, as events proved—refused. Instead, he assembled yet another invading force for Scotland, and, on September 8, 1310, advanced to Biggar in southern Scotland. Bruce, by now an old hand at this, refused battle and retreated north of the Firth of Forth, leaving Douglas behind to harass the English. The lowland Scottish peasantry, also by now experienced, collected all their seed corn and livestock, and headed for the hills, leaving the cavalry-heavy English force with no forage for their horses, as Bruce "lurked continually in hiding [and] did them all the injury that he could."

Edward was completely flummoxed. He stayed at Berwick until December, emerging only when Bruce let it be known he was planning an invasion—completely fictitious—of the Isle of Man, which allowed the Scots to open their eastern coastline for food and weapons. By then, a winter campaign looked so unappealing to Edward's generals, Sir John Segrave and Sir Robert de Clifford—in the words of the *Chronicle of Lanercost*: "the English do not willingly enter Scotland to wage war before summer, chiefly because earlier in the year they find no food for their horses"—that they signed a series of truces with the Scots, extending to June 1310. Even had they a taste for winter campaigning, they would have had to contend with another enemy: Edward could no longer avoid the restraints of the Lords Ordainer, whose first Bill of Articles explicitly observed, "you have lost Scotland and grievously dismembered your crown in England and Ireland ... whereas the commonalty of your realm give you the 20th penny from their goods in aid of your Scotch war ... all levied and foolishly spent." In July 1311, the king returned to Westminster, a month before the publication of the forty-one Ordinances that would ultimately lead to Gaveston's death.

Edward's departure left Bruce free to attack the garrisoned forts that were the basis of England's military power in Scotland. Though he lacked the siege engines needed to take the larger castles, nothing stopped him from nibbling at the smaller ones. James Douglas, in particular, proved adept at luring garrisons out from behind their walls by teasing them with cattle herds; when the English came out to seize them, he ambushed them. He worked the same magic at his ancestral castle of Douglasdale three times before he finally razed the castle to the ground. Bruce himself had taken half a dozen castles, most significantly the fortress and port of Aberdeen, which permitted the reestablishment of a trading entrepot with the Continent, particularly Flanders and the Hanseatic cities of the Baltic. In a little more than two years, Bruce was transformed from a hunted fugitive, never leading more than fifty supporters (and just as frequently only two or three) to the ruler of two-thirds of Scotland.

By trial and error, King Robert was perfecting his strategy of avoiding Edward's armies while destroying their supplies. The next step was forcing the English to finance their own defeat. After continuous raids through the fall of 1311, in February 1312, Bruce burned the village of Corbridge, but instead of continuing to ravage the rest of Northumbria, this time he reminded the rest of the county that, instead of paying their share—a bit more than £916—of what amounted to a national English property tax, they could pay him instead: with a modest enough increase, to £2,000.

Extortion was lucrative: at least £20,000 overall, from the bishopric of Durham, from Hexham, Cumberland, Coupland, and Westmorland. The "leading men" of Dunbar offered a payment of £2,000 for ten months' truce, to run until midsummer of 1313; Northumbria made an identical offer, £2,000 having become the going rate, with hostages taken as security for the "loan." By 1313, the whole enterprise was running like a real business, with careful record-keeping and even negotiated extensions; when Cumberland fell behind in payments, Bruce burned "many towns and two churches, taking men and women prisoners, and collect[ing] a great number of cattle" as a penalty. The total, according the *Chronicle of Walter Guisborough*, amounted to some £40,000 (more than £13 million today). Not only was Bruce raising the money he needed to purchase armor and weapons from Flanders and the Hanse, he was denying a similar amount to Edward.

This was not a trend that could continue indefinitely, though less for reasons of economic advantage than national pride. Whether Edward recognized Robert Bruce as a rebel or as a king was immaterial. In the first case, the north of England was the victim of a criminal insurrection; in the second, a foreign invasion. And a king who could not protect his northern border from either was no king at all.

CHAPTER FIVE

"Scots, Wha Hae"

1313–1315

The circumstances that led two kings into a decisive collision on the banks of a tiny stream in central Scotland seem, in retrospect, inevitable. To the participants, they were anything but. Though Edward's northernmost vassals were being bled dry by Bruce's "taxes," the far more populous and wealthy south of England was barely affected, which offered a good deal of insulation from Bruce's provocations. The English king, meanwhile, had plenty with which to occupy himself without venturing northward, since, after Gaveston's judicial murder, Edward had sworn vengeance on the earls he held responsible: Lancaster, Warwick, and Hereford (the earls of Pembroke and Surrey aligned with the king). King Robert, on the other hand, was making a very profitable art out of avoiding direct battle with Edward's armies. Neither had any strategic reason to pursue a winner-take-all battle with the other.

As a result, the path that brought them to the same battlefield, on the same day, meanders quite a bit. A good place for it to begin is September 1312, three months after the death of Gaveston, when Lancaster, Warwick, and Hereford marched on Edward, headquartered in London. The earls were forbidden entry to the city proper by a combination of loyalist troops and the city's militia, while the king sent envoys across the Channel—to Pope Clement, and to King Philip of France—hoping to achieve victory over his hostile nobles (and the end of the Ordinances) by diplomacy.

The pressure seems to have worked. In December, the king and his peers negotiated a treaty—carefully, and indecisively. Neither king nor earls appeared at the negotiations out of fear of treachery, and the document that emerged didn't resolve anything at all. The king still maintained, to anyone who would listen, that the Ordinances were null and void, contravening the Magna Carta, the Charter of the Forest, the king's own coronation oath, canon law, and the unified system of precedents and case law inaugurated in the reign of Henry II that had come to be known as the "common law." The magnates, on the other hand, continued to insist on confirmation of the Ordinances and pardons for the death of Gaveston. Given that sort of standoff, the final agreement was little more than a face-saving compromise: Edward was permitted to carve out some of the Ordinances with which he disagreed most vehemently (mostly on finance) while pardoning Gaveston's murderers, all the while proclaiming that Gaveston had not been a traitor. Of far more relevance to most of Edward's subjects was the matter of taxes. Unable to persuade Parliament to grant him a new set of tax revenues, the agreement freed Edward to impose his own, amounting to one part in ten of all revenues—essentially a national sales tax—and one part in fifteen of the value of all moveable goods, which, since it exempted the value of land, lay rather more heavily on England's peasantry than its aristocracy. Edward did not limit himself to simple taxes on sales and movables. With his credit restored, he was able to borrow again, nearly £100,000 from a variety of sources, each loan brokered by the Genoese banker Antonio Pessagno, who had taken over for Frescobaldi.*

It was enough to pay for Isabella and Edward to travel to France, in May 1313, hoping to settle a decent peace with Philip IV over the still-disputed territories of Gascony and Aquitaine; and not at all incidentally, to guarantee Philip's support of Edward in his conflicts with the earl of Lancaster and his supporters. It's not known whether the subject of Scotland was raised, though it seems likely. Certainly the latest in a long line of increasingly fragile peace treaties between France and England was an occasion for celebration. Amid great pageantry in

---

*Pessagno would, between 1313 and 1319, arrange advances to the king of more than £25,000 annually, which meant that a single banker was financing nearly one dollar in ten of all national expenditures.

Paris, Isabella's three brothers were each knighted, and the two kings, Edward and Philip, made vows to join each other on crusade.

While Edward was replenishing his treasury, King Robert was consolidating his sovereignty. The campaigns of the previous four years had given him control over almost all of Britain north of the Firth of Forth (as well as a fair bit of northern England) but the English still maintained garrisons in the most formidable castles in Scotland. As long as they remained in the hands of an occupying army, their recapture was King Robert's highest priority.

Without artillery to throw boulders at castle walls—fourteenth-century trebuchets used a counterweighted arm to sling projectiles weighing two hundred pounds nearly a quarter-mile—he was unable to batter his way to victory in the manner of Edward I at Stirling in 1303. Instead, he made a virtue of his relative military poverty, and developed tactics that typically involved surprise attacks on castle walls with nothing more than light scaling ladders. As related in the *Chronicle of Lanercost*:

> Now these ladders, which they placed against the walls, were of a wonderful construction . . . the Scots had made two strong ropes as long as the height of the wall, making a knot at the end of each cord. They had made a wooden board, also, about two feet and a half broad, strong enough to carry a man and in the two extremities of the board they had made two holes through which the two ropes could be passed.

With iron hooks intended as grapnels, and fenders to hold the ladder away from the wall, Bruce's soldiers used very long spears to hoist the hooks over the walls—rarely more than eighteen feet high—and then climbed up and over. This is precisely what they did at Perth on January 7, 1313, with Bruce himself swimming the moat at night and putting the first ladder on the wall. Not to be outdone, on the night of February 19, 1314, Scots under James Douglas captured Roxburgh Castle in an even more audacious attack: wearing black cloaks over their armor, his troops crawled to the base of the castle's walls on a moonless night, hoisted their rope ladders over the battlements, and surprised the garrison in the middle of its Shrove Tuesday celebrations.

The élan of Bruce's lieutenants was contagious. Thomas Randolph, who had been captured by Douglas in 1308—he had changed sides, briefly, two years before—had been welcomed back by King Robert, who made him the new earl of Moray in 1312. In March 1314, Randolph was sent by Bruce to capture Edinburgh Castle, which had been built on a scarp too high even for scaling ladders. Randolph's response was to recruit thirty highlanders with a talent for rock climbing, who ascended the cliff to the base of the wall, clambered over, and entered the castle to open the gates to the rest of his force.*

The 1313 attacks on English castles were so successful that by spring, fewer than six remained in English hands, two of them—Stirling Castle, which had been occupied by English troops since 1303, and Berwick, which Edward Longshanks had sacked in 1296—virtually invulnerable to any Scottish attack. Nonetheless, in the spring of 1314, Stirling was invested by Edward Bruce. When the king's brother was unable to take the castle by surprise assault, his lack of patience with siege work in general led him to an agreement with the garrison's commander, Sir Philip Mowbray: If, by midsummer of 1314, the castle hadn't been relieved—actually, unless an English army got to within three leagues of the castle, about ten miles—Mowbray agreed to yield.

Though neither the king of England nor the king of Scotland had been a party to the agreement, it bound them nonetheless. When King Edward learned, on May 26, about the deal between Mowbray and Edward Bruce, he was already traveling to Berwick, the strongest castle in Scotland still held by the English. He had already embargoed the export of all foodstuffs and requisitioned a wagon train of more than a hundred each of four-horse and eight-oxen carts. With a decisiveness that would have done his father proud, he immediately ordered the mustering of his army, sending a formal writ to his vassals

---

*Led by William Francis, a local who had apparently practiced climbing the castle scarp in order to visit his girlfriend in the town below.

commanding them to appear with their levies at Berwick on June 10. The total number of men summoned added up to 21,640 infantry from England and Wales, plus 4,000 from Ireland. Lancaster, Warwick, Surrey, and Arundel—essentially the anti-Gaveston party—couldn't completely ignore the command, but, citing the Ordinance prohibiting the king from going to war without permission, sent the bare minimum required by their feudal obligation.

They were, however, the only ones. Edward's host, between eighteen and twenty thousand (with at least two thousand mounted knights, and three thousand Welsh archers) included the earls of Pembroke and Gloucester; John Comyn, the son of Bruce's victim; the unforgettably named Sir Pain Tiptoft and Sir Marmaduke Tweng. Also in Edward's army, which was large enough, according to the *Vita*, "to traverse all Scotland," was Sir Giles d'Argentan, whom Barbour described as the "third best knight of his day" (the other two were the Holy Roman Emperor Henry VII, and King Robert himself). The newly affluent king's army also included a train of auxiliaries, including smiths, farriers, carpenters, and cooks (and prostitutes, of course), along with the king's household servants, needed to set up and take down the king's pavilions daily and set his table with both cloth and plates of gold hourly. The king had even hired a troubadour to write an ode commemorating the coming victory.

Robert prepared to meet them, though reluctantly; according to Barbour, his reaction to his brother's bargain was, "That was unwisely done, indeed." Summoning the commanders of secondary expeditions currently under way all over Scotland produced a total of no more than six thousand men, which the king separated into four divisions: One, the vanguard of approximately five hundred, was given to Thomas Randolph, earl of Moray; the second, of a thousand or so, was to be commanded by Edward Bruce; another thousand men, in the third division, were nominally under the High Steward (now Walter Stewart, upon the death of James Stewart in 1309) but actually commanded by James Douglas. The fourth division, some two thousand infantry, was commanded by the king himself, with a few hundred mounted skirmishers under Sir Robert Keith, Scotland's marischal.

The battle for which both sides prepared is a regular feature on lists of the "Great Battles of History." It deserves its place. Bannockburn, the site of the 1314 meeting between Edward and Robert Bruce, didn't merely mark a change in warfare itself, but revealed how deeply the conduct of war was a reflection of politics, economics, and culture.

Consider the asymmetry of the two armies. The English force's core of armored knights were not, after all, still the dominant force on fourteenth-century battlefields because of their intrinsic superiority in the application of violence. It was the very particular environment of medieval Europe that selected for the armored knight; knights were the way an entire culture formalized both the ownership of land and the defense (and sometimes the acquisition) of it, not because they were an *efficient* way of doing so but precisely because they were *inefficient*. The more expensive it was to produce a class of militarily trained landed gentry, the easier it was for those in that class to maintain their position.

What made the medieval knight so successful was actually his confidence in his trained skill. It's very hard, even unnatural, to make a vocation out of killing and maiming others, particularly in an era when the administration of violence was such an up-close-and-personal activity. Only a lifetime of training was likely to overcome the natural urge to avoid such violent encounters, and as long as the training was monopolized by those who could afford it, horses and armor made the mounted knights of the High Middle Ages unchallengeable.*

And the price of maintaining a knight in the field hadn't done anything since the Norman Conquest except get more expensive. The cost of a mount was almost unimaginably high for anyone other than a noble. An average warhorse—the "great horses" that were the product of longstanding breeding plans, and necessary for carrying an armored man in battle—cost more than £18, and 10 percent of them

---

*This was less true when European knights were matched against the more lightly armored and more maneuverable cavalry of the Arabs, Persians, and Kurds they faced while on crusade, but they were a non-issue north of the Pyrenees since the ninth century.

more than £40; one of Edward II's horses cost him more than £70, or nearly forty times the average wage of his subjects.

Knighthood was costly to the knight's psyche, as well as his wallet, even though the profession of arms in medieval Europe regarded violence as a kind of sacrament. Ramon Llull, the great Catalan philosopher and poet of the early fourteenth century, famously wrote that "God and chivalry are in accord," since the chivalric code demanded that knights only raise their swords on behalf of virtue. In the words of Gutierre Díaz de Gómez, the friend and biographer of Don Pero Niño, the Spanish "Unconquered Knight" of the late fourteenth century: "Knights . . . are forever swallowing their fear . . . they expose themselves to every peril; they give up their bodies to the adventure of life in death." A French knight of the early fourteenth century, Geoffroi de Charny, advised other knights that the best way to cope with things such as sleeplessness, uncontrollable memories, and depression was to tell oneself that the battle was just, and not for private gain, and thereby make it more tolerable.

The contemporary reflections of Llull, Díaz, and de Charny are something of a clue to the real advantage of mounted knights: preparation, more than horses, or even armor, which, like their swords, was two-edged: good for protection, not so much for fighting. The amount of effort required to move while carrying up to forty pounds of iron or steel armor literally doubled the metabolic requirements of its wearers. Once unhorsed, armored knights used at least four times the amount of energy as, for example, the foot soldiers who turned them into scavenger meat at Courtrai.

As the Medieval Warm Period reached its last decades, the vulnerability of armored horsemen to disciplined foot soldiers, the Achilles' heel of medieval knighthood, was exposed more and more frequently. Stirling Bridge and Courtrai are the traditional examples; Bannockburn would be another. What these conflicts had in common was the kind of cohesion that could make well-trained infantry the match for equally well-trained and disciplined cavalry. At Courtrai that cohesion was a secondary consequence of the population growth enabled by centuries of mild climate: the new towns and villages had grown large and plentiful enough to support militias that could regularly train together.* At Bannockburn, however, the source was more personal: the charisma and determination of Robert Bruce.

By 1314, Bruce had been at war for nearly twenty years, and had long since realized that his instincts as a tourney knight were useless in a real war against English cavalry. His only hope for success was the imposition of discipline on his infantry—enough that his spear-bristling schiltroms could be moved as units, rather than in wild charges, which would make them as useful in attack as they already were in defense. Some of this was made possible by the relatively egalitarian nature of the Scottish host. Unlike English (and continental) armies that were, by design, hierarchical in the extreme, "the gradations of wealth were less steep" in Scotland, which meant that both chiefs and men were likely to be armed with similar weaponry.

And disciplined foot soldiers were likely to be as fierce as any knight. Infantry weren't disposed to abide by anything like a code of chivalry, which regarded them, in any case, as less than worthless. Archers, killing from two hundred yards away with missiles that covered those two hundred yards in less than five seconds, had no way to accept surrenders even if they wanted to. The result was an enormous increase in the risk of death to mounted knights. In twelfth-century Flanders, after a yearlong campaign between French and Flemish barons, only five knights had died, only one of them in battle (one apparently died from blowing his horn too vigorously). At Courtrai alone, hundreds of knightly corpses littered the field.

Edward's knights, therefore, were in greater danger than they knew when they departed Berwick on June 17. They, and the rest of the English host, arrived in Edinburgh four days later; as recorded in the *Vita*: "like a pilgrimage to Santiago de Compostela, rather than an army on the march." Since the agreement between Edward Bruce and Mowbray obliged the relief column to arrive by midsummer, timing was tight. The English had one day to march the twenty miles to Falkirk, then one more for the remaining twenty miles to Stirling, where the

---

*This was also the case at the 1315 Battle of Morgarten. See chapter 10.

Scots waited, on the north side of the Bannock Burn, a stream that flowed north to the River Forth, and which crossed the Falkirk-Stirling road.

While a dozen different accounts of the Battle of Bannockburn are extant, it's worth noting that no one knows with any certainty where it actually took place. The likeliest candidate looks very different to-day from how it did that June day in 1314, when—significantly—the area just west of the road into Stirling was a tangle of sluggish streams, which would play havoc with the footing of the English cavalry.

Whatever their absolute location, their relative ones are fairly well established. King Robert placed Moray's division on his far western flank, and held the eastern one himself, with Douglas and Edward Bruce in between, and close enough that each could reinforce the other as needed. Their positions were fortified by digging "pottes" in the land where the road rose at a shallow slope—disguised pits in-tended to cause injury, but even more to channel an advance across a chosen front "to force the enemy to bunch at a single well-guarded spot."

On the twenty-third, the English arrived in sight of Stirling, thus satisfying the original agreement made by Mowbray and Edward Bruce: the garrison would not be required to surrender the castle. Upon learning this, the English almost immediately started fighting. With one another. The issue was command; Gilbert de Clare, earl of Gloucester, and Humphrey de Bohun, earl of Hereford, each asserted a claim on the title of "Constable" and therefore commander of the vanguard. Gloucester was Edward's choice, Hereford the hereditary Constable, so the king split the difference and made them joint commanders—a poor decision on its own merits, even without the ap-parently salient fact that Aymer de Valence, earl of Pembroke, was the finest soldier in the English army, and the one who had defeated Rob-ert Bruce in battle in 1306. The choice wasn't the sort that boosted the troops' morale, which may have been why one of the army's more impetuous knights, Henry de Bohun (Humphrey's nephew) took it upon himself to improve things. Seeing King Robert, easily identified by his crown, inspecting his troops, the young knight immediately

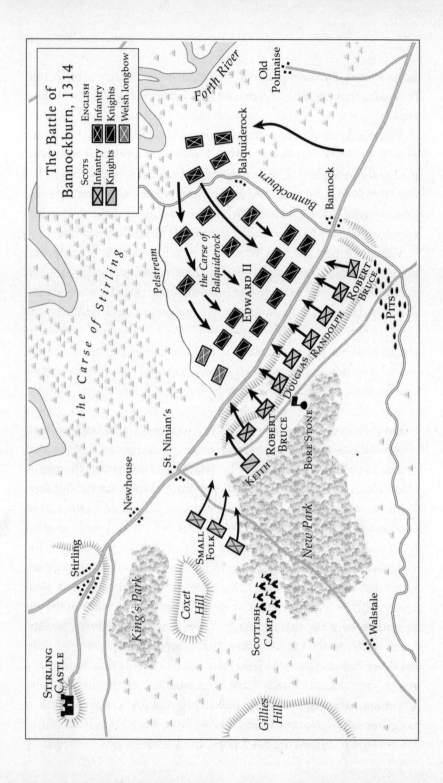

The Battle of Bannockburn, 1314

SCOTS
Infantry
Knights

ENGLISH
Infantry
Knights
Welsh longbow

Forth River

Old Polmaise

Balquiderock

Bannockburn

Bannock

the Carse of Balquiderock

EDWARD II

Pelstream

ROBERT BRUCE

RANDOLPH

DOUGLAS

ROBERT BRUCE

Pits

the Carse of Stirling

St. Ninian's

KEITH

BORE STONE

Newhouse

SMALL FOLK

Stirling

King's Park

Coxet Hill

New Park

SCOTTISH CAMP

Walstale

STIRLING CASTLE

Gillies Hill

charged, sword swinging. By the time he made it up the long and boggy slope to where his target waited, his horse was blown, he "myssit the nobile king," and King Robert contemptuously—the de Bohuns had been given the Bruce family lands in Carrick and Annandale when Robert was a fugitive—split Henry's skull with a single swing of a battle ax.

King Robert's skill at mayhem makes for entertaining reading, and certainly added to his legend throughout subsequent centuries as, indeed, it did during his own. But if battles had ever been decided by champions meeting in single combat, they weren't any longer. If Henry de Bohun's death had any meaning, it was a symbolic one: a demonstration that chivalric bravery wasn't nearly as important as terrain. It was a distinction that mattered. As the military historian John Keegan has noted, at the beginning of the fourteenth century it was widely regarded as unchivalrous to select a battlefield that would offer a topographical advantage; "taking the high ground" was, somehow, ignoble.

Not to the Scots, though. *All* of the skirmishes during the first day at Bannockburn were about terrain. When a patrol of a few hundred knights rode to the east of the New Park, trying to both flank the Scots and take the ground above them, Bruce rode furiously to his own division, and, forming them into *schiltrom*, marched out of cover to meet the English cavalry on ground where they had left themselves no room to maneuver.

Even so, the Scots weren't dug in behind a palisade of spikes on defense, but attacking in a moving formation, and it's a testimony to eight years of experience and discipline that they maintained the integrity of the schiltrom despite attacks from the cavalry. Hours of fighting later, King Robert had demonstrated that his infantry was just as formidable as an attacking force as it was on defense. That night, Bruce addressed his men:

> We have every reason to be confident of success, for we have right on our side. Our enemies are moved only by desire for dominion, but we are fighting for our lives, our children, our wives,

and the freedom of our country . . . See that your ranks are not broken so that, when the enemy come charging on horseback, you meet them steadfastly with your spears . . . You could have lived quietly as slaves, but because you longed to be free you are with me here, and to gain that end you must be valiant, strong, and undismayed . . . You know what honour is. Bear yourself in such fashion as to keep your honour.

The following day, Monday the twenty-fourth, dawn broke on the English cavalry, which found itself unable to maneuver, with streams to their right and left, and a very deep ditch behind them. They could not, therefore, have been happy to see three columns of Scottish infantry marching toward them in echelon, each one behind and a little to the left of the one in front. Their archers, who had broken the Scottish schiltroms at Falkirk, were still in line of march rather than perpendicular to the line of advance, which meant most of them couldn't even *see* the enemy, much less engage them. Sir Ingram de Umfraville proposed to Edward that the English feign a retreat, and so tempt the Scots to break ranks in order to plunder the huge baggage train that Edward had hauled from Berwick. The king, noting the Scots kneeling en masse, refused, saying, "Yon kneeling folk for mercy pray." Umfraville—in Barbour's telling, anyway—responded, "but not from you; from God for their sins. These men will win all or die."

The first Scottish division to advance was Edward Bruce's; the earl of Gloucester ordered a charge, and was killed almost immediately. Moray and Douglas followed suit, which finally brought them into the range of Edward's Welsh archers, who did some notable damage before the marischal, Sir Robert Keith, could get his small division of light cavalry into action, and broke them up. By then, the *schiltroms* had made contact with the cavalry, and were able to use their well-practiced tactic of spearing horses in their unarmored flanks and bellies in order to get them to throw their riders—and, even more destructively, to panic other horses as they ran around riderless. When King Robert finally committed his reserve division to the battle, it became a rout.

King Edward, by all accounts, fought bravely enough to have his first horse killed under him. No doubt he would have continued to fight had not the earl of Pembroke, realizing the danger of a king taken hostage by a Scots army, grabbed the reins of the monarch's second mount and dragged him off to Stirling Castle along with five hundred of the remaining cavalry. There, Sir Philip Mowbray refused to open the gates, making the perverse-but-persuasive argument that he was now obliged to surrender the castle, which would have meant surrendering the king as well. Faced with this unassailable logic, the king and the cavalry headed east, past Edinburgh all the way to Dunbar, then to Berwick, where he met Isabella on June 27.

The disaster was complete. In ten days, the largest English army to enter Scotland since Falkirk had been transformed into a rabble in retreat. Among England's captains, only the earl of Pembroke kept his nerve throughout the battle, returning to the field after rescuing the king, organizing a fighting retreat, and leading his men home on foot to Carlisle. Of those left behind, at least four thousand foot soldiers were killed, along with two hundred knights, against perhaps four hundred Scottish infantry, and no more than two knights. Thirty-four nobles were among the English dead, including John Comyn, the nephew of the earl of Pembroke and the son of King Robert's onetime victim. Thousands of prisoners were taken, including the earl of Hereford, who was exchanged for the long-imprisoned Robert Wishart, bishop of Glasgow, along with King Robert's queen, sister, and daughter. Valuables amounting to more than £200,000 were captured, along with both the Great Seal of England and the Royal Shield. The author of the *Vita Edwardi Secundi* was both merciless and accurate: "Indeed I think it is unheard of in our time for such an army to be scattered so suddenly by infantry, unless when the flower of France fell before the Flemings at Courtrai."

Edward, who was already regarded as deficient in martial virtue, was widely blamed for the disaster. From the *Vita*, again: "If he had employed himself in the pursuit of arms, [he would have] excelled King Richard [I]. Indeed, his make-up was fitted to this: he was tall of stature and a finely formed man of great strength with a handsome face . . . If he had given as much energy to the pursuit of arms as he spent in rustic pursuits, England would have prospered well." Even Edward's youthful enthusiasm for ditch digging wasn't forgotten: Robert de Newington, a messenger in the royal household, recorded that Edward's failure to win the battle of Bannockburn was because he spent his time in "making ditches, and digging, and other improper occupations."

Scotland, unsurprisingly, was exultant. As reported in *Fabyan's Chronicle* (and repeated in Christopher Marlowe's 1593 play about Edward's "troublesome reign") the victorious Scots, "inflamed in pride, in derision of Englishmen," made this rhyme as follows:

> Maidens of England, sore may you mourn
> For your lemans you have lost at Bannockbourn,
> With a heave and a ho [alternatively, a Heavelow]!
> What weeneth the King of England
> So soon to have won Scotland,
> With a rumbelow

Even better known than the "rumbelow" (likely a nonsense word) is the first stanza of Robert Burns's 1793 poem "March to Bannockburn":

> Scots, wha hae wi' Wallace bled
> Scots, wham Bruce has aften led
> Welcome tae yer gory bed
> Or tae victorie!

Bannockburn was indeed a great "victorie." As much as any battle in history, it was the great rallying cry in a struggle for national independence. For generations of military historians, it demonstrated the tactical value of disciplined infantry, in attack as well as defense. And for anyone still in doubt on the subject, Bannockburn proved how wide was the gap in talent for combat between Robert Bruce and Edward II.

Even more significant, for the population of both Scotland and England, was what occurred afterward. While Bruce had demonstrated his ability to win a great set-piece battle—to be sure, one he had not sought—his long-term strategy was to bleed not Edward's army but his subjects: to capture or burn the harvests of northern England's farms, to extort northern England's gold, and to destroy, as much as possible, northern England's food. In this, he was following a strategy of affliction explicitly described and proposed by a French nobleman named Pierre Dubois fourteen years before Bannockburn in a work that promised "Successful Expeditions and Shortened Wars."*

While Bannockburn had been as complete a victory as one could wish, it did little to shorten the war between Scotland and England, which would continue for another fourteen years. Since Scotland was far too small to conquer England, and, after Bannockburn, England couldn't envision defeating Bruce any time soon, the real result of the battle was not decisive victory but strategic stalemate. This was good news for Scottish independence, but very bad news for the farms and villages of northern England and southern Scotland, which would henceforth be the *only* battlefields on which the two nations could meet.

The deliberate attacks on those farms would have been hugely destructive at any moment in history. However, they didn't occur at just any moment, but rather a year before the worst storms in human memory appeared as if to announce to the farmers of Scotland and England— not to mention France, Flanders, Germany, and Scandinavia—that the four centuries of good weather were now at an end.

---

*The destruction of food supplies as a deliberate stratagem of war already had a long and dishonorable provenance. As far back as the seventh century, the *Strategikon,* written by the Byzantine emperor Maurice, gave very specific tactical advice on how to destroy crops, fields, and trees; how to poison wells; and so on.

CHAPTER SIX

"The Floodgates of the Heavens"

1315–1316

By the middle of 1314, Edward II had been King of England for seven years. Very nearly each one of them had been worse than the preceding one, with the lowest point to date coming on the fields of Bannockburn. The trend continued. If the first half of the year had been a disaster for Edward, the second half was a misery. In September, three months after Bannockburn, he called a parliament at York to deal with the changed situation in Scotland, but the only business it was able to conclude was the hostage exchange with King Robert. He did manage to assemble a mobile force under the earl of Pembroke and send it into Scotland to relieve the Bruce's siege of Carlisle Castle and temporarily buy a respite from Scottish raiders, but could do little to alleviate the sufferings of his northern subjects, who faced a more ruthless and powerful attacker than even James Douglas's *hobelars*—light mounted infantry (riding *hobbins*, or hobby-horses). The summer and fall of 1314, saw, according to the *Vita*, "such plentiful rain that men could scarcely harvest the wheat or store it safely in the barn."

To the world's farmers, drought is generally more feared than its opposite. But too much rain can be as terrifying as too little, since societies are built to accommodate normal amounts of rainfall, and roads, bridges, and especially farms in a region that receives less than five inches annually look very different than those in a place that gets more than two hundred.

Lacking satellite data, we cannot know the specific cause of any historical rainstorm. Any number of phenomena can cool air to its dew point, including contact with a colder surface—water to land, for example—or evaporation, or adiabatic cooling (the same thing that causes the air escaping a bicycle tire or the air you blow out of your mouth to feel cold). Gases expand when they move from a small chamber to a larger one, and since pressure and heat are proportional, lower pressure equals lower temperature. Because air pressure is lower at higher altitudes, it cools and condenses. But the mystery of the storms of 1315 and 1316 isn't their appearance but their duration, and especially their timing, so close to the estimated end of the Medieval Warm Period. A good guess is that when the very cold winters of 1309–1312, during which pack ice extended all the way from Greenland to Iceland, and polar bears could walk from one to the other, were whipsawed back into shape by a drop in the North Atlantic Oscillation in 1315, all the instability that had been held back by the high NAO index came flooding into continental Europe.* Some variety of large-scale atmospheric motion caused a huge mass of air to rise over Northern Europe, condense into water, and transport it to Earth. And so the rains began.

The Chronicle of Guillaume de Nangis, written by a monk at the Abbey of Saint-Denis, records their start in the middle of April. Other accounts have the storms arriving in Flanders around Pentecost, May 11. The abbot of Saint-Vincent, near Laon, noted that "it rained most marvelously and for so long." So long, in fact, that it didn't stop, except for a day or two, until August. By one count, it rained for 155 days in a row, virtually everywhere in Europe north of the Pyrenees and Alps, and west of the Urals: throughout France, Britain, the Baltic and German principalities, Poland, and Lithuania. A weather index prepared early in the twentieth century calculated the severity of winter frosts and summer rains throughout the Middle Ages, and not only found that the two decades 1310–1330 contained the worst winters on record but that the rainy years between 1310 and 1330 included the four worst winters in four centuries. Contemporary chroniclers from Nuremberg, Flanders, and Brittany all agree; one, writing in Salzburg, perhaps understated the case when he wrote that "the whole world was

---

*That is, less low pressure over Iceland; less high pressure over the Azores/Gibraltar/Lisbon.

troubled." In October 1315, four mills along the River Avon were swept away by floods; the same thing happened to fourteen bridges along the River Mur. In Saxony, more than 450 villages—people, cattle, and even houses—were washed away.

When it rains without a break for four months at a time, dikes and bridges disintegrate. Buildings with foundations flood; those without collapse. Quarries can't be mined. The two sources of fuel for heat and smelting—wood and peat—are too wet to burn. Meadows can't be mowed. Sod can't be cut.

But the biggest problem of all is that crops can neither be planted nor harvested. When seedbeds are too wet, pastures flood and grains rot. Bad as the rains were for bridges and roads, they were far worse for farmland itself, especially because the population growth enabled by the MWP had already pushed an ever-larger fraction of Europe's food production onto the region's poorest land. Soils that barely broke even in good years were about to be tested as never before.

It's been said that all of humanity is fed by ten inches of topsoil, and one constant theme of the four centuries of European history leading up to the rains of 1315 is the search for more of the valuable stuff. The dirt on which almost the entire food supply of the world depended—still depends today—is a sandwich of as many as eight distinct layers, resting on top of bedrock. The top layer isn't really soil at all, but not-yet-decomposed plant matter. Underneath is the true topsoil—a complex stew of light minerals, carbon-rich organic matter, and living things: worms, insects, and untold quadrillions of bacteria.* The very best soils derive from loess, essentially wind-blown silt that accumulates over centuries or millennia and whose constant weathering makes the topsoil rich in organics. In parts of China, the Russian steppe, and the American Midwest, the loess can be hundreds of feet deep.

All of the deforestation, draining, and cultivation of millions of acres in Europe had been, in this sense, a giant project for producing

---

*Under very wet conditions, the topsoil will turn into peat, itself useful as a fuel, and even more useful when a few million years, and a lot of pressure, turns it into coal.

topsoil. Among other things, feudal manorialism's system of crop rotation—one field in three allowed to "rest" each season—diffused throughout Europe by 1250, could raise productivity per worker by 50 percent. But in order for crop rotation to work its magic for a growing population, even more new land had to be found every year, which was a powerful spur to land reclamation: from forests, swamps, and pasture.

All those newly assarted lands didn't contain topsoils like those of the great river valleys, or even the Mediterranean littoral. The soil of northern Europe, for example, usually contained sufficient nutrients, but was so compacted that plowing it was just too much work. The soils that support old-growth trees tend to be extremely heavy, and even after the trees have been removed, a simple scratch plow or "ard" that farmers had been using for more than three thousand years to cut a furrow couldn't do the job. Most especially, it couldn't lift the bottom layer of topsoil to the top few inches; neither could it kill weeds, and so permit favored crops to prosper. The two-handled mold-board plow, which included a separate coulter (a kind of spike next to the plowshare), a horizontal blade behind the traditional vertical one, and the moldboard itself (a flat piece mounted at an angle to the share, which lifted the cut earth to one side as the plow moved), could easily turn a furrow in the newly revealed, rich-but-heavy soil of the north European plain.

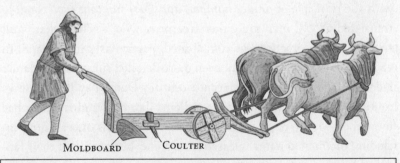

MOLDBOARD   COULTER

A Wheeled Moldboard Plow in the Fourteenth Century

A widely used medieval measure, the *virgate*, was the amount of land that could be plowed by two oxen in a season, approximately fifteen to twenty acres. This was the acreage thought to be required to support a single family of rural peasants.

However, a heavy wheeled plow wasn't an affordable expense for a single farmer. The new technology could only work in the open-field villages that, by the end of the thirteenth century, had become complex multigenerational organizations, with elaborate hierarchies of traditional occupations and folkways that had evolved for a single purpose: producing food. Cultivated village land was the foundation of all food production in Europe; plow teams, worked by a village's most skilled laborers (assisted by village smallholders, typically working for a day wage), accounted for virtually all production on Europe's manors, and anything that disrupted their productive capacity threatened the lives of millions of people.

In a typical village, the agricultural land was worked by both the tenant farmer on his own plot, paying his landlord for the privilege with a portion of his harvest, and by the landlord's employees—his plowmen, carters, cowherds, shepherds, and swineherds—farming the acres set aside for his personal use, his demesne, as salaried employees. The entire system required a wide assortment of transactions: payment in the form of produce, or crafts such as woven cloth, along with cash, and supervised by an even more complex set of managers— stewards and seneschals, bailiffs and reeves.

Underneath the village officers were the bulk of the rural population. A thirteenth-century jurist named Henry de Bracton is credited with the principle of *omnes homines aut liberi sun taut sevi*, roughly translated as "all men are either free or servile" . . . but what *"taut sevi"* meant in practice was complicated, particularly in England. In 1279, Edward I had ordered an even more detailed survey of England's land and laborers than the eleventh-century Domesday Book. In two centuries, the categories of serfs, villeins, bordars, and freemen had mushroomed into more than twenty fine gradations of peasantry, including *molmen* (tenants released from some, but not all, of their feudal obligations in return for rent), *customary tenants* (free tenants who received their holdings by being given a piece of earth), and *ecclesiasticals* (as expected: tenants tied to church property). Moreover, as the Medieval Warm Period began its long decline, the distinction between servitude and freedom had grown fuzzy. Status changed dramatically back and forth throughout the twelfth and thirteenth centuries, even within the lives of a single peasant. In some regions, such as northern France and Scandinavia, serfdom had nearly disappeared. In the German-speaking principalities that made up the Holy Roman Empire, it was widespread, but the status of serfs varied enormously, since some serf-born joined the imperial Civil Service (as *ministeriales*), intermarried with noble families, and even had vassals of their own. Land itself was frequently designated "free" or "villein" land (meaning that it could be farmed with either cash payment or labor obligation, respectively), with the implication that only freemen could own free land; but by 1300, thousands of villeins owned free land, and vice versa. A good estimate is that freemen, of some variety, outnumbered "pure" serfs by 1300, and 60 percent of tenanted land was held in free tenure. By the time the rains of 1315 arrived, a man's place in Europe's economic pecking order was more significant than his class; a wealthy villein had higher status in most villages than a poorer freeman. What villein and freeman had in common, however, is that both were tied to the soil.

And that soil was highly variable in quality. By the beginning of the fourteenth century, virtually all of the best topsoil had been reinforced and plowed with very long furrows, which meant it could absorb huge quantities of water without drainage problems, but, when the amount of annual precipitation increased fivefold—normal rainfall in England, France, and Germany is in the range of twenty-five to thirty inches annually; the storms of 1315 deposited at least a hundred inches—even the reinforced topsoil was washed away, leaving the clay subsoil behind. The newly revealed marginal stuff was too light and sandy to stand a chance. In England's midlands and the Scottish lowlands, from northern France to Poland, and in virtually all the farmland bordering the North Sea and the Baltic, as much as half of the arable land essentially disappeared, leaving behind not even clay, but rock. One study calculated that half of all the erosion suffered by cultivated land in Germany over the last fifteen hundred years happened during the decade that began with the rains of April 1315, during which the arable topsoil receded by an average of twenty-five centimeters: nearly ten inches.

Before the disastrous weather of April 1315 had even arrived, another set of storm clouds settled over England's royal court. Heartened by the success of King Robert at Bannockburn, a Welshman named Llywelyn Bren attacked Caerphilly Castle and ignited a near uprising; only his defeat at the hands of Roger Mortimer, one of the lords of the Welsh Marches, prevented a rebellion throughout Wales. Another revolt, this one led by the burgesses of the port town of Bristol, was put down by the earl of Pembroke before it could spread. But the real tempest was—as always—the work of Lancaster. The earl, who had sent the minimum number of troops to support his king in his march to relieve Stirling Castle, had already decided to spend 1314 building up his own army, putting himself in position to defend against a victorious Edward, or dictate to a defeated one. After Bannockburn, one can imagine him rubbing his hands together in glee at the opportunity, and his first blow was a successful revalidation of the Ordinances at a parliament meeting in Westminster in the spring of 1315.

The same parliament removed two of the king's most loyal supporters from the royal council, and, in response to the looming food crisis, pressured Edward to issue an ordinance fixing maximum prices for livestock, with a hay-fed ox at sixteen shillings, a cow twelve, and a pig three. England had already experienced an extraordinarily cold winter, so the torrential spring rains of 1315 made for a poor lambing year, and therefore saw a huge decline in the size of sheep flocks. Since prices had already been on the increase in England since 1305, the appropriate response was to control for another price increase in sheep, and therefore wool. Unfortunately, the royal revenues from wool exports fell from £12,200 in 1312–1313 to £7,100 in 1315–1316, which meant that the Crown's income stream was collapsing at a time when its expenses were essentially fixed. Supporting the garrison in Berwick alone was costing nearly £8,000 a year.

As the rains began, the oligarchs responsible for the welfare of

England—and everywhere in northern Europe—were, of course, unable to see the far larger dangers waiting a few months hence. Though they knew that crops must be sown in spring to be harvested in fall, they did not yet know that they were living through rains that would last longer than the ones faced by Noah, when "all the springs of the great deep burst forth, and the floodgates of the heavens were opened." By August, after four months of unremitting rain, even the least aware of England's rulers knew that there would be no fall harvest in 1315. The king's council, in response, required that no noble below the rank of earl would be permitted more than two dishes at any meal, at a time when members of the nobility were likely to eat five or more.

In an era that believed that natural disasters were punishments from heaven for misbehavior (the *Vita* was already blaming the rains on the English people, who "excel all others in three qualities: in pride, in craft, and in perjury") it no doubt seemed a good plan to limit opportunities for the sin of gluttony. It's not as if Edward was completely avoiding more practical measures. In December 1315, Edward asked his brother-in-law, Louis X (who had ascended to the French throne upon the death of his father, Philip IV, the previous November), to permit a number of earls, including Gloucester, Suffolk, and Norfolk, to buy grain from the farms of the Somme valley, around Caen and Dieppe. When he learned that the rains had been so widespread that northern France was in no better shape than southern England, the Crown gave safe-conduct to grain merchants from Spain, Sicily, and Genoa, in an attempt to restore grain supplies from the relatively untouched farms of the Mediterranean.

His strategy might have worked had not the same weather reappeared in early 1316. The hardships of one year were about to multiply sevenfold and transform into the Great Famine.

History's earliest recorded famines are chronicled in Egyptian stelae from the third millennium BCE. This was only to be expected in a region that was not only one of humanity's first to develop agriculture at all but also one whose farms depended on the annual Nile floods that carried the life-giving silt that made the river valley so fertile.

Too heavy a flood, or too light—and one year in five brought one or the other—and the risks of famine soared. But every ancient civilization experienced famine. The Babylonian epic of *Gilgamesh* tells of how the gods brought famine to cull the population that had annoyed them by "becoming numerous in the land [and] bellow[ing] like wild oxen." The Old Testament is very nearly a catalog of famines. One, in the twelfth chapter of Genesis, brings Abraham to Egypt; another, in chapter forty-one—the "seven lean years"—turns Joseph into Egypt's prime minister. Ruth and Naomi travel through a famine-struck landscape, and the prophets Elijah, Elisha, Nehemiah, Jeremiah, and Ezekiel constantly invoke the costs of famine. The Book of Lamentations warns, "those killed by the sword are better off than those who die of famine."

A millennium later, famine remained an ever-present danger and a regular feature in every contemporary history. The sixth-century CE *Chronicle of Joshua the Stylite* documents a famine in Edessa, in what is today southeast Turkey. In 499–501:

> there was a dearth of everything edible . . . everything that was not edible was cheap . . . the Emperor [Anastasius] gave no small sum of money to distribute among the poor. . . . [people ate] bitter vetches, and others were frying the withered fallen grapes . . . many villages and hamlets were left destitute of inhabitants [and] a countless multitude entered the city.*

Between 857 and 950, Europe experienced at least twenty famines large enough to be recorded in one medieval chronicle or the other. All of them were local, with local causes, such as the parasitic rust fungus that destroyed the Iberian wheat crop in both 915 and 929, with the by-now familiar lament from an anonymous Aragonese: "Destitution at last reached such a pitch that men began to devour each other, and the flesh of a son was preferred to his love."

No famine, however, is absolute. That is, there has never been a

---

*Vetches were ancient grain legumes, resembling red lentils, but so bitter that they are now only consumed by cattle.

famine where there was absolutely no food to be had. The modern Italian word for famine, *carestia*, comes from the Latin *caritas* or "dearth," which doesn't mean nonexistent, but expensive.* Both etymologically and practically, the nature of famine has always been economic, an explicit function of the cost of food. Famine is what happens when food becomes so expensive that a significant number of people cannot afford to buy it. Today, most major aid agencies break famines into different categories depending on the relationship between food and income, defining phase one as "generally food secure"; phase two as "moderately/borderline food insecure"; three as "acute food and livelihood crisis"; and four as a "humanitarian emergency." Only phase five qualifies as a "famine/humanitarian catastrophe."

Just as famines are categorized by severity, they are ranked by destructiveness, using the yardstick of "excess mortality": the number of total deaths greater than would have been in the case in the absence of famine. The greatest man-made famines are also some of the greatest famines in raw numbers: 9 million excess mortality during the Russian Civil War of 1921–22; 5 million more during Stalin's collectivization of 1932–33; and the biggest of all, China's Great Leap Forward of 1959–61, with an estimated 15 to 25 million excess mortality; though it should be noted that even these "artificial" famines were associated with droughts, floods, and harvest shortfalls. During the decidedly man-made famine of the Great Leap Forward, destruction was exacerbated by the fact that "eight of Shantung's twelve rivers had no water in them."

No famine is purely natural, or completely man-made. There are, however, degrees of responsibility. Modern famines are almost always at least man-accelerated; earlier ones, far more dependent on the vagaries of nature. Many appear to have been the consequences of extraordinary one-time events, such as volcanic eruptions (Laki in 1783, and Tambora in 1815 are the causes of two of Europe's most severe modern famines, while the so-called One Rabbit—the name of the year 1454 on the Aztec calendar—famine of pre-conquistador Mexico was

---

*In the early Latin of the Great Famine, *caritas*—which would later come to mean "charity"—acquired adjectives like *maxima*, *permaxima*, and even *intollerabilis*.

preceded by the eruption of the Vanuatuan volcano Kuwae in 1452) or ecological shocks, like the *Phytophthora infestans* that destroyed Ireland's potato crop in the 1840s. Usually, though, they have been driven by extreme versions of "normal" weather, as was the case after Ireland's Great Frost of 1740, when its people suffered a "year of carnage" or *Bliain an Áir*. And, of course, the rains of 1315.

Every famine, therefore, is to a greater or lesser degree a creature of changes in climate, or at least weather. One of the best known of those changes occurs most Decembers when an area in the tropical Pacific Ocean experiences a shift in temperature of about half a degree Celsius. When the temperature increases, the result is an El Niño (so-called because it's generally noticed around the same time that the west coast of South America prepares to celebrate the birth of Jesus).* This temperature change creates a huge turning gyre that displaces surface water largely east to west, while an equatorial countercurrent moves west to east along a line several degrees north of the equator.

Typically, an El Niño surges annually. But one or two times each decade, it is reinforced by the so-called southern oscillation—the temperature around Tahiti goes up when the temperature around Darwin, in Australia, goes down, and vice versa—and earns the acronym ENSO, for El Niño–Southern Oscillation.

ENSOs have their largest impact on nations and people that surround the Pacific, from China to Peru, but it's such a huge driver of worldwide climate that its effects are everywhere. The ENSO of 1876–77, for example, produced huge rains over Southwest Asia and the American tropics, with corresponding droughts in Brazil and southern Africa. Another ENSO preceded the Ethiopian famine of 1984–85. The "great drought" or *grande seca* of 1877–79 in Brazil killed at least half a million, and has been called "the most costly natural disaster in the history of the western hemisphere."

One artifact of researching famines is that almost everyone discovers fewer of them in antiquity; the fact that Ethiopia suffered "only" four famines between 100 CE and 1400 CE, and twenty-three between

---

*A comparable decrease, which usually follows a year later, is known as La Niña.

1900 and today, is almost certainly evidence of better documentation rather than greater hunger. Even for famines that can be found in the historical record, their effects are hard to quantify; claims that the Chinese famine of 209–203 BCE killed up to 90 percent of the population, or that the Bengal famine of 1770 resulted in a loss of one-third of the population, or even that the famine that accompanied World War I killed 40 percent of the population of Persia, are both impossible to verify and highly improbable. Nonetheless, there is some consensus around the numbers associated with the deadliest famines in history.

The first multiyear famine probably occurred in Egypt during the third millennium BCE, during which the Nile failed to break its banks for seven years in a row (the memory of which may be an inspiration for the biblical story of Joseph). The two worst collapses, in terms of the percentage of deaths among the pre-famine population, are both Irish: the frost-driven famine of 1740–41, in which 13 percent of the population died, and the "potato famine" that ran from 1846–52, with 12 percent mortality. But they were, of course, restricted to a single island. The excess mortality during the seven years of the Great Famine was somewhere between 5 and 12 percent *for all of northern Europe*.

In its geographic extent, in its duration, in the number of lives it touched and erased, the Great Famine was unprecedented. It wasn't merely a crisis of production, population, weather, or war. David Arnold, a historian at the University of London, has found that almost all famines tend to follow one of four different scenarios: (a) a brief but traumatic shock to agricultural productivity that pushes far beyond its best-case-in-good-weather output; (b) a sustained failure of weather, particularly rainfall; (c) a sustained problem of distribution, usually caused by war (including the special case of famines caused by siege, where food is not only scarce but can't be acquired elsewhere, at any price); or (d) conservatism in agricultural practice, which turns a modest problem into a cascade. The Great Famine followed all four. And it followed them year after year after year.

This matters even more than it seems. One season of poor weather could destroy an entire harvest. But a truly serious famine isn't caused by a single lost harvest; it is almost always the result of back-to-back losses, which means that its likelihood is the same as the probability of successive seasons of bad weather. Nearly four centuries of monthly mean temperature data in Europe reveal what a statistician would call *positive serial correlation*: good years tend to be followed by other good years. However, the weather that matters for famine isn't the average but the extremes. In Europe, for millennia, an extremely cold or rainy year is one that deviated from the average by more than 10 percent—an extra month of frost with five or even six times the normal rainfall—and such deviation has been recorded in successive years only twice since 1659, which makes the years 1315–1317 about a once-every-two-hundred-years event.

Nature wasn't the only enemy facing the rural peasantry. Even in non-famine years, European farmers learned to fear *disettes*—the time after the grain from one harvest had been exhausted and before that from the new one arrived. Any decade from the middle of the twelfth century on would see variations in harvest size of 10 to 20 percent just based on fluctuations in rainfall and sunshine, and a shortfall of 20 percent meant starvation for at least some people. The shortfall in 1315 was as much as 60 percent, and it would be more than 20 percent for at least two more years throughout Europe. Death records for the peasant population living on the manors of Hampshire, Berkshire, and Somerset show deaths in the range of 10 percent between 1316 and 1318. In Essex and Worcestershire, the same data show a mortality rate of 15 percent. Both were at least three times normal.*

Those who avoided starvation faced another threat: lawlessness, already rife in medieval Europe, but dramatically worsened after the failed harvest of 1315. In Kent, during 1316–17, a third of all thefts were of grain and grain products like bread and ale; 40 percent were livestock. Rioters took over the French town of Douai. Landless knights and men-at-arms, who had been well trained in looting as a necessity and tactic of war, were well positioned, in between battles, to put their skills to use in a more entrepreneurial fashion. Extortion

---

*Though relatively few actually starved to death. For more on hunger-related disease, see chapter 9.

became chronic, as armed men demanded the output of the peasantry, only occasionally using the cover of a (frequently fraudulent) royal warrant. One minor noble, William de Cotes, used a false commission to demand ten oxen, two horses, four cows, and £20 of assorted agricultural produce from the village of Saintbury; another, Richard de Richmond, blackmailed a parson for a ransom of £40. With thousands of men like de Cotes and de Richmond, few could feel free of the threat of extortion.

Crimes of all kinds are always one of famine's most reliable companions. Perhaps because, among all natural (or mostly natural) disasters, famines are by far the slowest moving, they are particularly able to undermine the more elevated human feelings, one hungry day at a time: Honesty and generosity don't disappear, but they become harder to find when people go without food. The same people who show enormous courage in the face of earthquakes and fires find their bravery exhausted by months with too little to eat. Hopelessness replaces hope. And hopeless people commit acts they would otherwise find unbelievable, even unthinkable. Such as cannibalism.

There are always stories of cannibalism during famines. Some are better documented than others; during a famine in third-century BCE China, the emperor officially granted parents the right to eat their own children; or, if too squeamish, to sell them for food. The frequency of cannibalism during the Great Famine isn't easy to document, but there is no doubt that it was widely believed *at the time* to be widespread: In Estonia, in *"Anno Domini 1315, tanta fames in Lyvonia et Esconia orta est, quod matres filiis vescebantur"* (the mothers were fed the children). An Irish chronicle recorded that between 1315 and 1318, "people used to eat one another, without doubt, throughout Erin" and, at the height of the famine, they "were so destroyed by hunger that they extracted bodies of the dead from cemeteries and dug out the flesh from the skulls and ate it; and women ate their children out of hunger."

The monk and chronicler Johannes de Trokelowe wrote, in his *Annales*, "Men and women furtively ate their children and even strangers in many places" while "jailed thieves . . . devoured themselves at the moment when they were half-alive." The fifteenth-century annals of the priory of Bermondsey—probably written around 1433—claimed (from earlier records) that *"pauperes enim pueros suos manducabant, canes, murelegos, stercus, columbarum."** Another contemporary chronicle, from Poland and Silesia, describes the same horrific scene: "in many places parents devoured their children and children their parents; also many ate the flesh from cadavers" hanging from gibbets.

The horrors of the famine that began with the lost harvest of 1315 were not a direct result of climate change. *Weather* is a nonlinear system, one in which a small change in initial conditions can have giant consequences in subsequent ones. *Climate* isn't, at least not in the same way. While some tantalizing research suggests that this phenomenon replicates itself in long-term climate change—that a graph displaying six months of weather can resemble a graph of six centuries of climate; a self-similar "fractal" like a coastline that looks the same for a hundred feet as it does for a hundred miles—it is a long way from widespread acceptance.

For one thing, long-term climate seems less sensitive to even dramatic changes in initial conditions. In 1257, a huge volcanic eruption, probably in Indonesia—the biggest in millennia—may have spread a particulate veil of sulfur around the planet and initiated a series of reinforcing feedback loops between Northern Hemisphere sea ice and the water surrounding it, with the result that ice caps in Arctic Canada and Iceland began advancing twenty years later. There is even a good argument to be made that this same volcanic eruption was responsible for a famine of its own: "In that year [1257]," according to the *Chronicles of the Mayors and Sheriffs of London*, "there was a

---

*Which translates, confusingly, as "the poor ate their children, dogs, cats, and bird dung." More than likely, the last comes from a mistranslation of a passage in Second Kings describing the siege of Samaria by Ben-Hadad, king of Aram, where "a donkey's head sold for eighty shekels, and a quarter of dove's dung for five shekels." The original Hebrew more likely meant something like "seed pods," though it is unclear why the Bermondsey writer thought that eating children, cats, and dogs wasn't repulsive enough.

failure of the crops; upon which failure, a famine ensued, to such a degree that the people from the villages resorted to the City for food; and there, upon the famine waxing still greater, many thousands perished." However, and despite an abnormally hot summer in 1262 (also related to the volcanic eruption, which messed up atmospheric circulation for at least five years), things reverted to normal. There were tremendously cold winters regularly between 1308 and 1312—dogs could hunt rabbits in the middle of the frozen-over Thames during the winter of 1309–10—but by 1312, the NAO index had shifted again, and the winter of 1312–13 was again mild.

Moreover, the weather systems that caused the Great Famine, and carried decades of instability along with a generally declining average temperature, were, like the Medieval Warm Period itself, largely confined to Europe, particularly northern Europe. Farther afield, the Indian monsoons, Nile floods, and other annual weather events that determined agricultural productivity continued to operate within normal boundaries. The rains of 1315–1316 were distinctively western European.

This doesn't mean that worldwide climate didn't change at all. Much of the world did experience a climatic downturn throughout the fourteenth century (really beginning in 1275). The Little Ice Age, as it has come to be known—the term dates to a 1939 paper by the geologist François Mathes on the growth of glaciers in California's Sierra Nevada Mountains—was real, even if its causes are even less well understood than those of the Medieval Warm Period that preceded it. There are respectable theories ranging from increased albedo (the amount of light reflected by the surface of the Earth) because of greater cultivated land to a drop in atmospheric CO_2 because of deforestation to variations in solar radiation. Sunspot activity started an astonishingly regular increase around the year 800, peaked just before the beginning of the fourteenth century, and then fell like a stone for the next century, reaching a minimum not seen since the third century BCE. One thing about long-term climate change not in doubt, however, particularly when the change is from a period of anomalous stability to something else, is that it brings with it far greater volatility.*

If the normal destructiveness of weather is amplified by underlying climate change, the great rains of 1315 were also magnified by human activity. Some of that activity was bureaucratic: By 1316, Edward's tax collectors were collecting grain and fodder from England's peasantry, as part of their "prises"—property confiscated at the prerogative of the king. The abuse was exacerbated through 1317, as both prises and taxes on "moveable" property, needed to support ongoing English garrisons and to repay the money borrowed from Antonio Pessagno to pay for the 1314 campaign that foundered at Bannockburn, were collected simultaneously despite the famine. It was a losing game: peasants cut back on consumption, which left even more grain and other movables to be taxed. But as much as the tax policy harmed the south of England, it was disastrous in the northern counties of Cumberland, Westmorland, and Northumberland, where residents begged the Crown for a three-year holiday from purveyors and other of the king's middlemen.

Nor were the Crown's attempts to control prices effective. The Ordinance of 1315, passed at Westminster in order to fix prices for commodities during the famine, failed so utterly that Edward ordered it repealed on January 14, 1316. He wasn't the only one to try price controls. The magistrates of London, on September 21, 1316, ordered a cap on the price of ale: no one was permitted to sell a gallon of the worst ale for more than three farthings, or the best for three halfpence, under threat of expulsion from the city for a third offense. Edward liked this one so much that in January 1317, he ordered that the price of the best ale in country towns couldn't exceed a farthing, which meant, of course, that brewers were obliged to pay profiteering prices for grain but to sell their product at a heavy, and unprofitable, discount. Contemporary chroniclers called the price regulations "beyond reason,"

---

*It's a lesson well worth repeating in the beginning of the twenty-first century, every time someone with a political ax to grind uses either a March blizzard or an August rainstorm to argue for—or against—anthropogenic climate change. It's true that weather is orders of magnitude more variable than climate; a particularly warm week in February doesn't argue for global warming any more than a particularly cold week in September.

stating "it is better to buy dear than to find in case of need that there is nothing to be had."

And there was, frequently, nothing to be had. Throughout 1315, the Scots continued to press their advantage by raids into the Tyne valley and other parts of northern England, burning everything they couldn't carry, and returning with enormous herds of cattle. So fearsome were James Douglas's raids that Northumbrian mothers sang their children to sleep with the lullaby, *"Hush ye, hush ye/Do not fret ye/The Black Douglas/Shall not get ye."*

The raids were destructive in themselves; in combination with the famine, they were devastating. An anonymous chronicler from Meaux Abbey in Yorkshire claimed that Northumberland was left a wasteland for fifteen years, "deserted by men and wild and domestic beasts." The *Chronicle of Lanercost* documents that the raids by Bruce and his lieutenants between 1314 and 1319 were tactics in service of deliberate starvation, "trampling down the crops by themselves and their beasts," burning the harvest "when the crop had been stored in barns . . . both the corn upon which the people depended for sustenance during that year and the houses where they had been able to take refuge."

By the end of 1315, moreover, the combination of Edward's taxes, the first of two lost harvests, and constant destruction of infrastructure—barns, farm equipment, and mills—by the troops of both Bruce and Edward was devastating not only the agricultural productivity but the entire economy of both northern England and southern Scotland. Literally dozens of lords in the Anglo-Scottish borderlands complained—loudly—to both Bruce and Edward of their near bankruptcies. As 1316 began, an inquiry into the value of lands held by lay lords in the borderlands described estate after estate as "waste." And not just cropland: the value of a typical fishery on the River Tweed, which might have been worth hundreds of pounds in 1300, fell by anywhere from 30 to 100 percent by 1315.

Bruce could ravage northern England, but he couldn't, by raids alone, force Edward to recognize an independent Scotland. He attempted to get the attention of the English king by authorizing privateers to act in the Irish Sea. It worked well enough to force Edward to pull back on his support for the campaign in Flanders being waged at the time by his brother-in-law, Louis X, but as long as most of the wealth of the nation was in the south, beyond the reach of Scottish hobelars, Edward could afford to lick his wounds, think about invading Scotland yet again, and contemplate the collapse of England's ability to feed itself.

The reliably melancholic writers of the *Vita Edwardi Secundi* tell us that "the floods of rain have rotted almost all the seed, to such an extent that the prophecy of Isaiah might seem now to be fulfilled, for he says that ten acres of vineyard shall yield one little measure, and thirty bushels of seed shall yield three bushels . . . in many places the hay lay so long under water that it could neither be mown or gathered." By the end of 1316, the rains abated—some—but the winter of 1317–18 was the harshest of all, lasting (in the record of a French chronicle) "from the feast of Saint Andrew or thereabouts until Easter" . . . which is to say, from November 30 to April 23, or just over twenty weeks. An English chronicle reads: "A thusent winter ther bifore com nevere non so strong . . . com never wrecche into Engelond that made men more agaste."

They were "agaste" outside of England as well. One consequence of the frighteningly volatile weather was sea erosion. As the Arctic Ocean becomes colder, it increases the temperature differential between it and the Atlantic Gulf Stream; the bigger the gradient in the oceans between about 50° and 65°N, the more storms in the North Sea basin. The more storms, the more frequent the storm surges; and geography dictated that Atlantic storm surges were narrowed and compressed like a funnel between Britain and the Continent—the Channel is only twenty-two miles wide between Dover and Calais—making the northern European coastline uniquely vulnerable.

Which is what the record shows: floods increased from fewer than five annually in the twelfth century and before to more than twelve by the end of the thirteenth and the beginning of the fourteenth, a peak in storm activity "unsurpassed in the last 2,000 years." The low-lying wetlands that had been reclaimed over the four centuries of the

MWP were inundated, in northern France, the Netherlands, and southeast England; more than two thousand acres of onetime marshland that had been converted to cropland in eight villages in Sussex alone were submerged. Dunwich, which was one of the five wealthiest ports in England in the late thirteenth century, was so devastated by one flood after another that 269 houses (including crofts and barns), 10 other buildings, and 2 shops had disappeared—fully a quarter of the entire port town. By the 1330s, most of five parishes of the town, and up to 600 houses, had been "reclaimed" by the newly unstable sea.

Without enough water, even the best soil is nothing but a desert. The perverse lesson of 1315 to the farmers of northern Europe was that too much water is as destructive as too little. Perhaps even more so. Lands parched by drought can return to productivity as soon as water returns; floods so extensive that they wash away the soil itself have a longer-lasting effect. Even five years after the rains began in the spring of 1315, contemporaneous German chronicles were still describing lands suffering from "an unheard-of barrenness." One French Cistercian monk called it a *sterilitas* "hitherto unheard-of in the realm."

CHAPTER SEVEN

"A Dearness of Wheat"

1316–1317

The Abbey Church of Saint Albans is located in Hertfordshire, about twenty miles north of London. It's named for Britain's first Christian martyr, a third-century Roman who assumed the identity of a priest and was beheaded in his place. And though the present-day church dates "only" to 1077, the site of the martyrdom has been a destination for pilgrims since at least the eighth century. As a Benedictine abbey— it's been an Anglican cathedral since 1877—it reached the peak of its notoriety in the early fourteenth century, famous for the gorgeous interiors painted by Walter of Colchester, and the thirteenth-century chronicles of the choir monk Matthew Paris. One of the most vivid accounts of the famine comes to us from a Saint Albans monk, Johannes de Trokelowe. Its most famous medieval abbot, Richard Wallingford, was a brilliant mathematician and the inventor of the most complicated astronomical clock in Britain.

Its best-chronicled *moment*, however, had nothing to do with monastic architecture, history, or even horology. On August 10, 1315, King Edward and Queen Isabella arrived at Saint Albans to celebrate the feast of Saint Lawrence. Even at what was then one of the largest churches in England, a visit from the royal family was a notable event, demanding the greatest hospitality any vassal could afford. Normally, fresh meat would be slaughtered and butchered, aged cheese brought up from cellars, and barrels of the rarest wine tapped. However, there was nothing normal about the summer of 1315; in the words of de Trokelowe, when Edward and Isabella arrived at Saint Albans, "The panic so weighed on the land . . . that scarcely any bread could even be bought."

The image—no bread for the rulers of England—remains an enduring symbol for the Great Famine. It's not that bread was medieval Europe's *only* food source. Cattle, sheep, and even goats were raised for their meat, though most of it was consumed after salting and drying. Fresh meat was, almost always, reserved for feasts—religious celebrations distinguished by eating rather than fasting; the word "festival" is an etymological cousin. Lamb, for example, was so precious that even wealthy aristocrats and churchmen ate it only once a year, at Easter. Every year, northern Europe fermented hundreds of thousands of pounds of cheese, the concentrated—and, more relevantly, storable—essence of milk; ocean fisheries produced huge quantities of protein in the form of smoked cod—*gadid*—and herring, at least in those parts of Europe with access to the North Sea. English kings were so famously fond of lampreys—an eel-like river fish—that a Christmas tradition of presenting the sovereign with a pie, in which the lampreys were cooked in syrup and covered with a crust, lasted until the nineteenth century.

But all of them, whether the luxuries only the wealthy could afford or commonplace foods like milk and cheese, vanish into insignificance next to the calories derived from grain. Between 80 to 90 percent of all the food calories produced and consumed across the entire Eurasian landmass during the Medieval Warm Period depended on the same seed-rich grasses that had launched the Neolithic agricultural revolution in Mesopotamia a hundred centuries before. In pre-famine northern Europe alone, records of the day show a single, moderately prosperous family of ten purchasing five and a half *tons* of grain annually; the earl of Leicester's household used three hundred pounds of grain *a day*, whether the earl's family was in residence or not. Most of it was milled into the flour used to bake the four-pound loaves that were frequently the daily ration for an entire family—at least those living north of the fourteenth century's vague poverty line: artisans and tradesmen in the towns, freemen and prosperous villeins in the country. Those a little further down the status ladder made do with the stuff known as *maslin* (or "horsebread"), which stretched out the wheat, rye, and barley flour with uncooked legumes, unmilled wheat, and lots of filler. The poorest families were likelier to get their daily rations in the form of *frumenty*—a gelatinized porridge of crushed and boiled seeds—and especially beer, which provided calories in an unfailingly popular form, down to the present day.

There are a dozen different reasons for a diet so dependent on grains, including the hardiness, disease resistance, and durability of grains in storage, and, not at all trivially, their ability to be fermented. But most crucially, grains possess a miraculous knack for assembling fat, carbohydrates, and protein in a single seed.

All of the grasses had their place in the human food chain. Rye, the hardiest of all, able to survive in the wet, cold lands of the post-glacial forests, was a huge part of the northern European diet from the days those forests were first cleared until it was displaced by potatoes in the seventeenth century. Rye's only real disadvantage was its vulnerability to the mold that causes ergotism—the same hallucinogenic ingredient found in LSD. A few historians even blame the frequency of mass delusions among the rural peasantry of the Medieval Warm Period—hysterical fits, epidemics of biting, demonic possession, the uncontrollable muscular chorea known as St. Vitus' Dance—on their heavy consumption of rye.

Barley is even more ecologically tolerant, particularly to cold, rocky soils everywhere from ancient Greece to Tibet, and could be sprouted in a kitchen garden, then boiled and served as pottage; the barley water left behind could be drunk, sometimes sweetened, or fermented into barley beer, which explains north Germany's strong preference for six-rowed barley (*Hordeum vulgare*). Millet is to hot, dry ecosystems—including Ethiopia, China, and West Africa—what barley is to cold.

The only significant Old World grain not found in medieval Europe—maize, or corn, is a New World grass—was rice, which provides a fifth of the calories and an eighth of the protein consumed in the modern world, but wouldn't be cultivated extensively in the Mediterranean until the fifteenth century.*

---

*Entire books have been written on the significance of grains to particular civilizations; by the fourteenth century, typical rice yields in east Asia were as much as five times that of Europe's cereal grains, didn't deplete the soil (because it's grown in river-watered terraces), and required

In medieval Europe, though, and throughout much of the modern world, the preferred method for eating those seeds was bread. Bread has been a synecdoche for food for millennia, and not just as the stuff breadwinners win; the word "lord" is derived from the Old English *hlaford,* meaning "keeper of the bread," and "lady" from *hlaefdigge:* "kneader of the dough." For the overwhelming bulk of Europeans, bread and beer were *the* food sources, providing between fifteen hundred and two thousand calories per person per day.

Though bread can be, and is, made using all sorts of grain, it still depends on the two-part protein that captures the gases released by yeast respiration, and is therefore necessary for risen bread: gluten. Corn and rice can't produce any true gluten at all. Other cereal grains produce some, but the one whose protein chemistry produces the most, by far, is wheat.

Wheat, which now covers more than 650 million acres of the Earth's surface, is—and has been for centuries—the world's most extensively grown and consumed crop. Throughout medieval Europe and Britain, the best land was reserved for wheat farms. The rivers were dotted with watermills for grinding it. European farmers grew any number of varieties of the precious stuff, including emmer wheat (*Triticum dicoccum*), einkorn wheat (*Triticum monococcum*), and spelt (*Triticum spelta*), but the favorite was, and is, bread wheat (*Triticum aestivum*).

Wheat's commercial value was matched by its ecological cost. Like all plants, it needs nitrogen to make chlorophyll, and like all plants, must capture reactive nitrogen from the ground. In the words of historian Fernand Braudel, "Wheat's unpardonable fault was its low yield . . . [it] devours the soil, and cannot be cultivated on the same land for two years running." In the wild, dying grasses keep the nitrogen in balance by returning their seeds to the soil. When humans cultivate those grasses in the form of wheat or any other grain, the whole point is to take them out of the soil, and put them into a flour mill.

Even without the catastrophic rains, wheat production was a tough

little manure and significantly less acreage. However, because of the tending needs of wet-rice farming, they were far more labor-intensive, and, in the minds of some more deterministic historians, a key factor in the growth of authoritarian government.

life; not merely because of the brutal demands of harvesting using nothing but muscle and a foot-long sickle, but the profound inefficiencies of medieval farms.

The farming manuals of the day weren't especially helpful. The most popular, the twenty-eight "Rules of Saint Robert," written by Robert Grosseteste, bishop of Lincoln, consists almost entirely of advice to lords about running household accounts, treating subordinates, and staying on the right side of the complicated laws regarding land tenure. A manual written in French by Walter de Henley was far more specific—"an acre of wheat requires three plowings, except lands which are sown yearly . . . each plowing is worth sixpence, and harrowing a penny, and on the acre it is necessary to sow at least two bushels"—but still used up pages advising landlords how to avoid being cheated by tenants: "one often sees the grange-keeper and barnkeeper join together to do mischief." The absence of practical information isn't terribly surprising. Widespread illiteracy, particularly among the peasantry, meant that no one who actually plowed a field depended on anything written in a book. Medieval technique was thus very much a matter of rule-of-thumb, if that, and depended on folk wisdom to describe how much seed to sow. Too little, and weeds choked out the crop; too much, and the crop choked itself.

The lack of any standard measure for seeding partly accounts for the frighteningly low productivity of medieval wheat farming. So does the constant pressure from even "normal" weather: autumn hail, for example, regularly knocked grain off the stalk. Wheat kernels also happen to be a favorite food for rodents—modern farms can be home to tens of thousands per acre—and birds. They're also subject to diseases like smuts and rusts. Combined with the widespread nitrogen depletion caused by the four centuries of expanding acreage, it's a wonder that anyone made a crop at all, even before the rains of 1315 washed away topsoils all over Europe. In England, at the time of the Norman Conquest, somewhere between 6.7 and 8.5 million acres of land were under cultivation, overwhelmingly with cereal grains. Those acres were able to feed a population of around 1.5 million fairly easily. By 1300, 11.5 million acres were struggling to feed 5 million.

The acreage simply couldn't expand fast enough to keep up with population. The reason wasn't always a deficiency of arable land—England had perhaps 26 million at least nominally arable acres available—but a lack of power to cultivate it. A clue is in the word "acre" itself, which originated by calculating the amount of land that could be plowed by one man behind a single ox in a single day. The *virgate*, another early allocation of land, was the amount of land that could be plowed by two oxen in a plowing season; the virgate—generally between fifteen and twenty acres—was also supposedly the amount needed to support a family.* A *hide* (averaging one-hundred-plus acres) might be as few as four virgates or as many as seven. The *furlong*, which survives today only around horse racing tracks, was originally the length of a single strip that oxen could plow without resting, or forty rods, each of five and a half yards. A *carucate* was the land that could be plowed by an eight-ox team in a plowing season, or four virgates. With so many measures in use at the time, calculating and comparing acreage was a complicated exercise, made even more so by the inability of medieval arithmetic to express a fraction with anything but a 1 in the numerator. An agricultural treatise described a plot of one acre, three and 9/16 roods (a rood is a quarter-acre, or a rectangle one furlong by one rod) as "one acre, and a half acre, and a rood, and a half rood, and a sixteenth of a rood." And if that wasn't complicated enough, the need to plow land in strips, as well as the legal tradition that made land inheritance "partible," resulted in fragmenting much of the manorial land in Europe into a crazy-quilt of dozens of parcels, sometimes two hundred meters long by as little as twenty feet wide.

Peasants who might know nothing of the boundaries of their country, or even their lord's manor, were well aware of those of their villages. An English tradition known as "gang-days" took an entire village's children out a-ganging: they would be dunked in boundary streams, and bumped against boundary trees and outcroppings, so as

---

*Thus, a village with eighteen hundred acres (like the well-studied village of Elton) would require about twenty plows to feed its 120 or so families . . . which, indeed, was the number it owned.

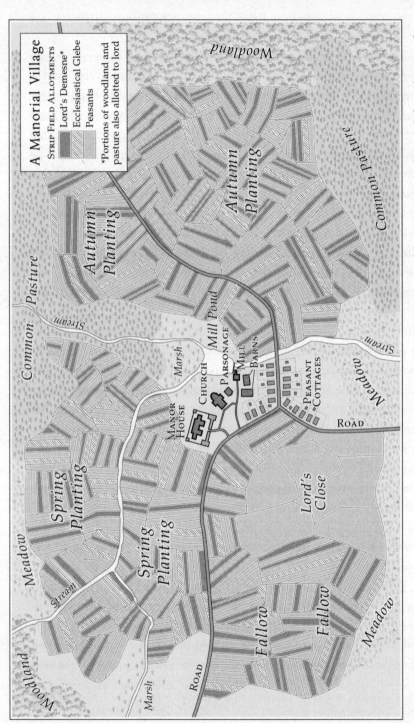

A Manorial Village

STRIP FIELD ALLOTMENTS
Lord's Demesne*
Ecclesiastical Glebe
Peasants

*Portions of woodland and pasture also allotted to lord

After generations of inheritance and subdivision, the narrow strips of manorial smallholdings were frequently barely wide enough for a plow to make a single back-and-forth circuit.

to define the borders of the village. They knew their place, in more ways than one.

But those children would grow up to be the freemen, villeins, and serfs who plowed the land, distributed the seed, and harvested the crops—a privilege for which they paid, typically one sack of grain in twenty. Even then, the remaining nineteen sacks of grain weren't especially useful for making bread (or even frumenty) until they were ground into flour. Milling grain was the source of every European landlord's *real* authority. The law may have given a baron or earl the right to tax his tenants, but the mills were what gave him the power. Not only was another sack of grain demanded as payment for turning the remaining eighteen into flour, but a monopoly on the water and windmills that did so gave each landlord a way of profiting from every kernel of wheat, or barley, or rye, grown on his land.

In retrospect, it seems obvious that the tool needed for producing 90 percent of the calories consumed by medieval humanity would be invested with such importance. Throughout continental Europe, one of the most valuable feudal privileges was a monopoly on the milling of grain produced by one's vassals; in Normandy, the *banalités* (which also included payment for use of the lord's oven and wine presses) were the single biggest driver of growth in landlord income. The reason was centralization, not efficiency: the lord could not supervise milling done at home by hand or (more rarely) by horse. But the capital needed to build a wind or watermill was available only to the feudal master of the land, who could supervise, and therefore tax, the produce of his vassals. This made milling a reliable arena of conflict. One of the chroniclers who recorded the history of the Abbey of Bury St. Edmunds tells the story of a tenant named Herbert the Dean, who built himself a windmill under the logic that the "free benefit of the wind ought not to be denied to any man." His lord responded with a vow that "by God's face I will never eat bread till that building be thrown down." In the words of the historian Marc Bloch, it was a "war of wind and water against human muscle," and the battlefields of that war were, literally, everywhere; 5,624 mills were surveyed in the Domesday Book of 1086. Every one of them was a constant provocation to the rural peasantry. The people of the village of Saint Albans, where Edward and Isabella could find no bread, spent more than a century fighting for the right to mill grain themselves, using querns and hand mills. During the famine, they actually invaded the abbey itself, where the stones of their hand mills had been taken for confiscation, and destroyed the floor that the monks had built with them.

By then, though, the floods of 1315 and 1316 had already done much of their work for them. The floodwaters had not only washed away the topsoil covering tens of thousands of acres of wheat fields, they had also destroyed thousands of the mills that turned the grain into flour.

Two years of rain left a mark everywhere. In a good year during the Medieval Warm Period, wheat might produce eight to twelve bushels an acre. In the fertile South Downs of southeast England, which used a variety of what were considered advanced agricultural practices, such as applying marl—lime-rich calcium carbonate—and planting legumes, the net yield was still only nine bushels an acre of wheat, and twelve for barley (today it's more than fifty). Of those eight to twelve bushels, between two and three were put back into the ground as seed corn for the next harvest. Those lousy yields were what the land was producing *before* the rains of 1315: in Winchester productivity dropped by at least 15 percent across the board; wheat that had produced net yields of 3:1 was now yielding 2.6:1. By 1316, wheat and rye harvests were only 60 percent of their historical averages, and they stayed at least 25 percent below those averages for at least another five years. Though barley and oats are less vulnerable to too much water—they are far more sensitive to drought—the rains of 1315 went on for so long that resistance to overwatering was beside the point: barley and oat seeds couldn't even take root in the flooded fields, and yielded only two-thirds of their pre-1315 harvests.

It may have seemed, to the farmers of northern England, that the rains were disastrous enough. They did not reckon on the Scots. Bolton Priory, in Yorkshire, was raided by Bruce's hobelars in both 1318 and 1319. Total grain production wasn't even recorded in 1319, because the raiders took the account roll, but even between 1320 and 1324, production was only a third of the level achieved before 1315. At some points, yields actually dropped below 1:1, which meant the population was literally eating its own seed corn, and, fearing even worse from the future than it had enjoyed in the past, the priory closed.

Cereals were the most important, but far from the only, foodstuffs produced and consumed in fourteenth-century Europe. The multiple traumas of weather, disease, and war were disastrous for them all.

For example, almost everything people ate required salt, either as a preservative or as an essential mineral. During the fourteenth century, most of it was produced in seaside salt pans: huge, concave, clay-lined depressions built between the lines of high and low tide. There salt "farmers" waited for it to evaporate, using both sun and fires set alongside the pans. However, during the rainy seasons of 1315 and 1316, the sun rarely shone, and the fuel for fires—wood and peat—was too wet to burn. Alternative ways of making salt, such as *briquetage*—pouring seawater into coarse pottery containers, then putting the containers in fires and, eventually, breaking the pottery to get the salt lining the interior, a technique dating to the Bronze Age— or boiling away the brine in huge cauldrons, were even more fuel intensive. But after four months of rain, fuel was even more difficult to find than food. The cost of salt skyrocketed, its average price in Europe doubling during the famine years. In England, the average price for twenty-five pounds of salt was three shillings in 1310; in 1316 it had quadrupled to between 11 shillings and 13 shillings.

And so, therefore, did the price of every commodity that depended on salt. During the Medieval Warm Period, huge schools of Atlantic herring massed in the North Atlantic every spring, and passed into the Baltic via the coasts of Scotland, and were so ridiculously abundant— and the seas so relatively warm and calm—that catching them in open boats became, for the first time, a practical business. Simultaneously, demand was accidentally increased by the Church, which had, by 1200, covered nearly half the calendar with meatless holy days, which promoted the eating of all sorts of fish.

By the thirteenth century, herring had developed into one of the most important protein sources throughout the North Sea and Baltic coastal towns. However, because herring is a fatty fish, it rots quickly if not salted, making salt an essential ingredient in the business of shipping protein from one part of Europe to another. Literally millions of herring were caught and sold in English ports alone, and every fall, the town of Yarmouth hosted a giant herring fair at which hundreds of thousands of barrels of salted herring—and, later cod—were brokered into ports on the North Sea. The most important fishery in Europe was, therefore, entirely hostage to the price of salt.

Between the years 1315 and 1319 fish prices were the highest in a century.

This was good news for fish brokers and salt producers, among them monasteries—nearly half of all the Cistercians in Europe were salt manufacturers—but very bad indeed for everyone else, and not just for consumers of fish. Milk, for example, was an even more popular component of the medieval diet, though its poor keeping qualities meant that it was usually consumed in the form of cheese. The rains didn't cause milk production to plummet immediately.* But without salt, cheese-making is nearly impossible. By September 1316, salt had become so dear that Louis X of France published an ordinance in which he ordered the exile (and confiscation of all the worldly goods) of salt hoarders for "avaricious cupidity," calling them "incapable of kindness, not knowing compassion, and devoid of charity."

The rains affected nearly everything. Wine, in the fourteenth century, wasn't laid down for years before drinking, so a poor harvest was felt immediately. A year with fewer than one hundred days of sun is a disaster for any fruit, and wine grapes are no exception. Without sun, photosynthesis produces less sugar, and less sugar means less raw material for fermentation. The result? In 1316 "there was no wine in the whole kingdom of France." Germany's Neustadt vineyards produced "a trifling quantity" in 1317. The rains, meanwhile, brought an epidemic of the funguslike parasite known as downy mildew that

---

*Though it would, soon enough. See chapter 8.

stunted European vines for a decade. In places where wine was levied as payment to lords, yields dropped as much as 80 percent by 1317.

Food production was battered everywhere in Europe; the grandest estate was as likely to be washed away in the great floods as the meanest freeholding. The effect on consumption was considerably less democratic. Since food shortages make themselves known mostly through higher prices for everything from beer to beefsteak, the severity of their impact on a family's diet depended on the rung that family occupied on the economic ladder. Since much of what was recorded about the medieval diet was written not only from its top rungs but by its most literate population—churchmen—popular accounts of the medieval diet have been confused for centuries. The feast-day consumption for one abbot included ducks, salmon, kid, geese, chickens at Easter, and a boar at Christmas. The cellarer at a prosperous abbey would require storage for bacon, beef, herring, butter, cheese, peas, poultry, eggs, and flour. The abbess of a Benedictine nunnery in Essex had two cooks providing food for her table exclusively, and even a "poding [pudding] wife." The cook at the Abbey of St. Augustine's, in Canterbury, was famous throughout England—at least, among England's gourmands—for a white ginger sauce (*blancgingvyre*) galantine, or green sauce (*vertesauce*). Even the more modest tables of lower-level ecclesiastics, such as monks, were enormously more varied than that of the typical peasant: "crispis" (i.e., pancakes) and crumb cakes on Shrove Tuesday; flans and cheese tarts on Rogation.

While it's difficult to find complete records of peasant diets for the era, it's a safe bet that flans and cheese tarts weren't a regular part of the bill of fare. Some rural peasants did cultivate kitchen gardens that produced some fresh vegetables for their own consumption, such as onions, garlic, lettuce, and parsley; they even had occasional access to fruits from cultivated trees as well as wild berries. And while it's well documented that grain dominated the diet of between 80 to 90 percent of Europe's population in the form of bread, frumenty, pottage, and ale, quantities are a little harder to tease out of the historical record. Peasants lacked stewards to record their monthly food bills.

Nonetheless, some evidence exists for an annual allotment of be-

tween twelve and twenty-four bushels of cereals and legumes annually per family. In the case of the former, most of the calories would
have been consumed as horsebread or frumenty; more prosperous
peasants would have enough grain to brew a considerable quantity of
ale, and might enjoy access to orchards, supplies of cider, and occasionally eggs, bacon, and dairy products. The food and drink given as part
of the wages of farm hands hired to provide labor during harvest time
on larger estates provides another clue. A normal breakdown might
pay the laborer half of his wages in the form of bread and oatmeal; a
bit more than a quarter in ale, and everything else—meat, fish, and
cheese included—a bit less. However, some simple nutritional arithmetic reveals that, since meat, fish, and cheese were so much more
expensive, they contributed far less as a percentage of calories. For every two pounds of bread paid to a harvest worker, he would receive
about two ounces of cheese, one ounce of meat, and possibly some fish.
At *least* 80 percent of those calories are, in one form or another, cereal
grains.

This remarkable level of dependence—80 percent of Europe's population getting more than 80 percent of their food in the form of
grain—is even higher than it appears, if a typical ration of ale (about
half a gallon) is factored in to the daily diet; and it should be. Ale, generally made from barley, was the most common drink throughout Europe, water being a very chancy beverage indeed for anyone wanting
to avoid intestinal parasites, and wine far too expensive for most families. Ale was also very cheap, traditionally three gallons for a penny in
England, with the brew typically served fresh, since it turns sour so
quickly (for the same reason, the ale consumed by peasant families
tended to be weaker in both flavor and alcohol than that produced by
the nobility).* By the ninth century, English monks had already fig-
ured out how to improve ale's keeping qualities: making it as beer.
Since beer requires fermentation to stop at some point—otherwise
the beer rots—hops, an antimicrobial agent, were added, and did the

---

*The household of Elizabeth de Clare—Piers Gaveston's onetime sister-in-law—used a bit
more than 200 pounds of barley and oats to make approximately 240 gallons of ale weekly . . .
twice as much grain as a typical peasant brew.

trick so well that by 1086, the monks at St. Paul's in London were brewing eighty thousand gallons a year.

So: How many calories, and in what form, were available to the average family during the fourteenth century? It's a nontrivial question, since the magnitude of a famine is at least partly a function of what people ate in non-famine times. Unfortunately, the calculations of "normal" food intake are all over the place. One regularly cited estimate comes up with an average of around four thousand calories a day. The French historian Michel Rouche actually calculated that the average fourteenth-century person consumed more than nine thousand calories a day.

Rouche's stratospheric number is derived from a statute dating back to the ninth-century Carolingian Empire that allocated approximately three and a half pounds of bread, one and a half quarts of wine, half a gallon of beer, a quarter pound of cheese, and half a pound of fat or meat per person *per day*. The recommended diet was more the product of hopefulness than arithmetic. Yields were so low that the amount of grain required to produce the bread and beer alone would have meant at least doubling the amount of land under cultivation throughout Europe.

Even if the acreage to produce a sufficient amount of grain had somehow been available, reaching anywhere close to Rouche's estimate would remain impossible, because of the inefficiency of all medieval agriculture. Dairy cattle, during the fourteenth century, might produce less than three hundred gallons a year (modern cows average around nineteen hundred), and it takes a gallon of milk to produce a pound of cheese. The numbers are even more daunting for meat. Domestic livestock were barely half as large as modern versions, though they required the same grazing territory; slaughtering a fourteenth-century cow or steer provided less than 140 pounds of meat, and another 40 pounds of fat. A good-sized pig might provide a total of 80 pounds. Providing the five million residents of 1300s England with half a pound of meat daily would have meant slaughtering a *lot* of cattle, and even more pigs (sheep were too valuable as wool providers to add much in the way of food). Getting a quarter of the total from beef cattle would require slaughtering more than 1.6 million cattle annually; and since it takes at least two years, on average, to fatten them up, that meant grazing somewhere north of 3 million cattle, each needing 2 hectares of grazing each, or 6 million total: nearly 23,000 square miles . . . in a country whose total area is only 50,000 square miles. The pigs, by comparison, were a bargain: at 80 pounds of meat and fat per fourteenth-century porker, and requiring only six months before slaughter, England would need "only" four million or so pigs to provide each person with about six ounces of pork a day.

In fact, pigs were far more widely held by members of the peasant class than either cattle or horses, partly because pigs were able to eat just about anything—acorns, slugs, worms, even the carcasses of other pigs. Pigs are also incredibly productive as agricultural assets, producing tallow, bristles, and leather, as well as food. Relatively prosperous peasant families could keep half a dozen pigs in sties and mark others and allow them to go feral in local woodlands, where swineherds would collect them in late fall or early winter—dangerous work, since wild pigs eat just about anything, and were just as likely to eat human children as acorns. Sometimes swineherds managed actual herds: hundreds of pigs, driven to market. However, their wide availability and relatively high resistance to both famine and disease made them extremely vulnerable to families seeking alternate sources of food— so vulnerable that the swine herd at Bolton Priory declined in the first year of the famine by 95 percent, to a single boar and six sows.

The most reliable estimates of actual livestock in fourteenth-century England, taken from sales and tax records, total 1.67 million cattle—580,000 of them dairy (feeding five million people using Rouche's estimate of a quarter-pound of cheese a day would have required at least 1.8 million dairy cows), 520,000 beef, and the remainder calves—8 to 10 million wool-producing sheep; 950,000 hogs; and 540,000 horses and 820,000 oxen, neither of which were raised for food. Rouche was wrong, by at least a factor of three.

In the 1980s, Jan Peter Pals, an archaeobotanist at the University of Amsterdam, did the heavy lifting in revising the estimates of medieval consumption. His model assumed that medieval farmers produced about 1,000 kilograms of grains and legumes for every acre under cultivation, along with another 1,365 kilograms of straw. With cattle and sheep fed on harvest residue, modest estimates of milk production from both cows and sheep, and pigs foraging, more or less for free, in surrounding forests, a reasonable range of actual daily provisions for an adult looks something like this:

· thirteen ounces of bread
· a quart of beer
· an ounce and a half of cheese
· a quarter-pound of peas, or other legumes
· a little less than four ounces of mixed fat and meat

This adds up to a more plausible total of between two thousand and twenty-one hundred calories a day—a pretty paltry ration for an adult who was required to perform substantial manual labor.

Since, however, almost everyone was, it's worth calculating their needs, as well as their consumption. In 2004, the Nobel Prize–winning economist Robert Fogel did just that, estimating the number of calories needed above the Basal Metabolic Rate, which is the amount of energy needed to keep vital organs functioning at complete rest, with some added for digestion of food and basic hygiene, but no other activities at all, not even preparing food.

For an adult male, 5'6" tall and weighing 140 pounds—that is, a fairly average fourteenth-century farmer—the BMR is 1,576 calories a day. Fogel's calculation for the additional calories needed to perform *any* sort of labor is 720 calories, for a total of just under 2,300 calories a day. The conclusion seems inescapable: for almost everyone living in the fourteenth century, hunger, not to say near-starvation, was constant.

Even when food was relatively plentiful (this is a relative term; the food supply was contaminated with insects, rodent feces, molds, and aflatoxins, the highly carcinogenic poisons produced by the fungi that contaminate stored grain) almost all peasant diets were lacking in protein; even if a family owned a cow, chickens, or other livestock, they would still be forced to use the meat, milk, and eggs to generate cash, rather than as food. The diets of at least half the population was deficient not just in calories (particularly for growing children) but in lipids, calcium, and vitamins A, C, and D; and they contained so much fiber as to block the absorption of minerals like calcium, magnesium, and zinc. This was a particular problem for women of childbearing age—and, since average age at death was under forty, it affected virtually all women. Half the adult population of Europe was constantly pregnant, and therefore constantly in need of vitamins B_{12}, C, and folic acid. And that was when things were normal.

When things weren't—when the lost harvests of 1315 and 1316 coincided with scorched-earth warfare everywhere from Scotland to Flanders to Germany—malnutrition became starvation.

In 1315, Edward II wrote a letter to the bishop of Durham, announcing his concern that the "poor and beggars were starving" to death in the Anglo-Scottish borderlands. By 1319, in Winchester, "the bodies of paupers, dead of starvation, littered city streets . . . and burial could not be delayed because of the foul stink, *'so miche and so faste folc deaden, that vnnethes men might ham bury'* [Folk died so frequently and so quickly that men could hardly bury them]."

Famines kill. But much of their killing is done indirectly. The most recognizable image from modern famines, the skeletal emaciation among infants known as *marasmus*, is a killer, though not nearly as dangerous as *kwashiorkor*, which is the same syndrome appearing in children older than a year and a half. Kwashiorkor, with its ulcerating sores and distended bellies, kills its victims by destroying their livers, which blow up like balloons when they can no longer process the body's waste products.

Both kwashiorkor and marasmus are caused by protein-calorie malnutrition, or PCM: pure calorie deprivation. But the body can be damaged just as severely when deprived of a few hundred micrograms of an essential nutrient. Too little vitamin A results in the disease known as xerophthalmia, which causes ulcers in the cornea, and, frequently, blindness. The progress of pellagra, a deficiency in niacin/

vitamin B$_3$, is still taught to medicine students as the so-called four D's: diarrhea, dermatitis, dementia, and death. Scurvy, a lack of the vitamin C necessary to produce the body's collagen proteins, causes teeth and hair to fall out, severe liver damage, and eventually a very painful death.

A famine can claim its victims just as easily from what they do eat as from what they don't. The typical response to profound hunger, for example, is the replacement of regular food with what are known as "strange diets." During the Great Famine, rural poor were said to have "gnawed, just like dogs, [on] the raw dead bodies of cattle" and "grazed like cows on the growing grasses of the field." In cities and towns, the strange diets were, if anything, even stranger, and more damaging: tainted meat, rats, insects, and bread bulked out with everything from straw to brick dust. The ergotism caused by eating moldy rye results in hallucinations and manic behavior when the fungus attacks the nervous system, and causes seizures when it attacks the muscles. In its most virulent attacks, it can cut off circulation and cause death by gangrene. Gastrointestinal anthrax is contracted from eating infected meat. Johannes de Trokelowe, the Saint Albans monk, wrote, horrified, that "men, poisoned from spoiled food, succumbed, as did beasts and cattle, dead from a poisonous rottenness of the grass. Nor does anyone remember so much dearth and famine to have prevailed in the past."

Even if the most acute poisonings could be avoided, one unavoidable result of eating so much with so little nutritional value is a profound lethargy. When there aren't enough calories to maintain even the basic functions of life—the BMR—the body's temperature drops and skin becomes pallid as the body reduces blood flow to its peripheries. People can, and did, die from lacking enough energy to find and prepare food.

Even more dangerous than the vitamin-deficiency disorders like scurvy and pellagra, or poisoning from badly prepared or toxic foods, was infectious disease. Malnutrition reduces the body's resistance to infection by impairing the immune response; white blood cells, for example, are less able to surround and destroy invading pathogens.

Famine victims died in the tens of thousands from opportunistic diseases, after their immune systems had been weakened to the point that a simple rhinovirus—the common cold—can become a killer.

But the relationship between infectious disease and malnutrition is complicated, and two-way. Infections shrink the appetite, and—when the gastrointestinal tract is targeted—reduce the metabolism of nutrients, at the precise moment when more nutrients are needed to fight the infection. But while all infections affect nutrition, not all infections are affected by malnutrition (or, for that matter, good nutrition). A number of studies of modern famines have demonstrated that malnutrition has a progressive increase on the likelihood of infection. However, it's just as common for malnutrition to actually *inhibit* the growth of pathogens, by denying them vital compounds. Many microorganisms that cause disease, for example, need iron to survive, and scavenge it from their host's blood and bone marrow. When iron is in short dietary supply—as, for example, during a famine—the body protects itself by storing it in places like the liver in order to keep it away from a pathogen.

As a result, not all infectious diseases are more easily spread, or made more virulent, by malnutrition. The ones that tend to see big spikes during famines include measles, tuberculosis, amoebic and bacterial dysentery, most intestinal parasites, cholera, and herpes. Others, more moderately promoted by nutritional deficiencies, include staph infections, influenza, syphilis, typhus, and diphtheria.

However, the world's most historically dangerous infectious diseases—smallpox, malaria, typhoid fever, bubonic plague, yellow fever, and poliomyelitis—are virtually independent of nutrition. Europe's best-fed populations during the Great Famine, monks in rich monasteries, died like flies during the Black Death thirty years later.

This particular fact is why modern increases in lifespan, and decreases in mortality at any given age, aren't mostly a function of improved nutrition. During the fourteenth century—during any century up to the present—the better you ate, the better you lived. Better, but not longer. The British peerage died at roughly the same ages as the British peasantry until the end of the eighteenth century, and neither was likely at birth to live much longer than twenty-five years in the fourteenth century, or even thirty-eight years in the eighteenth.

Nonetheless, not all the excess mortality of the Great Famine was a result of deficiency, toxins, or disease. Hundreds of thousands of people, from Ireland to Poland, simply starved to death.

It wasn't fast, to be sure. A typical adult stores up to one hundred thousand calories in fat reserves, and the body can live off nothing else for weeks or months. Even after consuming its stored glycogen, the body is remarkably adaptive; humans can use acetone, acetoacetic acid, and beta-hydroxybutyric acid—collectively known as "ketone bodies"—to run cognitive functions and some muscular functions for weeks in the absence of food, or even fat. Only then does it literally start consuming bone and skeletal muscle—the formal term is *catabolysis*. After a few days of this, *autophagy* is the result: cells cannibalize themselves. The structure of the diaphragm collapses, and lung function drops by up to 80 percent. Perversely enough, after weeks of agonizing digestive cramps and excruciating muscle atrophy from little or no food, a few minutes without oxygen supplies a relatively painless end.

The Great Famine brought starvation everywhere from the Atlantic seawall to the Urals, but nowhere suffered more than Flanders. As with Scotland, the famine was not an anomalous disaster in an otherwise happy era; the third horseman was preceded—and followed—by the second: war.

The rebellious province had been more or less at peace with France for over a decade in the spring of 1315. In 1305, Philip IV of France and Count Guy of Flanders had signed a peace treaty ending the war best remembered for the Battle of the Golden Spurs at Courtrai. After Guy's death later that year, his son Robert took the county, and spent the next nine years ignoring the treaty's terms.

Fed up, Louis X, who had been crowned upon the death of his father in November 1314, decided to invade the Flemish homeland, in partnership with Count William of Hainaut, Holland, and Zeeland (and Louis's nephew-in-law). In the narrow geographic confines of the

Low Countries, William was the perfect ally: located northeast of Flanders, Zeeland would cut the Flemish off from the North Sea and be the anvil against which the French hammer would smash Flanders into submission. On September 6, 1315, William and Louis invaded, sailing up the Scheldt past Antwerp, and made it as far as Courtrai.

Louis should have found the location an ominous place to give battle, given its historical associations. But he never got the chance. The rains of 1315, which hadn't stopped for more than a day at a time since May, completely stopped the progress of the combined Franco-Dutch army. Horses drowned every day. Provisions rotted. In less than a week, Louis's plans for solving the Flemish problem had sunk under the mud, and, on September 13, he began his withdrawal toward Tournai.

The Flemings were as cheered as they had been at Courtrai twelve years before. It was the only bright spot in what were, perhaps, their worst two years of the millennium. Within weeks of the French retreat, in Flanders "there began a dearness of wheat . . . from day to day the price increased." At Antwerp, the price for a *modius* of wheat (about two gallons) was £5 on November 1, 1315. By November 30, it was £7; by December 24, £10. By April 1316, it had increased to £12, and by June 24, £16—an increase of more than 300 percent in five months.

By 1316, a contemporary chronicler wrote, "people in many places began to eat less than sufficient bread, because they had no more." Jan van Boendale, a Brabant writer and chief clerk of Antwerp, wrote, "The cries that were heard from the poor would move a stone, as they lay in the streets with woe and great complaint, swollen with hunger." In the words of Gilles li Muisis, abbot of St. Martin's of Tournai, in 1316, men and women from every stratum of society "perished daily in such great numbers that the air was fetid with the stench." The abbot further noted that "so many poor beggars were dying in the street, on dung-heaps" that the city was compelled to hire a force of laborers to dispose of the corpses in the surrounding countryside.

Burials, traditionally and literally the last stage of European class distinction, became exceedingly democratic, given the need for common burial of everyone. In Louvain, hospital wagons carrying half a dozen corpses each made three round-trips daily to a new cemetery opened outside the city's limits. In Brussels, two new cemeteries were created during the first years of the famine. The mortality among Flemish ecclesiastics was especially brutal, though possibly it appears so only because the *Monasticon Belge* were so diligent about keeping records. Literally dozens of heads of monastic houses perished in 1315–1316, decimating the leadership of the Cistercians and Benedictines. Only the Black Death itself would kill more abbots and friars, and not by much.

Flanders—northern Europe's richest region—suffered a 10 percent population drop in 1316 alone. The burghers of the city of Ypres recorded the weekly death count from the famine—specifically, the number of corpses buried at town expense—between May 1 and November 1, 1316. In the week beginning May 8, 54 people were buried. By May 21, the number was 173. During the week of August 7, it was 191, before declining in October back to a few dozen. The thirty-week total was nearly 3,000, in a town with about 25,000 inhabitants. Bruges lost at least 5 percent of its own inhabitants—I say "at least" because it recorded only those "collected" not "buried." In Tournai, the death rate increased nearly fourfold over a "normal" year, losing one adult out of every ten.

Not that France was all that much better off, particularly in the northern provinces of Normandy and Brittany. But because France was, in European terms, the nation furthest along the path toward modern statehood, it could take remedial action more decisively, and more effectively, than the more feudally backward nations to the east. One of the most cherished of lordly privileges, the right to create protected areas for hunting, put them in direct conflict with France's rural peasantry, whose distaste for hunting preserves was partly economic— lord's land was, obviously, unavailable for either pasture or farmland— and partly a strong emotional regard for what they saw as their traditional rights: the even longer-standing common rights to common land. This conflict was endemic throughout Europe, but only in France was the king strong enough, once the famine made the issue urgent, to solve it by requiring that the nation's lords receive a royal authorization in order to create a *"parc à gibier,"* or "game park."

Regarding the basics—grain and, to a lesser degree, salt—the Crown was even more active. By the summer of 1315, King Louis had authorized the importation of grain from Gascony and distribution to the northern provinces (and, in September, the king publicly scolded merchants for their "avaricious cupidity" in his published *Ordonnances*). The Crown, able to read the political winds, scapegoated the merchant class without mercy. Despite acknowledging that the rising price for salt was determined by the rainy weather, he ordered his officers to find supposed hoards of salt and to prosecute the hoarders in question by confiscating all their goods and inflicting pretty much any punishment they wanted.

By the time Louis was succeeded by his brother, Charles V (technically, he was succeeded by his son, John . . . for five days), the French ruler was unquestionably the most powerful in Europe. He was able to settle the long-standing feud with Flanders and rule a country that was, for reasons of geography, still able to produce sufficient quantities of food to feed her eighteen million people, since the change in the North Atlantic Oscillation that dropped hundreds of days of rain on northern France, Flanders, and Germany in 1315 left the farms of southern France largely untouched.

And his sister was the queen of England. Which would have its consequences, as long-lasting in their way as the famine itself.

"She-Wolf of France"

1313–1320

The twelve-year-old who had celebrated the nuptial mass in Boulogne-sur-Mer in 1308 had been a girl; a royal princess, to be sure, but still a girl. Five years as queen of England transformed Isabella. She improved her position with her husband after the murder of the despised Piers Gaveston, and did so without alienating any of the opposing sides in the Gaveston affair: the king, his earls, and even her father, the king of France, who had let it be known that he would support Gaveston's enemies, even to the point of offering £40,000 to the earls trying to depose Gaveston. The young queen survived two failed expeditions to Scotland, not to mention near capture by Robert Bruce, and had even fulfilled her most important royal duty: giving birth to the future King Edward III in November 1312.

Yet she was still seen by her subjects as a luxury-loving spendthrift—and not unfairly. Even by the standards of medieval queens, few of whom could be called frugal, Isabella was remarkable. In addition to the royal wardrobe keeper, John Faleise, and the five dozen seamstresses required to drape the royal frame in the latest fashions, her household counted 180 servants, 70 of whom were of the "upper rank," including a physician, two apothecaries, three cooks, a chaplain, a steward, a comptroller, a cofferer, and an almoner, whose only job was to dispense alms on feast days and holy days, using "the Queen's great silver alms dish."* Reporting to them were

---

*A century later, the Lord Steward, the Comptroller of the Household, and Cofferer of the Household (who was responsible for paying the wages of the royal household staff) would become offices sanctified by time and custom, their occupants members of the king's privy

lower servants such as butlers, pantlers, a "clerke of spicerie," a saucerer, ushers, marshals, chandlers, watchmen, eight knights, twenty-eight squires, bailiffs, castellans, a variety of senior and junior clerks, ladies-in-waiting, and a fool called Michael. To manage the household stable's dozens of horses (plus eight greyhounds, and half a dozen falcons and hawks) required six carters, thirty-nine grooms, twenty-five palfreymen, and assorted (and uncounted) pages.

Such an extensive domestic staff made it easy for her enemies—and, as it happens, some of her modern biographers—to paint her as a profligate, even to the point of spreading gossip that Isabella's October 1311 pilgrimage to the tomb of Saint Thomas Becket at Canterbury was so lavish that it cost the treasury £140,000. The scandalmongers missed the far more important and valuable asset that the queen had become. On May 23, 1313, Edward and Isabella sailed for France, landing first in Gascony, and then traveling north to Paris. There Isabella was now old enough to be included, for the first time, in the negotiations between her father's and her husband's royal houses, and all three—Philip, Edward, and Isabella—formally accepted the cross of a crusader from Cardinal Nicholas, the papal legate, which technically obliged all three to enlist directly in the pan-European campaign to liberate the Holy Land.

In one of the more curious episodes in medieval European history, the bishop of Rome for whom Cardinal Nicholas was a representative wasn't, at the moment, actually residing in Rome. In 1305, after a decade of vicious fighting between Philip IV and Pope Boniface IX and his successors, a Frenchman, Raymond Bertrand le Got, had been elevated to the papacy as Clement V.* The new pope was, by design, far more pliant than his predecessors, especially where the French Crown

---

council, and otherwise powerful bureaucrats. In the early fourteenth century, their hierarchy hadn't—quite—been set in concrete, but in Isabella's household, the steward hired the comptroller, who hired the cofferer, who hired everyone else.

*Among other things, the French accused Boniface of simony, which is the source of the unfortunate pope's most durable notoriety: Dante Alighieri, who had his own reasons for hostility toward Boniface (he had intervened on the other side of an internal Florentine dispute), wrote him into the *Divine Comedy* as a future resident in the Inferno's eighth circle. The charge was repeated by both Boccaccio and Rabelais, a reminder that the power of kings and popes doesn't outlast the revenge of poets.

was concerned, and in 1309, he decamped, along with the entire papal court, to the Comtat Venaissin, in Avignon, beginning seven decades of ruling the entire apparatus of western Christianity from southern France.

The Avignon papacy was mostly a contingent historical event, the consequence of particular circumstances and decisions. It would be a mistake to see it as another piece of historical flotsam, floating on the same centuries-long wave that brought the Vikings to Europe and North America, turned Europe's forests into farms and meadows, and trebled the continent's population: the Medieval Warm Period. It would likewise be a mistake to see it as free from the effects of that wave. The medieval papacy had become the most powerful "state" in Christendom (its preferred name for Europe, for obvious reasons) on the back of the same feudal system that had emerged to manage and defend the millions of acres of newly arable land needed to feed a larger and larger population. But the medieval Church had an unfair advantage in a feudal system, since ecclesiastical vassals, unlike secular ones, were effectively immortal, with their lands, in particular, held by the "dead hand" of mortmain. Abbots died, just like any lord, but the abbey remained a fief, ultimately owing homage not just to a king but to the bishop of Rome. As much as anything else, the drive for secular sovereignty in any given country was a drive to oppose the Church on a more equal footing. It is no coincidence that the European nations that were slowest to become modern states were those where the papacy had the greatest ability to undermine secular rulers: in Italy by geography—the so-called papal states cut the peninsula in half—and in Germany by control over the title of Holy Roman Emperor.* And it is even less coincidental that the first modern European nations were those least dominated by the popes: England and France.

The Avignon papacy—subordinate to the French king, but wealthier than ever, from increased tithes and taxes, aggressive requests for "donations" from those seeking Church offices, and the highly profitable business of selling indulgences, or absolution from sin—was only

---

*Italy and Germany did not take on their modern borders until the nineteenth century. For more about the HRE, see chapter 10.

five years old when Isabella returned to France in February 1314, ostensibly to make pilgrimage to Boulogne and Chartres, really on behalf of her husband. She arrived almost to the day that the most notorious victim of both the first Avignon pope and the king of France was being burned at the stake.

Jacques de Molay, the twenty-third and last Grand Master of the Poor Fellow-Soldiers of Christ and of the Temple of Solomon, better remembered as the Knights Templar, had been a member of the order for at least thirty years when he ascended to its highest position. It wasn't the best of times for the Templars, the first of the dozen or so Catholic military societies—others included the Knights Hospitaller, the Knights of Calatrava, and the Teutonic Knights—organized to defend the Church against its enemies, from Iberia to the Baltic, and especially on Crusade in the Levant.

The First Crusade had been called in 1095 by Pope Urban II with two explicit objectives: first, to liberate the Holy Land from the Islamic armies that had conquered it four centuries before; and second, to unite Christendom. On both fronts, initial success was followed by long-term failure. Not only had the crusading armies lost the short-lived Kingdom of Jerusalem, the Templars, like other knightly orders charged with expelling Islamic influence from the Holy Land generally, and Jerusalem especially, had been expelled themselves, and ruled only parts of the island of Cyprus. And though the Crusades, by reestablishing trade in commodities and ideas with the east, had done nearly as much as the Medieval Warm Period to revive the growth of Europe's population and economy, the result wasn't a united continent but the opposite: the emergence of nation-states like France and England.

Thus, by the time de Molay became its Grand Master, a supranational organization like the Templars wasn't exactly sailing with the winds of history at its back. Even worse, the Templars weren't simply an affront to a secular king like Philip IV, they were also one of his largest creditors, with the Temple in Paris acting as the royal treasury as far back as the reign of Philip Augustus. The combination would prove deadly. In 1307, de Molay was summoned to the papal offices to discuss merging the Templars with other military orders like the Knights Hospitaller in preparation for a new crusade to liberate Jerusalem. He found himself the subject of an investigation into charges that his order had broken the canon law of the Church, including engaging in idolatry and fornication, and in violating the sacraments. The original five charges eventually grew to nearly a hundred, including bestiality, denial of sacraments, selling souls to the devil (whom the Templars were accused of worshipping in multiple forms: sometimes as a head with three faces, sometimes as a giant cat), sodomy, corruption, intercourse with succubi, and witchcraft. The expansion of the indictment was the work of Philip, who could not avoid seeing a successful prosecution of the Templars as an opportunity to clear his debts. On October 13, 1307, he ordered the arrest of all Templars in France, and the confiscation of all their possessions. Pope Clement obediently followed suit, ordering the same for every Templar in Christendom.

Over the course of the next seven years, de Molay and other Templar officers were tried at least half a dozen times, and each time testimony was extracted by torture. Hundreds were subjected to the rack, or to thumbscrews. Others had their fingernails pulled out at the roots. Thirty-six died under torture; 122, including de Molay, confessed. Most of the confessions stuck, but not de Molay's. Neither did his recantation. Nor his next confession. The Grand Master would admit, for example, to "denying Christ" only to repudiate his admission months later. Admission, recantation, repeat, again and again. In 1310, Philip lost patience and sentenced sixty-seven of the recanting Templars to be burned at the stake. In 1312, the Templars were dissolved by papal decree, and de Molay, along with the remaining Templar leadership, was condemned.

On the morning of March 18, 1314, de Molay and a number of other senior Templars were brought to the Île de la Cité in the middle of the Seine to hear sentence passed by a group of cardinals commissioned by Pope Clement for the task. All present believed that the accused would admit guilt in return for life imprisonment. Instead, de Molay and his lieutenant, Geoffroi de Charny, standing in front of the church of Notre Dame de Paris, confessed only to betraying their own order to save their lives: the charges, they vowed, were false. While the cardinals departed to consider their next move, King Philip did not. He ordered the accused transported to the Île des Juifs, an island on the Seine just west of the Île de la Cité.* By sunset, a pile of wood was constructed, and the two unrepentant Templars slowly burned to death, refusing a final offer of pardon, and—apparently—screaming no more than was necessary in order to produce one of the more enduring pieces of the Templar myth: through his dying screams, de Molay supposedly pronounced a curse on both the pope and the entire royal family, to the thirteenth generation.†

The folk memory of de Molay's execution has survived even longer, partly because of the viselike grip that the Templars continue to exert on historians, popular novelists, aficionados of the Shroud of Turin (whose image is supposed, by some, to be not Christ, but de Molay), Freemasons, and assorted conspiracy theorists. But part of the enduring power of the scene, the one that greeted Isabella upon her return to her father's capital, is how well it illustrates the ascendant power of secular rulers over religious authority.

Within days of Isabella's father's exhibition, in the most direct form imaginable, of his power over the Templars, she was to demonstrate a very different talent for influencing events—in the palace intrigue that became known as the Tour de Nesle Affair.

Like so much else, the story of the Tour de Nesle can be traced back to the beginning of the feudal era. When Charlemagne's brief Carolingian empire was divided among his three grandsons, the result was three proto-states: the western one became the nucleus of modern France; the eastern one, a patchwork of German-speaking principali-

---

*The island acquired its name not, as some casual historians report, because of the number of Jews executed there, but because it was where one of Paris's early Jewish families settled. Since the construction of the Pont Neuf in 1607, it's been connected to the Île de la Cité as the Place Dauphine.

†The Templar curse, for those who believe in such things, had legs. De Molay had, it was said, predicted that both Pope Clement and King Philip would join him before God by year's end. Clement barely survived de Molay, dying on April 18, to be succeeded by John XXII, and Philip IV died on November 13, 1314, at the relatively young age of forty-six.

ties that wouldn't be unified until the nineteenth century. In the middle was the kingdom, later the duchy, of Burgundy. Its strategic location, and enormous wealth, meant that, for five hundred years, no French ruler had ever forgotten the importance of neutralizing, or even better, annexing, the province.* Isabella's father, Philip IV, had gone further than most, marrying each of her three brothers to Burgundian princesses: Louis, the eldest, married Margaret, daughter of the duke of Burgundy; Philip married Jeanne, daughter of Otto, count of Burgundy; and Charles married Blanche, another of Otto's daughters.

None was a love match, particularly not those of Louis and Charles. Few dynastic marriages were, as Isabella had every reason to know. She was, therefore, perhaps particularly astute in detecting evidence of infidelity, and her family wasn't especially discreet about such matters. When Edward and Isabella had traveled to France in 1313, Isabella had presented distinctive purses to each of her sisters-in-law, two of whom immediately gave the gifts to their respective lovers: the brothers d'Aulnay, Gautier and Philippe.

If they thought no one would notice, they didn't know Isabella. During an encounter at court, she recognized the embroidery on the purses, and, after her return to France in February 1314, told her father of her suspicions. Her motives for doing so remain unclear. A good guess is that she was engaged in her own game of thrones; by removing the mothers of every potential heir to the French throne, she opened a path for her own son, the future Edward III of England.† Her father was considerably less concerned about his daughter's strategy than he was furious at his daughters-in-law. The king had all three of them followed, and in less than a week, Blanche and Margaret led the king's agents to the tower of Nesle, or Tour de Nesle, a structure on the left bank of the Seine that the king had purchased from

*Five hundred years or even longer. In 532, two of the sons of the Frankish king Clovis, Childeert and Chlotar, annexed Burgundy to the Frankish kingdom.

†If so, it worked, sort of. Even though Charles and Philip remarried, both died without male heirs, which encouraged Isabella's son to claim the throne of France, which ignited what became the Hundred Years' War.

the nobleman Amaury de Nesle in 1308. There, the two princesses—at first, it seemed that Jeanne was involved as well—entertained the d'Aulnays, and were entertained in their turn.

Adultery was bad enough; adultery with a royal princess, the very definition of lèse-majesté, was treason. In April 1314, the Paris Parlement—the highest court in France, essentially the king's council—found both princesses and both brothers guilty. Each of the princesses had her head shaved, and was sentenced to life in prison, at Château Gaillard in Normandy, the great castle built by Edward's great grand-uncle Richard Lionheart. There, each died, coincidentally, not to say suspiciously, within weeks of the date their cuckolded husbands ascended the throne: Louis in August 1314, and Charles in February 1322.

Their lovers didn't have it quite so easy. Both of the d'Aulnay brothers confessed after unspecified tortures, were castrated, and their testes fed to dogs. Each was flayed alive, then spread-eagled on a wooden cartwheel, where they had their arms and legs broken with iron cudgels while the wheel slowly rotated. Finally, after both torturers and audience had tired of their entertainment, they were decapitated and their shattered bodies displayed for all to see.

The brutal drama was memorable on its own terms—in 1832, Alexandre Dumas turned it into a play named, perhaps a little unimaginatively, *La Tour de Nesle*—but it is also the first real evidence of the true character of the onetime French princess, grown to be an English queen. Until 1314, Isabella's impact on events had been largely anodyne, when it had been noticed at all. That was about to change. Isabella had started to earn the epithet that the poet Thomas Gray gave her in one of his eighteenth-century Pindaric odes: the "She-Wolf of France, with unrelenting fangs, that tears't at the bowels of thy mangled mate."*

The rains of 1315 made Isabella's talent for royal intrigue, at least temporarily, irrelevant. As England was attempting to recover from a

---

*It was an enduring nickname—Bertolt Brecht used it in his *Life of Edward II of England*, as did Maurice Druon in a 1960 novel—but not a particularly original one. Gray was copying Shakespeare, who'd coined it for Margaret of Anjou, wife of Henry VI.

completely lost harvest (really two lost harvests, though Edward didn't know that yet), Edward was obsessively trying to repair the army that had been defeated by Bruce's infantry. Among other things, he ordered that his Irish footmen wear chain mail and, to pay for it, required that freeholders with property in excess of £2 provide themselves with iron gauntlets and helmets. He didn't stop there. The king introduced a new set of levies on each manor—in the terminology of the day, on each "vill," essentially every rural community smaller than a township—requiring them to provide a specified number of soldiers, which cost the agrarian population not only men but money: approximately 24 shillings for even the lowliest footman, of which 7 to 8 shillings went to equip him with the most basic tools of the trade: a sword, knife, or bow, or sometimes all three. During the worst famine in centuries, Edward was requisitioning men at an unprecedented pace; some cities were required to provide men for forty days' service, armed with padded doublets, chain-mail hauberks, basinets, and iron gauntlets, thus putting the heaviest burdens on the population least able to cope with them. And he did so during the two years of 1315, and 1316, when the torrential rains had destroyed the roads on which his armies would have had to travel. England was taxing its peasantry to pay for an army that it could not afford, at a time when it was unable even to deploy it.

Edward's defenders (and there are more than a few) might respond that it's unfair to chide the king for these seemingly dissonant policies. Sovereigns confront crises as they appear, and they can't ignore any of them completely. At the same time he was, however unwisely, rebuilding the army destroyed by Bruce, Edward faced the worst inflation in British history as the pound lost more than half its value from the beginning of 1316 to the end. He also had to manage his increasingly deteriorating relationship with the earl of Lancaster, as a series of councils increased the earl's direct involvement in government throughout 1316. The earl (who, careful readers will recall, had declined to join in Edward's 1314 expedition) even planned his own invasion of Scotland . . . and this time Edward played turnabout and refused to join in.

Those same defenders could, with even more justice, point out that Edward's concerns with Scotland and his own nobles certainly didn't mean that he was unaware of the famine afflicting his realm. In April 1316, the king wrote to the bishop of Durham complaining of "an unaccustomed dearth of grain" and accused his subjects of hoarding "an immoderate amount." The realm's poor, he continued, were "daily dying from famine and starvation." The king published a plea to the English clergy, asking them to persuade hoarders ("with efficacious words") to sell at a reasonable price, encouraging them to use any method up to and including excommunication to get the message across, "lest the cause of such ruin and death be imputed to those having grain and refusing to sell it."

The real problem, however, wasn't hoarding but supply. Efficacious words were going to be insufficient, which even the king recognized. So, since England's waterlogged fields couldn't grow grain, the king offered promises of safe-conduct for grain merchants in order to encourage them to find their supply elsewhere in Europe. The storms of 1315 were so outrageously large, though, that "elsewhere in Europe" meant "somewhere in Europe that was still able to harvest its crops." Northern France and the Low Countries were just as affected by the weather as England. The trading cities along the southern coast of the Baltic were better able to supply salted fish than grain, and those on the northern shores were experiencing their own shortfalls in everything from grain to meat and dairy. In the winter of 1316–17, the tax collectors of King Birger II of Sweden (which had already been subject to decades of "difficulties and afflictions of wars and oppressions, of taxes and tribulation") attempted to transport taxes in kind—cheese, meat, and so on—out of Swedish territories surrounding the Gulf of Bothnia, and met a full-blown tax revolt, followed by mass executions and confiscations. England's only likely sources of grain were as far away as Spain and Italy.

Along with an increase in the distance traveled by seaborne grain came its companion: piracy. During the fourteenth century, the piratical trade was dominated by three maritime communities: the Gascon city of Bayonne, at the very southern tip of Aquitaine; and the Cinque

Ports, towns on the coast of Kent and Sussex, including Dover and Rye, that were traditionally obliged to provide ships for the defense of the English Crown and just as traditionally winked at the smuggling and piracy that fueled their economies; and Normandy.

Though Edward I and Philip IV had asserted sovereignty over their own territorial waters, each king intended it as a keep-off sign for the other—certainly not for pirates. During the feudal era, piracy was less a matter of eye patch–wearing, cutlass-wielding thieves than an informal bit of maritime commerce (or, occasionally, a part of irregular warfare; one of Bruce's privateers, Thomas Dun, was practically a legend, attacked in England as "a cruel pirate").* To the degree that it made its way into the courts, it was treated as evasion of debt—a kind of legal self-help carried out by individuals. Four years before the rains of 1315 initiated the Great Famine, Edward II announced a schedule of fines for piracy, but they were to be paid by the pirate's home port, not the pirate himself. Pirates wouldn't typically be hanged from yardarms for another three hundred years.

Like their seventeenth-century cousins, fourteenth-century pirates preferred targets with holds filled with cargoes such as gold and jewelry. The disastrous years of 1315 and 1316, however, weren't normal in any sense. During the spring of 1316, so many southern English ports were regularly attacked, ships burned, and warehouses ransacked, that on April 4, 1316, Edward took the extraordinary step of commandeering dozens of ships "for the repulse of certain malefactors who have committed manslaughter and other enormities on the sea upon the men of this realm and upon men from foreign parts coming to this realm with victuals."

Like almost all of Edward's tactics, it had little effect. England was starving, unable to feed itself, and even when able to purchase grain from elsewhere, barely able to ship it home. It was also very nearly bankrupt, facing the biggest financial crisis in a century, as England's loans from both Edward's Italian bankers and the pope came due at the same time. The events of 1315 and 1316 are a litany of catastrophe:

---

* The term "pirate" is anachronistic; though England had admiralty courts from the reign of Richard the Lionheart, none of its laws explicitly prohibited piracy.

Two lost harvests. A near total destruction of England's roads. Northern cities subject to constant raids by Bruce's lieutenants, especially James Douglas. It seems almost farcical that one of Edward's best-remembered efforts for dealing with the famine was aimed more at restoring his own image than his subjects' farms. That's what appears to be behind his decision to commission a spectacular psalter: a luxuriously illustrated manuscript bound in red velvet and featuring not only the Book of Psalms but more than two hundred scenes from the Old Testament. The so-called Queen Mary Psalter—though composed around 1316, it wasn't named until it was presented to Queen Mary I in 1553—is notable not just for its beauty but the extraordinary amount of attention it paid to the story of Joseph: the one about the seven fat years and the seven lean years. The devotional was an unsubtle public-relations stunt intended to promote Edward's ability to cope with the failed harvests; predictably, however, the "curious image of Edward II as the good pharaoh never achieved much currency outside the circle of his sycophants and clients."

Given Edward's affinity for bad choices and worse luck, it's no surprise to learn that when the king sent his most loyal vassal, the earl of Pembroke, on a mission to Avignon to renegotiate the outstanding loans from Pope John, things didn't work out as planned.* Pembroke, the only English general to defeat the Scots since Falkirk, the king's rescuer at Bannockburn, and one of the few genuine heroes of an unheroic age, was taken on his return from Avignon by a French nobleman and disgruntled onetime vassal of Edward I whose list of grievances included unpaid wages dating back as far as 1296.

The king had to pay the enormous ransom demand: £10,000. He needed not only Pembroke but the nobles who had coalesced around him. The group, which included the earls of Surrey, Hereford, and Arundel; a number of bishops; and Bartholomew de Badlesmere—a former steward of the royal household who had been named a baron in 1309 after marrying into the powerful de Clare family—joined

---

*The earl was also charged with getting a papal dispensation allowing the king to postpone the hasty promise he (and Isabella) had made two years before to go on crusade; and to secure support from the pope against Robert Bruce.

together to offer a middle way between the king's favorites and Lancaster's party. The "middle party" (a later name that suggests they were both more organized and more independent than they actually were) provided the only barrier remaining against civil war, which was becoming uncomfortably probable, though the proximate cause was an untraditional one: adultery.

In the spring of 1317, the earl of Lancaster's wife, Alice de Lacy, was either abducted by, or ran away with—plausible evidence exists for both—her lover, a squire, Eubulo (sometimes Ebulo) L'Estrange. When the two were offered refuge by the earl of Surrey, Lancaster armed for battle, and his troops attacked Surrey's. Skirmishes turned into battles, which drew the attention of the king, no doubt looking for anything to distract him from famine, debt, and Scotland, and decided that punishing Lancaster was just the ticket.* Accompanied by fifteen hundred men-at-arms, the king marched to within a mile of the earl of Lancaster's castle at Pontrefact, where at least one report has the king actually challenging Lancaster to single combat, in support of the earl of Surrey, only to be prevented by the ever-prudent earl of Pembroke.

The alliances among England's earls, always a mess, were about to become even more complicated. The earldom of Gloucester had been vacant technically ever since the death of Gilbert de Clare at Bannockburn in 1314. Or, would have been vacant, if his widowed countess hadn't been contending that she was pregnant with the earl's child at the time of his death. After three years of increasingly unkind speculations about the countess's weight and sanity, his widow finally gave up the fiction of her pregnancy in November 1317. The title of earl disappeared, but not the estates associated with it. Those were divided among the earl's sisters: Elizabeth de Clare, the youngest, who had married a member of King Edward's household, Roger d'Amory; Margaret de Clare, the second youngest, and the widow of Piers Gaveston, who had remarried another of the king's favorites,

---

*Though the torrential downpours of the previous two years had not returned, and planting for 1317 had more or less returned to normal, no one in England—or, for that matter, northern Europe—was likely to relax until the fall harvest.

Hugh de Audley; and the eldest, Eleanor de Clare, who was married to Hugh le Despenser.

In the conflicts that defined Edward's first years as king, Despenser—usually called the Younger, to distinguish him from his father, Hugh Despenser the Elder, one of the most loyal supporters of Edward I—backed the Lancaster party, evidently more out of pure opportunism than any conviction. Which explains why, when the informal but powerful position of favorite-to-the-king became vacant following the death of Piers Gaveston in 1312, Despenser dropped his connection with Lancaster and presented himself as a king's man; specifically, in the words of the *Chronicle of Lanercost*, as "the King of England's right eye and, after the death of Piers de Gaveston, his chief counselor against the earls and barons."

Despenser was just as ambitious as Gaveston had ever been, and far more capable. He had already served in some of the highest councils of state, and was one of the relatively few English lieutenants to emerge from Bannockburn with more glory than he had going in. And he needed money. Though he had been granted the revenues from some of the manors controlled by his father, he was still deeply in debt. Once the king resolved the status of his wife's inheritance, Despenser was able to turn toward the most valuable of Gloucester's lands, in Wales.

After Edward I's Welsh conquests, the king granted the various nobles who had established their feudal manors on the border between England and Wales—the Welsh Marches—an unusual amount of freedom from royal supervision, in return for maintaining the border's security. These "Marcher Lords," the barons and earls of the Welsh Marches, were, as a result, none too happy about the king's new favorite assembling a series of Welsh estates. Not only did Despenser persuade the king to grant him the largest of Gloucester's estate—castles at Cardiff and Glamorgan, including Caerphilly, one of the strongest fortresses in Britain—but attempted to seize the rest of it from his brothers-in-law: in the words of the *Vita Edwardi Secundi*, "thus, if he [Despenser] could manage it, each would lose his share through trumped up accusations and he alone would obtain the whole earldom." His aggressive empire-building, sanctioned and supported by the king, made Despenser a powerful set of enemies. One of them was Roger Mortimer, a powerful Marcher Lord, and the former Lord Lieutenant of Ireland.

Another was the queen of England.

Like Piers Gaveston a decade before, Despenser was an enormously powerful rival to Isabella. Just as with Gaveston, Hugh the Younger's sexual habits have produced several centuries' worth of tittle-tattle. Most of the contemporaneous (or near-contemporaneous) chronicles, such as the *Vita* and the *Chronographia regum francorum*, are accusatory: The *Vita* quotes Isabella identifying Despenser as "someone [who] has come between my husband and myself" and who wanted to dishonor her "by every possible means." But if Despenser was a new version of Gaveston, Isabella was no longer a teenage girl, which made her single-minded animus far more dangerous, as events would prove.

Meanwhile, as if to reproach the aristocracy for their squabbling over abductions, infidelities, and false pregnancies, the rural populace of England stubbornly continued suffering from famine and other attendant miseries. Beginning in 1317, according to Thomas Walsingham's *Historia Anglicana*, gangs of *schavaldores* (a local dialect term meaning "robbers") terrorized Northumberland, and "robbed rustics in their homes and their neighbors in the fields, releasing their oxen from wagons and plows and killing them for their food. Indeed, they left nothing behind in the villages that seemed suitable as food, for bread, grain, cows, sheep, pigs, . . . they plundered for themselves."

The food shortages that plagued England were even more destructive in the rest of the British Isles. Scottish soldiers, led by Robert Bruce's brother Edward in a 1315 invasion of Ireland—an attempt to divert Edward's attention from Scotland—were, by 1316, suffering from such extreme food shortages that they were destroyed as a fighting force. By 1317, at Offaly, the Scottish army "suffered from so great a famine that many of them died of hunger." In October 1318, the Scots were finally defeated at the battle of Fochart (sometimes Faughart), and they had long since worn out their welcome among their Irish hosts. The *Annals of Connacht* report that when Edward Bruce died at the battle—subsequently to be beheaded, and carved into quarters, one of which would be sent to the four corners of Ireland—"never was there a better deed done for the Irish . . . in this Bruce's time, falsehood, and famine, and homicide filled the country, and undoubtedly men ate each other in Ireland."

In January 1318, the Baltic froze, for the third time since 1303 (the second time was during the winter of 1307–08). This time, the rivers leading into the sea froze as well, isolating coastal cities from what is now Estonia to Denmark. King Robert, who had returned to Scotland long before his brother's defeat, chose to wait out the brutal winter at the walls surrounding the eastern port city of Berwick, which had been the pivot point for Anglo-Scottish warfare for more than twenty years.

Bruce's troops had been fitfully besieging the town, and the English garrison ensconced in Berwick Castle, for three years. Because of Berwick's location—on the Scottish border, without access to its own hinterlands—the town could not be easily supplied by land.* With Bruce's raiders operating nearby, Berwick was vulnerable even in years when harvests were good; and after the two lost harvests of 1315 and 1316, Scottish and English farms had no grain to sell at any price. And not just grain: even if the waterlogged fields could be mowed, the grass couldn't be turned into hay.† Grass needs to be dry to serve as provender for ruminants like cattle and sheep; and by 1316, the sun hadn't shone consistently in much of Britain and northern Europe for nearly two years. As each rain-soaked spring was followed by a failed harvest, which was in turn succeeded by bitterly cold winters, cattle and sheep died in droves. Bolton Priory counted three thousand sheep in its herd in 1316; by 1317, there were only 913.

The obvious solution was to supply the city by sea. Or would have

---

*The word "hinterlands" literally refers to the amount of farmland contiguous to a town or city.

†One thing that happens to uncured hay when it is stored wet is that it rots; so much so that it outgasses methane, which has a distressing habit of spontaneously combusting.

been, if the town's ability to import food by sea hadn't been severely limited by the destruction of the port facilities during the vicious punishment that Edward I had visited on Berwick in 1296. Ships from Gascony bound for Berwick were regularly captured not just by Bruce's privateers, but also pirates from England, the Low Countries, and even the cities of the eastern Baltic. Those that weren't jettisoned their cargoes within sight of the Scottish coast. By 1318, Berwick had been slowly starving for two years.

The result was what always happens in a siege: a substantial black market; accusations of speculation and profiteering; and, perhaps inevitably, conflict between garrison and townsfolk, as both began living on starvation rations. As the English soldiers were forced to eat their own horses, the cavalry saw its mounts dwindle from more than three hundred to fewer than fifty.

It took until April 1318 before the forces of King Robert "captured" the town. Peter of Spalding, one of the town's leading citizens, was a distant relation to Robert Keith, the marischal of Scotland and King Robert's general commanding the besieging forces. Spalding got word to the marischal that he would find the city gates open when he next had the watch, and, on April 1, Berwick's inhabitants, suffering from a combination of two years of famine and siege, welcomed Bruce's soldiers into their town. The English garrison continued to resist for another three months, but surrendered Berwick Castle on June 18 to James Douglas, whose father, William, had surrendered it to the English twenty-two years before.

The spring of 1318 marked a dramatic improvement in the fortunes of nearly everyone in western Europe. The harvest of 1317 was a rich one, and with supplies of everything from wheat and barley to milk and wool increasing, prices fell enough that even the rural peasantry could afford to feed itself. Isabella's brother had become King Philip V of France in 1316, and two years later had not only reconciled with his wife Jeanne after her conviction-by-association in the Tour de Nesle affair but, after another disastrous attempt to conquer Flanders by his brother, Louis X, in 1315, was close to a peaceful resolution of the conflict with the Flemings.* Robert Bruce, despite his setback in Ireland, had finally taken Berwick, and his position was unquestionably stronger in 1318 than it had been at any time since Bannockburn.

Predictably, the outlier in this litany of good news was the luckless king of England. In June 1318, he was still challenged by the increasingly formidable earl of Lancaster; his wife was becoming an independent power in her own right; and his chief counselor, Hugh le Despenser the Younger, was proving to be more adept at making enemies than even Gaveston at his worst—and, because of his closeness to the king, Despenser's enemies were de facto Edward's as well. In the zero-sum game of royal politics, the growing strength of everyone surrounding the king made his relative weakness even more obvious.

Even the king's piety, which no one doubted, had a hapless cast to it. Edward spent years, beginning in 1317, pursuing the Holy Oil that had supposedly accompanied his favorite saint, Thomas Becket, to his exile in France in 1164. The legend of the oil—that it would anoint the fifth king to follow Becket's nemesis, Henry II, who would then recover the Holy Land—obsessed Edward, partly because he was, in fact, the fifth king, and partly because he was, also in fact, remarkably credulous. He sent knights on missions to discover the oil's whereabouts and (after believing, wrongly, that it was in papal hands) dozens of entreaties to Pope John XXII. Rejected by the pope, and realizing that the legend was nothing more, he was compelled to forego his hoped-for anointing, and apologize to his closest advisers for his gullibility.

While all this was unfolding, in June 1318, a deranged man, the son of a tanner, appeared in Oxford, claiming to be the true king, swapped in the cradle for Edward. He declared that Edward "was not of the blood royal, nor had any right to the realm, which he offered to prove by combat with him." The man, John of Powderham, who evidently resembled the king, claimed that, as an infant, he had been attacked by a royal sow, which had bitten off his ear, and that his nurse, fearing

---

for her life should her carelessness become known, switched him with the son of a carter. Edward had the man arrested, and, apparently attempting to make light of the whole thing, greeted him at Northampton saying, "Welcome, my brother," to which the imposter replied, "Thou are no brother of mine." At this, Edward's common touch deserted him, and John of Powderham was tried and tortured into confessing that the devil had appeared to him in the guise of a housecat, had seduced him, and compelled him to his imposture. With his admission that he had committed not only treason but sorcery, he was sentenced to be hanged and burned.*

Had John of Powderham attempted to impersonate Edward I, his outcome would have been the same. But his effect would have been very different. No one would have accepted him as evidence that Longshanks was a weak and ineffectual king; but, given the succession of embarrassments experienced by his son—from Gaveston to Bannockburn to Berwick, to say nothing of the famine—the English nobility were all too ready to wonder about Edward II. Most notably, the episode was a crisis for Isabella, who was "troubled beyond measure" by John of Powderham—not the validity of his claim but the readiness of her subjects to believe in him, which sowed a seed of doubt in her husband that would germinate for the next nine years.

At the same moment that his authority was being undermined by a madman, the king, via the earl of Pembroke, was negotiating at great and tedious length the Treaty of Leake with Lancaster and his allies, which, among other things, provided for a standing council to advise the Crown, its composition more or less evenly divided by the king's supporters, and Lancaster's. The treaty wasn't ideal, but it did allow Edward to turn his attention northward, and Edward, whose one consistent objective as king had always been the preservation of his father's Scottish conquests, began laying the groundwork for a new expedition, requesting a tax to pay for it, and calling for a parliament that would authorize it to be held in May 1319.

If, however, the king believed that a new year would bring a change

---

*As, indeed, was the cat.

in his fortunes he was, as so often, mistaken. In the Easter season of 1319, the cattle brought to market day in the town of Sussex started dying. Edward, who commissioned the Saint Mary's Psalter in order to style himself as Joseph in the Book of Genesis, was, like Pharaoh in the Book of Exodus, ruling a land afflicted with a great murrain.

Plagues of cattle, or murrains—a generic term for pastoral disease, from the Latin for death, *mori*—are as old as pastoralism itself. The Kahun Petrie Papyrus from 3000 BCE Egypt records the deaths of bulls with labored breathing, inflamed gums, and swollen necks. A similar plague seems to have occurred in Ireland around 2048 BCE, and in Egypt in 1300 BCE, the latter of which was easily the most famous in history, the fifth plague of Exodus 9:3: a "very grievous murrain . . . throughout all the land of Egypt" (though one that affected only Egyptian-owned cattle, and spared those of the Hebrews). In 29 BCE, Virgil, in the third book of the *Georgics*—the greatest poem ever written on animal husbandry, not that there is much competition—refers to a "piteous season" when

> Every tribe of cattle, tame or wild, it swept to death . . . when the fiery thirst had coursed through all the veins and shriveled the hapless limbs, in its turn a watery humour welled up and drew into itself all the bones, as piecemeal they melted with disease.

Severus Sanctus Endelechius, the fourth-century author of the morbidly titled *De Mortibus Bovum* (On the Deaths of Cattle) describes a plague that accompanied the Hun invasions in which "cattle died of a plague all over Europe." Other outbreaks are recorded from ninth-century "Germany" (at the time, eastern Francia), tenth-century Ireland, and eleventh-century Florence.

However, as with all such historical epidemiology, the actual disease causing all the trouble is hard to name definitively. Throughout history, the deadliest of cattle diseases has been caused by the bacterial pathogen *Bacillus anthracis*; the best known may be the viral disease known variously as hoof-and-mouth or foot-and-mouth disease.

But neither is very specific in its targets. Anthrax is deadly to humans as well as just about all herbivores. *Aphtae epizooticae*, the virus that causes hoof-and-mouth, is generally not a hazard to people, but deadly to pigs. The one that arrived in Sussex in 1319 was a different disease altogether.

Though epidemiologists have traced rinderpest back at least nine thousand years, the first definitive appearance in Europe of the viral disease also known as steppe murrain occurred in 1223, initially in what is now Hungary, then Austria, and then Italy and Germany. That first outbreak lasted for at least three years, recurred in 1240, 1249, and 1299, and is only one of the enduring pathogens left behind by the Mongol invasions of the thirteenth and fourteenth centuries. Unlike its close cousin, measles, rinderpest is harmless to people but deadly to cattle. Though it isn't very hardy—it can only survive within a fairly limited range of temperatures, and is easily killed by sunlight—it still spreads wherever ruminants such as cattle, sheep, and goats are in close, indirect contact: places like the paddocks and corrals used by medieval cowherds.

The rinderpest virus is little more than a bit of free-floating genetic code, and in order to replicate, it needs host cells. A rinderpest particle—a *virion*, a single strand of RNA surrounded by a protein envelope—invades a host cell, unwraps itself from its own protein shell, and hijacks the cell's machinery to produce more of both the viral RNA and the viral protein. It then reassembles itself and signals its daughter virions to break out of the host cell to do the same thing all over again. This alerts the host's immune system, particularly the proteins that are always present in the circulatory system, to summon cytokines, proteins shaped to latch onto invaders like rinderpest, and they, in turn, set off an alarm that summons specialized white blood cells, the B and T lymphocytes, that are designed to respond to specific pathogens: B cells have "hands" that are custom-made to hold on to the proteins of invading pathogens, while T cells puncture the invaders' shells.

Or they would, if rinderpest hadn't already evolved a counterstrategy: The virus has what epidemiologists call a "core affinity" for lymphoid tissue, which means that the cells that rinderpest virions invade and take over first are the same B and T lymphocytes that are specially designed to kill them. Only after the immune system is rendered irrelevant does the virus attack its secondary target: the epithelial cells lining the walls of the host's respiratory, alimentary, and gastrointestinal tracts.

The result: a high fever, usually lasting two to three days, followed by anorexia, constipation, congestion, and nasal discharge—unpleasant, but not disabling. During the second phase, however, things get truly ugly. Animals develop necrotic mouth lesions, followed by enormous gastrointestinal distress: bloody diarrhea, alternating with tenesmus—the desire to defecate, even without any material need—which results in cramping, and even muscle tearing. Diarrhea leads to dehydration. In their terminal stages, animals can no longer stand, and fall in untidy heaps, dying within days.

But before even the first signs of disease, infected animals first shed huge quantities of the virus through tears and saliva, thus ensuring a ready supply of new hosts. The disease has been living in reservoirs of such hosts for thousands of years—the formal term is *enzootic*—but for not very well understood reasons, sometimes the reservoir overflows its banks, and the disease becomes *epizootic*: an animal epidemic.

Which is precisely what happened in 1319, in a region that was particularly vulnerable to epizootics. For four centuries, European agriculture production and population growth had become a pyramid scheme that relied on putting more land under cultivation every year. More land meant more dependence on plows. And more plowing meant more animal power. Both horses and oxen (the generic term in Europe for castrated bulls) were used throughout Europe as plow animals; horses more productively because of an improved horse collar developed in Asia and diffused to Europe by the eleventh century, and which multiplied the load horses could pull nearly fivefold. But while horses could plow faster, oxen were much cheaper to feed; they can survive on hay, which just needs to be cut and dried, and they don't demand oats, which need to be planted and harvested. Oxen remained the optimal choice wherever the cost of provender—hay/straw—was low, such as large demesnes and manors, where grass grew wild.* In such traditional villages, the typical plow was pulled by a team of eight oxen—a communally owned team, since only a village could afford such a capital investment. In others, horses and oxen were frequently harnessed together.

For the overwhelming majority of Edward's subjects, therefore, a cattle plague was a life-and-death issue. During 1319, attacks of rinderpest killed 65 percent of England's bovids—cattle, sheep, and goats. The consequences were both wide and long-lasting, since the disease killed not just plow animals but dairy producers as well. And it did no favors for the ones that survived; the 35 percent of cattle remaining were so undernourished that their milk production fell from 142 gallons per animal annually to 45 gallons. And because animal populations bounce back far more slowly than cereal production, it was 1327 before the flocks recovered. All by itself, the lack of milk was bad enough. Combined with a deficiency in other protein sources, it resulted in widespread malnutrition that lasted for—in another nod to the Book of Genesis—seven very lean years.

Though Edward had tried, with limited success, to address the horrific first two years of the famine—price controls, import subsidies, exhortations to his subjects to forego hoarding—he had little to say about the destruction of millions of pounds' worth of livestock. For whatever reason, his attention was directed elsewhere. Despite the Treaty of Leake, things between the king and Lancaster weren't exactly resolved; the earl continued to assert his claim to be Steward of England, and used the purely nominal title to try to approve everything from appointees to the royal household to control of royal castles. And it wasn't just Lancaster: Two of the king's closest advisers,

---

*The actual economic calculus is even more complicated: Horses were valuable when armies were on the march because of the constant need for replenishing mounts. In addition, horses could also be sold when old, their hooves used for glue, their tails and manes for horsehair, though not their flesh for human food, since Pope Gregory III had forbidden the consumption of horsemeat in the eighth century. Plow horses therefore could be sold only for about 5 or 6 shillings, less than half their cost when new. Europe's agricultural peasantry was poor, but could not afford to be economically unsophisticated, and made such choices daily.

the earl of Pembroke and Antonio Pessagno, quarreled so fiercely that Pessagno left England for Paris. And he was no closer to liberating Berwick.

The only "good" news—good in the king's eyes, anyway—was that, at the end of 1318, Hugh le Despenser the Younger was confirmed as the king's chamberlain, serving as Edward's official spokesman and as liaison to the kingdom's highest nobility.*

The new chamberlain's first task was to prepare for a new Scottish expedition. Despenser, acting in the name of the king, demanded a new set of subsidies and taxes from Parliament, asked the episcopate for contributions, and applied to the Italians for loans. His coffers replenished, in the spring of 1319, the king summoned 23,000 soldiers to muster at York (though only 8,000 appeared). England's earls and barons supplied their usual contingent of men, notably 140 knights and 350 men-at-arms from the earl of Lancaster, along with a decent number of archers. Perhaps 10,000 men, along with a siege train, followed Edward north to Berwick.

The English arrived in the first week of September 1319 and immediately began assaulting the town and castle from both land and sea. They continued hammering at the city's walls, and sapping, or digging under them—one of Edward's siege engines was a "sow," a long covered shed on wheels, intended to allow sappers to approach a castle's walls—until September 17. Then, just as the Scottish garrison, under Walter Stewart, was about to surrender, Edward learned he had been duped.

While Edward was marching north, King Robert had sent ten thousand hobelars under James Douglas and Thomas Randolph, the earl of Moray, south; at just about the moment that the English arrived at Berwick, Douglas and Moray entered England, and headed for York. Their plan was not to capture a castle but a queen. When the king took his army on the hundred-mile journey to Berwick, Isabella had stayed near York with her three children—Edward, John, and Eleanor; Joan,

---

*The title, formally Lord Chamberlain of the Household (to distinguish it from the Lord Great Chamberlain, a state office held, in 1318, by the earl of Oxford), was still somewhat informal at the beginning of the fourteenth century.

the youngest, wouldn't be born until 1321—which meant that the king had left behind a much bigger prize than Berwick. The authors of the *Vita* even wrote that Douglas "would have inflicted great loss and immeasurable damage on us . . . if the Queen had at that time been captured."

The "would have" is a giveaway, of course. One of Douglas's scouts was captured just outside of York and brought to William Melton, the archbishop. None of the English authorities had any idea what a Scottish scout was doing in Yorkshire, and told him that he would be "put to the question"—that is, tortured—in order to find out. The scout immediately gave up everything he knew of Douglas's plan, only to be greeted with disbelief. Melton "laughed his intelligence to scorn," though he did take the precaution of sending his own scouts to where the Scottish prisoner directed. Finding ten thousand heavily armed hobelars, the archbishop alerted the queen and arranged for her to escape by boat to Nottingham. It cannot have failed to occur to the queen that, seven years after stranding her at Tyneside at the mercy of Scottish raiders, her husband had abandoned her yet again. Neither was she likely to forget that he had done so at the behest of the man who had taken Gaveston's place in his inner circle.

With their primary objective unattainable, Douglas and Moray marched toward York and met up with the English defenders in the village of Myton-on-Swale, though "defenders" suggests a level of martial skill that was in short supply. Virtually the entire English force had never picked up a weapon before, and at least a quarter of them were men in religious orders: priests, friars, and clerks. On October 20, Melton's twenty thousand men attempted to surprise the Scots, encamped on the west side of the river Swale, by crossing over Myton Bridge. However, the experienced hobelars saw the English advancing in nothing like a military formation, and formed a wedge-shaped *schiltrom* behind a smoke screen created by setting three haystacks on fire. As they slowly marched toward the priests and townsmen, the Yorkshiremen broke, then started running back toward Myton Bridge, where they found that Douglas had sent a force of horsemen to block their retreat. At least one thousand men of

Archbishop Melton's "army" died there—some sources say four thousand—three hundred of them priests, and one of them Nicholas Fleming, the mayor of York. Another thousand died trying to swim across the Swale. In the words of the *Chronicle of Lanercost,* "Had not night come on, hardly a single Englishman would have escaped . . . many were taken alive, carried off to Scotland and ransomed at a heavy price."

Douglas and Randolph had landed a heavy enough blow on the north of England at what became known as the "White Battle" (or "The Chapter of Myton"). The defeat, and especially the number of clerics involved, gave Edward no choice but to break off the siege of Berwick, not least because Lancaster used the excuse of the attack on York to depart. On September 1, 1319, Edward II and the rest of the army followed him back to Newcastle, and eventually York, where an attack of rinderpest killed virtually all the oxen in Edward's siege train and baggage. Meanwhile, Douglas carried out "the most savage raid yet seen on the west side of the Pennines, cruelly waiting until after the harvest"—only the second decent one in five years—"and on about November 1 destroyed the corn and seized great numbers of men." "Then, after ten or twelve days [Douglas's troops] fared through part of Cumberland, which they burned on their march, and returned to Scotland with a very large spoil of men and cattle."

A disaster as monumental as the Berwick campaign of 1319 called out for scapegoats, and there were many to choose from: Some blamed Hugh le Despenser the Younger (who *was* responsible for spreading rumors about the rift between the king and Lancaster). Others pointed the finger at Lancaster himself; a rumor in wide circulation had the earl taking as much as £40,000 from Robert Bruce to allow James Douglas free passage on his expedition to capture the queen.

But the real blame lay with the king himself. Defeated at Berwick, and with Douglas and the earl of Moray raiding in Yorkshire, Edward had no choice but to offer a truce. And, just before Christmas of 1319, he had one, guaranteeing no further battles for two years while the Scots were barred from building any new castles in specified territories, a compromise that fooled no one; the Scots had won a decisive victory in their struggle for independence. Four months later, King Robert sent a grandiloquent letter to Edward proposing negotiations between the two kings, and another reminding Pope John XXII—who had already placed him excommunicate, and generally opposed his rebellion—that "while agreeable peace prevails, the minds of the faithful are at rest, the Christian way is furthered, and all the affairs of holy mother church . . . are carried on more prosperously."

King Robert's letter to Edward was a demand for the recognition of his own royal status; the one to the pope, a call for the blessings of peace. On April 6, 1320, thirty-nine Scottish nobles—eight earls and thirty-one barons—put their names to a far more consequential document.* They signed, at Arbroath Abbey, on the North Sea south of Aberdeen, Scotland's true charter of independence. The so-called Declaration of Arbroath wasn't simply a piece of political symbolism, intended to promote the interests of King Robert Bruce. It was also a powerful argument that his claim on the throne was validated by the fact that he had been chosen by the Scots themselves—by the "community of Scotland"—and that he could even be replaced by the nobility if he proved unable to defend them against the English. By the standard of the day, it was as revolutionary a document as the Magna Carta, an argument that a king wasn't selected by God but elected by man; or, at least, noblemen. It ends, "As long as a hundred of us remain alive, we will never on any condition be subjected to the lordship of the English. For we fight not for glory nor riches nor honours, but for freedom alone, which no good man gives up except with his life."

---

*The original, sent to the pope at Avignon, has since disappeared; other versions claim up to fifty-one signatures.

"The Dearest Beef I've Ever Seen"

1320–1322

On the last day of the month of June, in the year 1320, dozens of the most exalted members of France's nobility congregated in a church eighty miles north of Paris to witness the most familiar ceremony in feudal Europe: a vassal kneeled, and presented his clasped hands to his lord, who wrapped them in his own. This church wasn't just any place of worship, but Amiens Cathedral, the largest in France, reputed home to the head of John the Baptist, which had been part of the booty taken by French knights on the Fourth Crusade. And the participants weren't ordinary men but the kings of France and England. Edward, accompanied by Isabella and Hugh le Despenser the Younger, had come to pay the long-delayed homage for the fiefs of Aquitaine and Ponthieu to Isabella's brother Philip V, who had been waiting since he ascended the throne in 1316.

Homage was the connective tissue of feudalism: its bones, tendons, and ligaments. Its oaths bound one man to another, most especially vassal to liege. When they involved two of the most powerful men in Europe, these connections, as sacred as any religious obligation (and even more legally enforceable), were the occasion of a formal ritual as solemn as a Mass and as strictly choreographed as a coronation. Unfortunately, the ritual began better than it ended, when Philip surprised Edward by demanding not just homage, but fealty.

The distinction was subtle, but important. Homage was a surrender of a particular fief by vassal to lord, who then formally returned it, usually by handing over some object that symbolized the property in question: a baron could give a bag of salt to a freeman; an earl might receive a jewel from his king. Fealty, on the other hand, was an oath of fidelity: a promise that the vassal would harm neither the lord nor his property, and that he owed his lord military service. Symbolically and literally, they represented the two sides of feudal manorialism—land, in exchange for protection. Fealty was generally regarded as the less consequential of the two. Though vassals were required to make homage directly to their lords, fealty could be made to his representative—a bailiff, perhaps—and one could even declare fealty to more than one lord.

When the ceremony involved two kings, however, it became a more fraught affair. When Duke William of Normandy was crowned on Christmas Day, 1066, he became the last link in a chain of feudal obligations touching every family in England, and owed homage only to God. But because he retained his dukedom as a fief from the king of France, in Normandy he occupied the middle of a different chain, between his own vassals and (at the time) King Philip I. By 1177, Henry II, William's grandson and Edward's great-great-grandfather, finally agreed to pay homage to King Philip's grandson Louis VII as duke of Normandy and count of Aquitaine—another fiefdom held from the king of France, acquired by marriage to Eleanor of Aquitaine. However, he rewrote the normal oath to make it "only for lands held overseas," and commenced the tradition that obliged the succeeding dukes of Normandy—and, therefore kings of England—to meet French kings under a tree at the southern border of Normandy, there to acknowledge their feudal obligations. Henry's objective, and that of his successors, was avoiding the trap of offering fealty *as the king of England,* and thereby acknowledging the French king as overlord. Edward, however feckless in other matters, recognized the trap well enough that when Philip attempted to force him to swear an unqualified oath of fealty, Edward exploded, "as to the fealty, we are certain that we should not swear it."

By the time Edward returned home in July, his brief and inconsequential victory over Philip had been pushed into the background. The Declaration of Arbroath had reached the papal court at Avignon while he was balking at swearing fealty to Philip in Amiens, and Pope

John XXII had written to the English king, pressing him to end the conflict with his northern neighbor. Simultaneously, King Robert had sent a letter offering to send representatives to a peace conference. Having avoided Philip's fealty trap, Edward was caught in an even more knotty one by the combination of church pressure and Scottish diplomatic ingenuity.

Though Edward managed to stall until the beginning of 1321, he had to agree to a meeting or risk provoking the pope and, worse, his lord-in-all-but-name, Philip V, who was not only already angry enough after Amiens but had considerably more troops surrounding Edward's French fiefs than he had to defend them. However, a willingness to meet didn't make Edward any more flexible about Scotland than before, which guaranteed that the peace conference, at which the king was represented by the earl of Pembroke and Hugh le Despenser, was doomed to failure. No parties ever give up at the peace table what they think they can still win militarily, especially with such an intractable issue at the core of the dispute: Edward was unprepared to even recognize Bruce's kingship, and without such recognition, King Robert was unwilling to sign anything but another truce.

Perhaps unfairly, Hugh's failure to return with a peace treaty served to solidify the battle lines between the Despensers and everyone else. Partly this was resentment toward the Despenser family for its control over access to the king; a contemporary account records that "no Baron could approach the king without their [the Younger and Elder Despensers'] consent, and then a bribe was usually necessary." Partly it was the anger of the earl of Lancaster over accusations that his early departure from Berwick had been purchased by a bribe from Robert Bruce.

Lancaster had already refused to attend the parliament that Edward had called the previous year, thus ending the brief reconciliation outlined in the Treaty of Leake, and by February 1321, the earl had decided to attack Hugh the Elder. In May, Lancaster's allies, including the earl of Hereford and the Mortimers (who, as Marcher Lords, were especially hostile to Despenser's acquisition of nearby real estate), attacked the Welsh lands of the Young Despenser, plundering Newport, Cardiff, and

Swansea. By July, Lancaster, after instigating the first attacks, joined in at the head of a fragile coalition of northern peers and Marcher Lords, and (perhaps more provocatively) in his capacity as Steward of England: the same dubious position from which he had attempted to control Edward's access to his own castles four years before.

Edward called a parliament to resolve the dispute. On August 19, 1321, Lancaster and the Marcher Lords, including Hereford, the Mortimers, and Baron Badlesmere (who had deserted the compromisers of the so-called Middle Party, and broken with both the earl of Pembroke and the king), argued strenuously against the Despensers. They weren't alone. Isabella begged the king "on her knees, for the people's sakes" to banish the Despensers. And the earl of Pembroke advised his king to cut them loose: "Neither brother nor sister should be dearer to thee than thyself. Do not therefore for any living soul lose thy kingdom: 'He perishes on the rocks that love another more than himself.'"

Whether it was the force of their oratory or Lancaster's five thousand armed retainers* that proved more persuasive, Parliament found against the Despensers, and ordered both Elder and Younger banished.

One reason for Edward's posthumous reputation as one of England's most feckless kings was his uncanny talent for repeating his own disasters. In April 1308, under pressure from his own earls—preeminently Lancaster—the king had exiled his favorite, Piers Gaveston, to France with less-than-stellar results. Now, an unlucky thirteen years later, the king did exactly the same thing, exiling both Hugh the Elder and Hugh the Younger to France. To anyone who could remember the years between Gaveston's exile in 1308 and his murder in 1312, this could not have been a good sign, and Edward was nothing if not consistent. Just as when Gaveston became the target of his intransigent barons, the king's immediate reaction, thirteen years later, was not compromise but combat. Only two months after Parliament banished the Despensers, Edward's casus belli was indirectly handed to him by his onetime supporter, Baron Badlesmere.

On October 10, 1321, Queen Isabella arrived at Badlesmere's home,

---

*In order that their presence would be obvious to everyone, the retainers were uniformed in green tunics with one yellow sleeve.

Leeds Castle, a stopping point on one of her pilgrimages. The baron was away, so the castle was under the authority of his wife, Lady Badlesmere. When, for unknown reasons, Lady Badlesmere denied the queen admittance, Isabella insisted on confronting her, at which point the baroness ordered her archers to fire on the queen's retainers, killing six of them.

Edward's reaction was fierce. He summoned his own household troops, hired several hundred mercenaries, and immediately besieged Leeds Castle, which fell after only a week. Edward hanged the castle's constable and thirteen others, and imprisoned Lady Badlesmere and her children in the Tower of London, all without benefit of trial. And his subjects loved him for it. After fourteen years on the throne, three major (and even more minor) defeats in his Scottish wars, nearly constant rebellion from his greatest vassals, livestock epidemics, and, most tellingly, five years of famine, Edward was the object of an unfamiliar outpouring of loyalty and affection. In fact, support for the king was so widespread that historians have speculated ever since whether the entire incident was a lucky opportunity, or a planned provocation—a put-up job intended to rally his realm against his rambunctious nobles—though it seems far too clever for this particular monarch.*

However unexpected the king's newfound support, he needed it.

The fall of 1321 marked yet another catastrophic harvest. This time it was occasioned not by torrential rains, as was the case six years before, but drought. Europe's harvest of barley, which needed more water than either oats or wheat, suffered a worse failure in 1321 than it had in either 1315 or 1316.

If Europe's farmers were surprised by the lack of rain in 1321, they were tragically familiar with the year's temperatures: cold, and colder. By one measure, the winters from 1303 to 1328 represent one of the coldest twenty-five-year stretches ever recorded. Using a complex system collating both tree-ring and impressionistic records—impressionistic here meaning descriptive, such as "the Rhine froze before Christmas" or

---

*A lucky opportunity, that is, for the king. No one would call the retainers killed at Leeds anything but unlucky.

"the Danube was dammed for four weeks by ice"—only one year of the twenty-five qualified as "warm." Warm was defined as two warm months with little or no snow activity. Meanwhile, eleven were "cold" (two cold months, ground snow for weeks, and rivers frozen for one to three weeks), and four years made it all the way to "severe" (snow all winter, rivers and lakes frozen for at least a month). The winter of 1321–22 was one of the severe ones. Before January, the Baltic had frozen over once again, and a Danish chronicle recorded that horsemen and coaches could travel on the frozen sea all the way to Sweden.

Such weather is especially hard on sheep; lambing is highly sensitive to cold. Though cold weather results in heavier individual fleeces (the average ram produced 1.93 pounds in 1321, up from a more typical 1.35 pounds), it also decimated the flocks. Wool prices, like that of nearly every other agricultural commodity grown, raised, or processed in Europe, hit a three-century peak in the decade 1310–1320.

But wool *wasn't* like any other agricultural commodity. It was at the center of the most dramatic change in the European economy since the fall of the Roman Empire.

By the fourteenth century, four centuries of weather-enabled population growth had transformed the medieval economy from a static collection of self-contained (and self-sufficient) communities into a network that needed trade to survive. In northern Europe particularly, the towns that had emerged during the Medieval Warm Period couldn't be fed by their surrounding fields and pastures, even when the weather was good, which meant that they needed to produce something that they could trade for grain. Textiles were the first and overwhelmingly the most important "something." And though linen could clothe the wealthy families of northern France, and silk the great tradesmen of Italy, for everyone else the textile that mattered was woolen cloth.

However, the regions that spun wool into thread and wove it into cloth were geographically separated from the ones that produced the best wool. The part of Flanders along the Scheldt River in possession of good clay for the "fuller's earth" needed to bleach and filter wool before carding it into fibers, as well as many plants that could be used to make dyes, happened also to be home to sheep capable of producing only inferior coats. As a result, Flanders' near monopoly on cloth manufacture in northern Europe was utterly dependent on sheep raised in Spain—the flocks of sheep that Don Quixote confuses with two attacking armies were part of the hundreds of thousands of merinos making their annual trek from the uplands of northern Spain to the plains of Andalusia—and especially Britain.

English and Scottish wool was so good, and so plentiful, that the phrase "carrying wool to England" (coined by a thirteenth-century French poet) was a medieval aphorism precisely analogous to the later cliché about coals and Newcastle. The long, silky fibers of Cotswold and Lincoln sheep in Shropshire, and Leicester sheep in the Midlands and north, produced the most important cash crop and most valuable export commodity in all of Britain. Since fleeces were far more valuable than meat, *wethers*—castrated males—were kept alive for years as long as they could be shorn of their thicker-than-female fleeces. This was both good and bad. The fact that wool was worth more than grain meant that pastoral lands dedicated to sheep farming got farther and farther away from those used for cereals. Though East Anglia was well suited for grain production, it was almost entirely devoted to livestock by 1300, which detached the biggest producers of manure from the lands that needed it most.

And they needed a lot of it. England's economy, in any practical meaning, *was* the wool trade; wool has such a powerful meaning in England that, to this day, the seat of the presiding officer of the House of Lords is known as the "woolsack," and has been so since the fourteenth century, when it was an actual bale of wool. As a result, the wool trade was also central to the taxing authority of every English king from Richard the Lionheart onward: the most valuable and, when exported, the easiest thing to tax. Wool was also the collateral for the Italian loans that financed the Scottish wars of both Edwards. In 1275, Edward I established the "Great and Ancient Custom" of an export tax on wool, originally 7 shillings 6 pence per sack—a "sack" was twenty-six stone, or 364 pounds—which was tolerable enough, as long as Flemish clothmakers were buying sacks for £18 each. In 1297, however, when Longshanks needed to finance wars in both Scotland and Flanders, and announced an export duty of 40 shillings a sack—effectively, the value of one sack in ten—he created a constitutional crisis. His own earls argued that "the whole community feels itself burdened by the tax on wools, which is exceedingly burdensome, for the wool of England *amounts almost to the value of half the whole land,* and the tax which is paid thereon to a fifth part of the value of the whole land."*

Which is why the lost harvest of 1321, bad as it was, wasn't the worst of it for Edward, or his subjects. Two years after rinderpest wiped out most of northern Europe's bovids, an epidemic of inch-long parasitic worms—*Fasciola hepatica,* also known as the sheep liver fluke—reduced its sheep and goat flocks by as much as 70 percent.

The impact of this disaster—yet another in a long series—was felt most disastrously in England's towns rather than villages. Even though townspeople neither raised wool nor (until the end of the four-teenth century) produced significant amounts of woolen cloth, they depended on the trade surpluses generated by the export of wool to purchase food. A declining supply of the nation's most important commodity at the same time that food prices were on a sickeningly steep upward trend affected everyone, but the rural peasantry could at least grow some of their own food. Townsfolk could not.

As a result, town mortality was orders of magnitude higher than anywhere else. As measured in the sale of properties in order to pay the taxes due when their owners died, the death rate in towns—Winchester is a good example—tripled during 1316–1320, resulting in a net reduction of population of close to 15 percent. Over the entire decade from 1310 to 1320, the mortality rate was at least 25 percent greater than normal.

And "normal" wasn't especially good. In modern industrialized economies, for every thousand people living at the beginning of a

---

*By the end of the fourteenth century, England recognized fifty-one different grades of wool, selling for a much as a shilling a pound and as little as two pence. Still, with at least eight million sheep, each producing at least a pound of wool annually, England could count on more than £250,000 every year.

typical year, about eight will die—a significant improvement over the number in 1900, when it was more than seventeen. During the last half of the thirteenth century, the crude death rate in Britain was approximately 27/1000. From 1300 to 1348—which is to say, *before* the Black Death made its reappearance—it regularly reached 50/1,000. In towns, more than 100/1,000: one in ten.

Bad as this was, it could have been worse. At the time of the Great Famine, only 10 to 15 percent of Europe's population lived in towns and cities—what M. M. Postan, the eponymous author of the thesis about Europe's "internal colonization" of marginal farmland, called non-feudal islands in a feudal sea—from one in four in Flanders to fewer than one in twenty in Scandinavia. The boundary is a little slippery, however; depending on who is doing the counting, at the beginning of the fourteenth century Europe as a whole had only between fifty-six and seventy-nine towns and cities with populations greater than ten thousand. Britain had very few; London, by far the largest, had about forty thousand to fifty thousand permanent residents. Some provincial towns, like Norwich in England, Dublin in Ireland, or Berwick in Scotland, counted between three thousand and ten thousand people, but even the most densely populated parts of Britain were home to no more than four hundred people per square mile.

Continental Europe was considerably more urbanized. Paris was its largest city, with population estimates ranging from eighty thousand to two hundred thousand, but others were, even to a modern eye, true cities. Lille had more than twenty thousand residents; Calais, fifteen thousand; Bruges, at least thirty-five thousand; Ghent, perhaps sixty thousand. Farther east, Leiden and Strasbourg were each cities of more than ten thousand; Cologne, forty thousand.*

Despite being a small fraction of Europe's fourteenth-century population, or perhaps because of it, residents of towns and cities were far wealthier on a per capita basis than their rural cousins, which bred, as it always does, resentment. Even in modern societies, the virtues of

---

*The world's largest fourteenth-century city was Hangzhou, China, with a population of at least 400,000, though some estimates go as high as 1.2 million, perhaps as many as Rome had in the first century BCE.

trade—of buying low and selling high—are frequently seen as criminal profiteering, so it's no surprise that a precapitalist, preindustrial world looked askance at it, particularly during times of famine. Disapproval of profiting from the misery of others was reflected in statute and traditions, sometimes both at the same time. A modern business is lauded for discovering new customers; during the fourteenth century, finding a new market in which to sell, for example, grain, was known as *forestalling*, and was not only illegal but shameful: "stealing" from the rightful, traditional vendor. Even worse was hoarding for purposes of speculation, which featured in dozens of stories in wide circulation by 1316: a woman denying she had bread to share with her sister, only to have God turn her hidden loaves into stone, for example.

Even in times of plenty, towns and villages had a problematic relationship. Villages depended on towns to supply a market for their entire surplus production, which made the income of rural peasants hostage to the decisions of townsfolk. During a famine, these positions were reversed, since it wasn't their prosperity for which towns depended on villages, but their very lives. And it took a *lot* of rural acreage to feed even a small town.

Consider grain: in Devonshire, the town of Exeter, with about five thousand people, received its grain shipments from as much as twenty-five miles inland; Dijon—at least twice as large as Exeter—from a roughly circular area reaching more than fifteen miles in every direction, or more than twenty-three hundred square miles. London's hinterlands comprised nearly a quarter of England's stock of arable land.

Even though towns were obliged to buy all their raw materials from their own hinterlands, they still prospered. This sort of economic leverage worked both ways, however, and during any shortage, inflation hit a cash-and-wage economy far harder than one that still included a large element of self-sufficiency and barter. The giant price increases caused by the lost harvests of 1315–1316—when output drops by half or more, prices go up by at least as much—affected towns an order of magnitude more fiercely than villages. In Valenciennes, for example, the price of cereal was twenty-four times higher in 1316 than in 1320; in Mons, thirty-two times higher. Even when compared with other nonabundant years, from decades later, prices remained five to eight times higher. The royal town of Hull, in England, was already in severe trouble before the famine; in 1310, more than a quarter of the town's agricultural rental properties were "decayed" . . . that is, not being worked. By 1315, that number had increased to a third; by one calculation, to half. So bad did things get that Edward II ordered his men to reduce rents ruthlessly in order to preserve at least some of the crown's income—a desperate and ultimately doomed measure, since the town, on the banks of the Humber River, was not only practically flooded out by the rains of 1315–1316 but dependent on its flocks of sheep, which were utterly destroyed by the murrain of 1320. In Hull, and in dozens of other towns, the burghers could barely afford food, much less rent.

Those who lived in towns were also more vulnerable to both food shortages and infectious disease, since high population density increased exposure to every sort of pathogen that could be transmitted from one person to another. In the worst year of the famine, 1315, "the year of the mortality," as many as a third of the residents of Ghent—twenty thousand men, women, and children—died from either pestilence or hunger.

Not every aspect of the "evil times" was more ruinous for Europe's urban population than its rural peasantry. True, they died in huge numbers from infectious disease and suffered brutally from the cold, rain, and, of course, incompetent monarchs and rebellious nobles. But they were at least better insulated than their country cousins against the ravages of war. Moreover, they were wealthier, even in the poorest of times, which meant they had a far larger arsenal of strategies for coping with disaster. Flemish and German cities regularly bought food with money raised in the bond market. They even went into the insurance business, by selling life annuities: promises to pay pensions tomorrow for cash today. So "successful" were the annuities as a hedge against famine that an annuity bubble formed; and, like all bubbles, it burst. After pledging their properties during the years

1315–1320 as collateral for the promised annuity payments, Europe's towns, cities, and churches were left holding a highly toxic bag. The town of Stralsund, Germany, offered life annuities of 10 percent of the amount invested, and, when they were compelled to default, lost a large number of municipal properties pledged as guaranty.

It's a mistake, though, to assume that a typical resident of Edinburgh or London (or even Paris) believed that the famine could be relieved by better food-distribution systems, prosecution of speculators, or even annuities. The almost unfathomable series of weather-linked disasters could not have been the work of man, after all. If, on the other hand, God was testing his people, the only way for His blessings to return was by contrition: the putting aside of vanities, which meant, perversely, that fasting by those with enough to eat was viewed as a direct appeal to heaven. Another was what can only be called expiatory marches. By the fall of 1315, Parisian guilds and religious societies tried to placate God by means of barefoot processions: A contemporary French eyewitness reported, "We saw a large number of both sexes, not only from nearby places but from places as much as five leagues away, barefooted, and many even, excepting the women, in a completely nude condition, with their priests, coming together in procession at the church of the holy martyr, and they devoutly carried bodies of the saints and other relics to be adored." The archbishop of Canterbury even went so far as to order Friday barefoot processions by all religious orders in London, so pervasive was the belief that appealing to God's mercy could only be secured through the most public sort of contrition.

Whatever the direct consequence of prayer and procession, charity was asked for and occasionally received. In 1318, a wealthy Londoner named Robert de Lincoln left £10 in his will to buy a meal—at a penny each—for two thousand poor people. Others with the funds to do so founded monasteries and even hospitals. Of course, private charity was easier to raise in the first years of the famine, as, year after year, economic pressure started to tell on even the wealthiest.

The most important direct strategy for coping with famine was by importing food. Despite the ongoing war with France, and the embargo of all imports from its closest and wealthiest neighbor (and the fact that everywhere in northern Europe was suffering from the same flooding and lost harvests), municipalities were far more sophisticated in their management of a grain policy than rural estates. The Flemish were especially good at it, partly because their own territory was so dependent on trade of all sorts. The municipal council of Bruges bought stocks of grain—more than fifty-five thousand bushels of wheat alone in the spring of 1317—from Genoese, Venetian, and even Spanish middlemen, suspending the free market in grain for the duration of the emergency, and selling the grain at cost to the city-licensed bakeries, which was probably the single reason that famine-related mortality was only half as high in Bruges as in Ypres.

The bakers of Bruges recognized a responsibility owed to their fellow citizens, either out of public-spiritedness or fear of retribution. Not everyone was so lucky. The bakers of Paris, for example, were frequently accused—and convicted—of not just increasing the price of bread but adulterating its content. In 1316, according to the contemporary chronicler Jean de Saint-Victor, the Parisian bakers

> put many disgusting ingredients—the dregs of wine, pig droppings, and other things—in the bread that the famished people were eating . . . when the truth was known, sixteen wheels were placed on stakes in small fields of Paris, and the bakers were set upon them with their hands raised and holding pieces of the loaves so tainted. Then they were exiled from France.

And so it went, in town after town, year after year, as rains were succeeded by drought, accompanied by murrains of cows, sheep, and horses. And while most towns and cities were safe from the widespread destruction of the armies of Scotland, England, France, and Flanders, they were still subject to self-inflicted episodes of violence.* A typical, though late, example occurred in Douai on October 28, 1322—past the worst years of the famine, but at a moment when grain

---

*This applies generally to any of the rival claimants to the throne of the Holy Roman Empire; see chapter 10.

hoarding and profiteering were still widely practiced and even more widely suspected. So, when two women named Jacquette Espillet and Margot Cauche appeared in the town market and, without evidence, denounced the hoarders, a riot broke out: the granary was raided, barges ransacked, burghers' houses invaded. When justice was finally meted out, the women were sentenced to have their tongues torn out for their "evil and outrageous" words, and were banished forever, along with dozens of other rioters.

While towns and villages throughout Europe and Britain continued to experience the torments of weather and war, Edward II resolved to use his newfound popularity against his own tormenters. In January 1322, he recalled the Despensers, father and son, from exile, assembled several thousand troops, and pointed them at his rebellious nobles, advancing up the east bank of the Severn to Shrewsbury, where the earl of Hereford and the Mortimers had retreated. There they surrendered to the king without a fight, leaving Edward free to turn north in pursuit of the peer who had been his most reliably hostile vassal for the preceding fourteen years: the earl of Lancaster. He would never have a better opportunity to land a decisive blow. Letters between Lancaster and both James Douglas and the earl of Moray (in which Lancaster was referred to by his code name, "King Arthur") had appeared, in which the earl offered to swear fealty to Robert Bruce— as clear evidence of treason as any king could ask. Lancaster's plan to sell his honor, however, was a failure, since his potential customer doubted he had any worth buying: King Robert is supposed to have responded, "How will a man who cannot keep faith with his own lord keep faith with me?"

Lancaster was neither a gifted soldier nor, except by accident of feudal inheritance, a formidable political force, and the circumstances of his last rebellion seem scripted to make Edward look good by comparison. Whatever plan he had when "King Arthur" marched south from his castle at Pontrefact to besiege a royal castle at Tickhill is lost to history and certainly isn't obvious in retrospect. Having neither the siege engines needed to batter down the castle's walls nor the time to starve the garrison out, he stayed only a few days (perhaps hoping that the garrison was even less adept at analyzing the tactical situation than he was) before continuing south to Burton-on-Trent. With Edward and the royal troops on the move, however, Lancaster was in danger of being cut off from his northern home, and retreated, first back to Pontrefact, then farther north, one step ahead of the king.

His backing-and-forthing eventually came to an end in Borough-bridge, at the River Ure, north of the city of York. There Lancaster, leading perhaps seven hundred knights, plus their retainers and men-at-arms, found himself on the southern end of the bridge over the river staring at the opposite shore, where four thousand light cavalrymen held the bridge's opposite end. They were under the command of the sheriff of Cumberland, Sir Andrew Harclay, an experienced soldier who had been fighting on the Scottish borders since at least 1304, when he was a lieutenant of Robert de Clifford—decidedly not what the earl had hoped to find blocking his retreat north.

With Edward marching rapidly from the south, Lancaster was out of options. On March 17, 1322, and for the last time, he unfurled his banners and ordered the attack.*

The battle was a replay in miniature of Stirling Bridge, if not Bannockburn. Harclay had dismounted his cavalry into a formation that mimicked the Scottish schiltroms, and placed archers on the flanks so that when Lancaster's cavalrymen tried a frontal assault across the bridge they were broken by Harclay's spears, and their attempts to flank the position allowed his archers to decimate them. The earl of Hereford was killed by a Welsh infantryman hiding under a bridge as he crossed. At least he tried. Lancaster simply surrendered.

Harclay brought the earl back to his own castle of Pontrefact, where Edward was now ensconced. On March 22, without bothering with any formality such as a trial, the king sentenced the grandest noble in England, lord of four different earldoms, to death as a traitor, but out

---

*Just his. Earlier attacks on the Despensers had featured the king's banners as well, in order to maintain the fiction that the attacks were legal. Marching on Harclay under only his own banners made Lancaster an admitted rebel and traitor.

of deference to Lancaster's rank, he commuted the traditional punishment—drawing, quartering, and so on—to a simple beheading.

On the same day twenty-four of Lancaster's followers were executed in various, more grisly, ways; the following day, six more. The king's justice continued for a month, during which 118 of Lancaster's men were executed, exiled, or imprisoned. Six other high nobles were executed, including Baron Badlesmere, who was dragged through the streets of Canterbury before being hanged and beheaded, with his head mounted on the city gate. The Mortimers forfeited all their properties and were sentenced to death, a sentence commuted by the king. The murder of Piers Gaveston had been avenged.

Those who weren't punished were rewarded. Harclay was made earl of Carlisle and Hugh le Despenser the Elder earned the title of earl of Winchester a few months later. Hugh the Younger was given no new titles but much property, including spoils from the lands of Mowbray, Damory, the earl of Norfolk, and, of course, Thomas, the erstwhile earl of Lancaster. Lancaster's widow lost not only manors but additional lands comprising 175 "knight's fees," which was the amount of land thought necessary, ever since the Norman Conquest, to provide the revenue that would keep, arm, and armor a single knight, his retainers, and horses. Given that knight's fees were financial measures and not geographical ones, each represented a highly variable bit of property, ranging from as little as fifty acres to more than a thousand; one estimate calculates a knight's fee to be as much as twenty-seven *hides*, each of one hundred-plus acres. Which meant that the widow Lancaster was being fined perhaps ten thousand acres. On the other hand, she did get to marry her longtime lover, Eubulo L'Estrange.

Thus, the spring of 1322 saw one of Edward's rare high points. At a parliament called by the king to meet at York in May, the Ordinances of 1311 were repealed; the Lord Ordainers were no more, though the king's actions and establishments would "be treated, granted and established in Parliament by our lord the King and with the consent of the prelates, earls, and barons, and of the commonalty of the realm, as has been hitherto accustomed." The king's position was restored. Edward even refrained from using his newfound strength to establish himself as a tyrant, instead showing both moderation and magnanimity to his formerly rebellious barons. Given the king's history of snatching defeat from the jaws of victory, it's no shock to learn that the real result wasn't to promote affection but to invite criticism of his lack of ruthlessness.

If the Lancaster rebellion of 1322 was notable for how it restored Edward's fortunes—at least temporarily—it is even more remarkable for just how much it hammered the already fragile agricultural economy of Britain. After three relatively good years, the harvest of 1321 had been another disaster, compounded by the king's confiscation of grain at far below market price. Moreover, looting was widespread, an explicit tactic of both the king's party and Lancaster's. In response, when the Despensers were restored to power, they wasted no time in seeking redress. Hugh the Elder claimed recompense from the confiscated rebel lands for two years of lost harvests: one burned on the ground, the other in the barn. And, with remarkable specificity, he demanded repayment for 38,000 lost sheep, 1,400 oxen, 1,700 cows, 420 horses, 2,400 pigs, and 300 goats taken or destroyed on his lands in England and Wales.

And as in 1315, what was left by rebel raids and royal demands was taken by the weather: a winter that was so harsh that the royal lands in Herefordshire were reduced to what the royal custodian called "sterility." Once the snow and ice started to melt, in spring of 1322, rivers like the Severn rose so high that they flooded half the lands in Gloucestershire. Neither were the cities immune, not even London: desperation caused fifty-two deaths as people were crushed at the gate of the Preaching Friars, fighting over alms.

It was an omen of worse to come. At the end of the summer of 1322, the truce with Scotland having run its two years, Robert Bruce raided into England as far south as Preston (more or less as far from Edinburgh as Leeds). In response, Edward summoned a very large force—thirty-eight thousand English infantry, six thousand Irish infantry, another thousand cavalry, along with ten thousand Welsh archers. The summons wasn't exactly ignored so much as approximated. The army that Edward led north in August comprised twenty thousand infantry (including archers), four thousand light cavalry, and about two thousand heavy cavalry. Another war was about to amplify a famine that was now in its seventh year.

Once again, the English encountered Bruce's scorched-earth tactics. In Barbour's poem *Le Brus*, the only provender the English could find was "one lame cow," called by the earl of Surrey "the dearest beef I've ever seen . . . for a fact, it cost a thousand pounds or more." Unable to feed his own army, Edward made it only as far as Holyrood Abbey before retreating back to England, harried by Black Douglas all the way. In the words of Sir Thomas Grey's 1836 *Scalacronica*:

> The king marched upon, where at Leith there came such a sickness and famine upon the common soldiers of that great army, that they were forced to beat a retreat for want of food; at which time the king's light horse were defeated by James de Douglas. . . . before they arrived in Newcastle there was such a murrain in the army for want of food, that they were obliged of necessity to disband.

Grey was citing, five centuries after the fact, the many chronicles that recorded that Edward's troops were starving, but this is probably an exaggeration; soldiers are among the *last* to starve in a famine, as long as they are able to take food from those who grow it.

Their four-legged companions were another matter. Beginning in the summer of 1319, the rinderpest outbreak, followed by the epidemic of sheep liver fluke, had already killed two-thirds of the cows, oxen, sheep, and goats in most of northern Europe, but had left horses—non-bovids—largely alone. They survived just long enough to encounter the bacterium known as *Burkholderia mallei*, the carrier of the respiratory disease known as glanders, which is a killer of horses, mules, donkeys, dogs, cats . . . and, frequently, humans. Nearly half the horses in Europe died between 1320 and 1322. Edward invaded Scotland with an army that was a quarter cavalry; he retreated with one that was virtually all infantry.

A chronicle written in that year by a monk at Bridlington Priory in

Yorkshire noted that the Scots carried "a true famine, so that many villeins of those parts, who possessed a very full abundance of sheep and cattle on their farms and among their goods, now are compelled to go through the countryside, begging." In July, as if to prove him correct, King Robert led an incursion down through Cumberland, burning and taking all cattle while ordering all the food stocks he couldn't carry destroyed. The tactics were brutal; the strategy, effective. Slowly but surely, Bruce was raising the cost to England of Scottish invasions while simultaneously reducing the income available to pay for them.

It was likely the prospect of further damage to northern England's productivity that inspired Bruce, along with the earl of Moray and James Douglas, to enter Yorkshire again, in October 1322. If so, he must have been pleasantly surprised to find not just grain and cattle but England's king and queen.

Edward and Isabella had been touring the important monasteries of Yorkshire, and had just arrived at Rievaulx Abbey, the Cistercian monastery near the River Wye, when they learned that several thousand of Bruce's hobelars were less than ten miles away. The royals weren't necessarily trapped; the only approach available to the Scots was a narrow and apparently defensible path, strongly held by knights and foot soldiers of the earl of Richmond. On October 14, nonetheless, King Robert sent Douglas (later joined by Moray, who realized that it isn't every day that you might be able to capture a king and his queen) straight up the hillside between Rievaulx and Byland Abbeys, while a group of the same mountaineers that had taken Edinburgh eight years earlier climbed the escarpment on the English flank. Trapped, the English defense collapsed, though in truth, it wasn't much of a scrap.

To elude capture, Edward and his queen took separate routes. Isabella and her retinue rode northeast to the Benedictine priory at Tynemouth, just ahead of Douglas's light cavalry. In 1312, Isabella had been left at Tynemouth while the king and Gaveston were chased by Lancaster. Seven years after that, she had been abandoned by her husband in precisely the same place while being pursued by the same

Black Douglas (who, once again, captured the king's household silver, his clothes, and—again—his Royal Seal). In 1319, she had taken ship from the banks of the Tyne; in 1322, she was compelled to do so again. Isabella was furious; Edward, merely humiliated.

A king's authority depends utterly on the loyalty and faith of his people. Faith in Edward, which had never been higher than after his victory over Lancaster in the spring, had virtually disappeared by year's end. The *Chronicle of Lanercost* described him as "chicken-hearted and luckless in war." The Archbishop of York, demonstrating that discretion is the better part of loyalty, permitted his monasteries and other houses to treat with Bruce for immunity. After the defeat on the hills between Old Byland and Rievaulx Abbey, Andrew Harclay, the new earl of Carlisle, followed Bruce back to Scotland and, in January 1323, presented the Scottish king with an unauthorized peace plan. In return for recognition by Edward of his sovereignty over Scotland, King Robert would agree to pay England a war indemnity of 40,000 marks, or £27,000, over the next ten years. A commission of twelve lords, six of them English, six Scottish, would negotiate a final peace treaty, which would be followed by a royal marriage between the two houses.

Bruce promptly agreed to the terms. However, Harclay's insistence on a clause providing that Harclay's own estates would remain untouched in the event that Scotland were to invade England in the future gave the agreement a self-serving flavor. The earl must have been suffering from political tone-deafness, because he still presented the agreement to Edward on his return in February 1323, Harclay immunity clause and all. It looked more like treason than diplomacy to the king, who refused to renounce his claim to overlordship of Scotland (most of Edward's passions for kingly privilege were directly related to rights he felt he had inherited from his father, and Scotland was one of them). He did agree to a truce, brokered by Pembroke and Hugh the Younger, this one to last thirteen years. To Harclay, he was brutal: the old soldier was removed from the rolls of knighthood, and his earldom was revoked before he was hanged, drawn, and quartered on March 3, evidence that the reign of Edward II was capable of being as stern and vindictive as that of Edward I; toward his own subjects, even crueler.

Isabella, still furious over her near capture at Tynemouth Priory, certainly thought so. With the royal union by now so severely strained that the king was publicly asserting that he had been forced into his marriage, it's probably not too much to suggest that this was the moment that Isabella's conspiracy against her husband began.

CHAPTER TEN

"The Mouse Tower of Bingen"

800–1323

It was meteorologically inevitable that the clouds that covered England and France (and Scotland and Flanders) at the beginning of the fourteenth century would spread, in due course, across the Rhine and, eventually, the Elbe. It is metaphorically satisfying to note that the prevailing winds that brought massive floods and bone-crushing cold to the European continent were also winds of war. But while Isabella's husband and brothers went to war over territory, and their opponents in Scotland and Flanders were fighting for their independence, the German casus belli was all about titles. Specifically, it was about the most confusing and contradictory title in the history of European sovereigns: Holy Roman Emperor.

The untidy birth of the Holy Roman Empire is incomprehensible to anyone without an understanding of the decline of the original version, and barely so even then. Voltaire's famous 1756 slur—"the body that was called, and still calls itself, the Holy Roman Empire was neither holy, nor Roman, nor an empire"—isn't false, but it isn't completely true, either. The Imperium Romanum Sacrum, to give the institution its Latin name, wasn't especially holy, but the word "sacrum" can just as easily mean "ordained" as "holy"; and the empire—technically, any territory ruled by an emperor, which makes the third part of Voltaire's mockery a reverse tautology—was certainly ordained by Rome.

By the time it got around to doing the ordaining, however, Rome hadn't really been the Rome of the Caesars for more than four centuries. The fourth-century empire did not adopt Christianity as a state policy for some decades after the conversion of the future emperor, Constantine, in 312, but by the end of the century, Constantine's successors were the defenders of Christianity; and since Rome was the place where St. Peter was—in legend, at least—martyred, the security of the Bishop of Rome was one of their clearest responsibilities.

That responsibility was discharged from Constantinople, the "New Rome" that Constantine had built on the Sea of Marmara and dedicated in 330. For the next century and a half, the empire periodically divided itself into eastern and western zones of imperial responsibility, but the emperor in Constantinople was nearly always the senior partner. By 476, when the last Roman emperor in the West was deposed by one of his own generals, Constantinople was home to the only emperor left, who remained nominally responsible for the safety of the bishop of Rome—for another century, anyway.

In 568, a Germanic tribe known as the Langobards, or Lombards, invaded the Italian peninsula and established their own "kingdom"— the term tends to flatter; better to regard it as several dozen quasi-independent dukedoms—controlling the Piedmont, Tuscany, the Po Valley, Naples, and Calabria. The emperor's provincial capital in the Italian peninsula—the formal term was "exarchate"—had been pushed into a coastal strip surrounding the city of Ravenna on the Adriatic, and a corridor reaching from Ravenna to Rome.

The decline in imperial influence in Italy after seven centuries meant de facto abandonment, not just of the north—the city of Venice was built as a refuge against the Lombards—but the papacy itself. The very existence of a Lombard kingdom in Italy was a powerful reminder that the emperor had higher priorities than protecting the empire's birthplace; with an aggressive Bulgarian kingdom to its north, and facing the powerful and dynamic armies of Islam to the east, Constantinople was an undependable protector. By 751, when the Lombards finally conquered Ravenna and executed the last exarch, it was an impotent one as well. It was time for Rome to seek one elsewhere.

The most attractive option was to be found even farther north than the Lombards: the Franks, then mostly living in what today are the

Low Countries. In 752, a year after the Lombards defeated the exarchate, Pope Stephen II traveled to Quierzy, in northern France—he was the first pope to cross the Alps—to persuade the Frankish king, Pepin the Short, to accept the duty of protecting Rome, and the papacy. His plea worked. In 754, Pepin invaded Italy, defeated the Lombards, and gave Ravenna back to the papacy in the so-called donation of Pepin. The pope, in return, anointed Pepin and his two sons, Carloman and Charles, *patricia Romanorum:* Roman "patricians." Subsequent historians would, rightly, mark this as the inauguration of the "Frankish papacy."

The orthodox Franks, now ruled by a Carolingian dynasty, came as a salvation to the besieged bishops of Rome. In 772, another pope, Hadrian I, invited Charles to continue his father's work. He did just that, in 774, with the complete defeat of Lombard power in Italy. Twenty-six years later, on Christmas Day, 800, Pope Leo III crowned Charles—by then "the Great": Carolus Magnus, or Charlemagne—as the "most serene Augustus, crowned by God, great and pacific emperor, governing the Roman Empire."*

Just as feudalism owes its emergence to Charlemagne—some historians date it to the lands granted to soldiers who followed Charlemagne back across the Pyrenees after the failed invasion that is memorialized in *The Song of Roland*—so, too, does the medieval papacy owe him its survival. Even before his Augustan elevation, Charlemagne had created the so-called papal states: mostly the old Rome-Ravenna corridor, plus parts of Tuscany and Lombardy, all of them directly ruled by the bishop of Rome.

Charlemagne's son and successor, Louis the Pious, had three sons of his own—Pepin, Louis, and Lothar—and announced his intention to have the Carolingian Empire ruled by them in partnership. The westernmost portion of the Frankish world, what would become France, would be the responsibility of Pepin; the east, Louis. Lothar, the eldest, received the title of Augustus Romanum, formal sovereignty over his brothers, and direct authority over of what is now a

---

*Or at least its western half; the emperor in Constantinople, ruling what modern historians call the Byzantine Empire, was likewise known as the Emperor of Rome.

The Holy Roman Empire
in the 14th Century

The Holy Roman Empire

The Papal States

large part of Germany and the Low Countries, along with Burgundy and Provence. When Louis the Pious died in 840, the results were predictable. The brothers went to war; and after the dust had settled, the Carolingian Empire was no more.

The collapse of Charlemagne's empire remade the map of Europe. During the four centuries of the Medieval Warm Period, while the German-speaking areas of Europe enjoyed a population explosion identical to that of the French-speaking areas to their west—by 1300, the population of the Germanophone areas of the Holy Roman Empire was about 13 million—they saw nothing of the same political consolidation. At a time when the temporal power of the popes was never higher, they were determined to keep any emperor from becoming so powerful as to become a threat to, rather than a defender of, Rome. Part of this was simple geopolitics: the papal states were easily surrounded, both north and south, particularly after the Arab armies conquered Sicily in the ninth century and were conquered in their turn by Normans—those aggressive Norsemen again—in the eleventh. But part was a dedication to what might be called antinationalism: the belief in a European polity, Christendom, that was unified by religious belief *and nothing more.* Ten years after Charlemagne's death in 814, Agobard, the archbishop of Lyon, described a Europe in which, paraphrasing Galatians 3:28: "There is now neither Gentile nor Jew, Scythian nor Aquitanian, nor Lombard, nor Burgundian, nor Alaman, nor bond, nor free. All are one in Christ." This vision remained the fundamental and enduring dream of the papacy for the next five hundred years.

The dream didn't anticipate the nation-building talents of leaders like King Henry II of England; or, for that matter, King Robert Bruce of Scotland. The centrifugal forces of nationalism proved stronger than the centripetal pull of Catholicism. One modern historian has observed that "by 1300 it was evident that the dominant political form in Western Europe was going to be the sovereign state . . . the universal Church had to admit that the defense of the individual state took precedence of the liberties of the Church . . . [and] loyalty to the state was taking on some of the overtones of patriotism." The earliest evidence appeared in the western third of the old Frankish empire as well as in the territories conquered by Duke William of Normandy. It is no coincidence that France and England (and, somewhat later, Castile, as the germ of a reconquered Spain) were far enough from Rome to germinate the first European versions of modern nation-states. Nor that Germany and Italy, largely because of their predecessors' vulnerability to papal intereference, never coalesced into something approaching their modern forms until the middle of the nineteenth century, nearly a millennium after Otto the Great, the Duke of Saxony, was crowned Otto I in 962.

Otto was the first of a long line of Germans to wear the crown of Holy Roman Emperor, which by then included the Kingdom of Italy and (from 1032 on) Burgundy. For each emperor, another crown preceded the imperial one; a group of German princes named a "King of the Germans" who would also be known, in the period between his election and his imperial sanctification, as "King of the Romans." Though technically an elective office, dynasties emerged; Otto's line, the "Ottonians," was succeeded by another extended family, the Salians, and eventually, the Hohenstaufens, from the coronation of Frederick Barbarossa in the early twelfth century until the death of his grandson, Frederick II, in 1250.

The second Frederick embodied the highest aspirations of medieval society: he spoke half a dozen languages; was a gifted soldier, scholar, and musician; was the founder of the University of Naples and leader of the most successful and least bloody of all the crusades, which concluded when he negotiated a treaty that returned Jerusalem, Bethlehem, and Nazareth to the crusader "Kingdom of Jerusalem." After centuries of intermarriage, Frederick was not only King of the Germans and Holy Roman Emperor, but ruler of Burgundy and (through his mother) King of the Two Sicilies—that is, both the island and the southernmost portion of the Italian boot. He was, in short, the papacy's greatest threat since the Lombards: a single monarch who ruled all the territories surrounding the papal states. By an accident of history, the sovereignty of Germany had become the most important strategic concern of the bishops of Rome.

As the thirteenth century turned into the fourteenth, they weren't shy about expressing that concern. Adolf of Nassau was elected King of the Germans in 1292 but never crowned by Boniface VIII, who took time off from his long-running feud with Philip IV of France to accuse Adolf of being the "mercenary knight" of Edward I of England. Albert of Habsburg defeated Adolf in battle in 1298, and was subsequently elected his successor, but wasn't invited to Rome for a coronation until 1303—an invitation that Albert declined. When Albert was killed in 1308, months after attending the marriage of Edward and Isabella in Boulogne, Henry VII of Luxembourg became the new King of the Germans.

Henry *was* crowned Holy Roman Emperor four years later, the first since the death of Frederick II, more than sixty years before. The ceremony was held, as tradition demanded, in Rome, though the pope was not there; Clement V had already moved to Avignon. Henry's reign started so well that Dante Alighieri extolled his virtues in *De Monarchia*, though not in a way that the pope might have chosen. The Florentine poet's argument—that the imperium was derived from God, rather than the pope, and any proper emperor, like Henry, should reduce the Church to its spiritual duties only—was not the sort of thing that endeared any emperor to any pope.* It's easy to imagine the sighs of relief that attended Henry's death, only fourteen months later.

A vacant imperial—not to say German, or even Roman—throne meant an election. Though the empire comprised dozens of duchies, principalities, counties, and Free Imperial Cities (free from rule other than that of the emperor, including Basel, Worms, Mainz, and Cologne), the King of the Germans was traditionally chosen by seven electors. Those electors were archbishops of Cologne, Mainz, and Trier, as well as the four highest princes in the fractured territory: the

---

*One of the longer-standing consequences was that Dante's book stayed on the Vatican's banned list until 1921, three years after the last Hapsburg ruler in Europe had finally been removed from his throne—a lesson in the durability of papal grudges.

king of Bohemia, the margrave of Brandenburg, the count palatine of the Rhine, and the duke of Saxony.* The first candidate to win four out of the seven was the victor.

If only. While the *titles* of the legitimate electors were clear enough, the names of the men entitled to vote on behalf of those titles was not. Which is why, on October 19, 1314, five months after Bannockburn and six months before the start of the rains of 1315, the electors assembled at Frankfurt-Sachsenhausen to choose their new king, and four of them cast their votes for Duke Friedrich IV of Austria, known as the Fair. Which would have been conclusive, except that the following day the archbishop of Mainz demanded *another* election. And in that one, a different majority of electors chose Frederick's rival, Ludwig IV of Wittelsbach. Just as the rains began their destruction of northern Europe's agricultural core, the Holy Roman Empire was about to embark on an eight-year-long civil war.

The lesson from the Great Famine most easily recalled, because most frequently repeated, is that "natural" disasters are most disastrous when humanity gives them a push. All of rural England suffered through the floods and murrains of the famine years, but the territories that played host to the armies of Robert Bruce and Edward II experienced the very worst of it. The grain harvest failed all over the Kingdom of France, but Flanders—at war with a succession of French kings for decades before the rains began—starved. And all over northern Europe, the farther you were from the land—that is, the likelier you were to live in a town or a city—the more you suffered when it was no longer able to grow sufficient quantities of food.

So it was farther east.

Germans and western Slavs were just as dependent upon buying and selling foodstuffs as their western neighbors. To connect villages and manors throughout the region and to facilitate trade between

---

*The term "count palatine" derives from Charlemagne's *paladins,* and is a more or less honorary title in Germany; in England, it actually has some more precise meanings, specifically used by a noble who has some of the powers of the king within his domain.

locals, they created a reasonably well-integrated system of fairs and markets for people living within a day's travel of one another. The buyers and sellers weren't locked into long-term relationships as they were in the English wool trade; many, perhaps most, were essentially barter arrangements that effectively served their purpose of bringing together producers and consumers of food.

When the farms of Saxony, Alsace, and the Rhineland lost their harvests to the rains of 1315, the manorial lords who depended on the rents from those farms for gold, as well as the townsmen who depended on them for food, were strapped. They couldn't replace lost income by shifting to other activities, and neither could they purchase food from anywhere nearer than the Mediterranean. For most, the best available option was alienation: essentially pawning property to raise cash, which happened dozens of times between 1315 and 1320. Literally hundreds of pieces of real property (and, sometimes, just the rents from them) were alienated during 1315–1317, often at fire-sale prices. This was true at every level of society; Duke Otto I of Pomerania, the margrave of Brandenburg—one of the empire's seven electors—alienated enormous parts of his estates in 1317 for a fraction of their earlier value. Both buyers and sellers knew that the property was producing no income at all. The most frequent descriptive word in bills of sale was *nihil*: nothing. Princes and barons pawned their properties an acre at a time. Monasteries and other ecclesiastical properties regularly sold their farmlands to others, less destitute, who just as frequently resold them in their turn, all while they were being taxed to pay for the armies of two outstanding aspirants to the imperial throne, and to finance planned Crusades at the behest of their own liege lord: the pope.

The most obvious solution to the food shortage was trade. But though some high-value trade goods traveled up Europe's inland waterways like the Rhine, and overland from northern Italy and points east (raw wool was exported from England to Flanders, to return as cloth), and England was importing thousands of tons of salted fish annually from the northern Baltic nations, most of northern Europe's traditional trade in food traveled less than ten miles from source to consumer.

An economic disruption of the magnitude of the Great Famine, extending, as it did, well beyond the German-speaking areas of Europe, upended such traditions. Once the combination of flood, famine, and self-inflicted destruction drove up the price of grain by several hundred percent, some of the Holy Roman Empire's merchants did take advantage of the prices England (and, to a lesser degree, France) was willing to pay—and, the eagerness of both to keep Baltic grain out of the mouths of Scots and Flemings. The most audacious, and by far the most important, of those merchants were part of a seagoing consortium that would become known as the *Hansa*, or Hanseatic League.

The advantage of conveying goods by water rather than land is startling. The Roman Empire is rightly lauded for the roads it built from Syria to Spain, but from its beginnings Roman commerce was far more dependent on seaborne trade, for the obvious reason: it cost less to ship grain from Alexandria to Cartagena than to send it seventy-five miles by oxcart. Egypt was the Mediterranean's granary for a thousand years not just because of its farms' productivity but their locations: none of its cultivated land was more than a few miles from either the Nile or a canal.

And since Roman roads were virtually nonexistent east of the Rhine, the rivers that led to the Baltic were obvious choices to serve as the great arteries of central European commerce. During the ninth and tenth centuries, colonies of Norsemen appeared everywhere from the Seine to the Vistula, but they marked the high point of Scandinavian trade into Europe, as German-speaking merchants started to overtake them by the beginning of the twelfth century. In 1157, King Henry II of England granted the merchants of the city of Cologne a charter with special trading privileges. In 1159, Duke Henry of Saxony founded the city of Lübeck on the western shore of Baltic entirely to compete with Danish and Swedish merchants; two years later he signed a treaty with the rulers of the Swedish-controlled island of Gotland to establish a trading partnership in the town of Visby, largely for trade in Russian furs from Novgorod. Within a decade, the

men from Lübeck were clearly the senior partners, establishing trading posts—*kontors*—everywhere they could, including Bruges and
even London.*

Other cities, watching the first Hanseatic cities grow rich on the
exploding Baltic trade, were eager to join in. A road network was built,
connecting Lübeck with Luneberg and Hamburg. Cologne and Bre-
men became, like Flanders, authorized trading centers for English
wool. The territory between Lübeck and Novgorod—the settlements
around the Gulf of Riga (modern Latvia, Lithuania, and Estonia)—
was transformed from a sleepy farming region into a huge market for
buyers and sellers of the raw materials of shipbuilding: timber, flax
(for sails), and hemp (for ropes). In 1252, the countess of Flanders
granted the eager Germans yet another set of trading privileges.
Though it wouldn't be formally established as the Hanseatic League
until 1369, the merchants of Cologne, Lübeck, Hamburg, Riga, and
half a dozen other Baltic port cities formed the Hansa.

The Hansa depended on trade. However, trade depends not just on
buyers and sellers, but some mechanism to enforce contracts, trade
agreements, and the like. The Hanseatic League was that mechanism,
a response to the vacuum caused by the chronic inability of the Holy
Roman Empire to assert political control over its independent cities.
Like the Italian city-states that dominated the Mediterranean during
the same era, the cities of the Hansa were walled ports in regions
without an overlord—and even when feudal lords thought about conquering them, walled port cities were virtually impossible to besiege
or even intimidate. The cities of the Hansa weren't a true political confederation; they fielded no armies, and were likelier to outfit pirates
than naval vessels. But they could, and did, defend their interests. In
1294, Eric II, king of Norway, tried to take back the privileges his father, Magnus VI, had granted to the Hanseatic cities. He was forced
by embargo and blockade to give the Lübeck merchants the right to
trade; they graciously allowed him to keep all trading rights to the
north of Bergen, offering, as a consolation prize, the commerce

---

*In 1988, archaeologists uncovered the original site of the London trading post the *Stahlhof*,
or "Steelyard" underneath the Cannon Street tube station.

between Iceland and Greenland, which had peaked during the days of Erik the Red and been on a steady decline ever since.

Yet the Hanseatic League was safe from neither the era's climate change nor the Great Famine itself. The great ports of the Baltic froze in 1303, 1307, 1318, and again in 1321. German-speaking Europe weathered similar dramatic price increases for all foodstuffs, from grain to beer to cheese. Anyone reading the chronicles of the day can't avoid being struck by how often the word *"penuria,"* or penury, appeared. In 1316, the chronicler of Würzburg noted "the poor beset by penury and hunger were greedily eating the carcasses of cattle." His opposite number, in Salzburg, described 1317 as "the year of penury and the severest hunger."

German weather was as terrifying as it was in France or Britain: the floodwaters of the Mulde River at Grimma, southeast of Leipzig, were so violent that the entire church of the Austin Canons was lifted off its foundations and swept away. The Moldava River in Bohemia was frozen solid by November 20, 1315—and it remained solid enough for travel by sleigh until March 28 of the following year. Northern Europe, from the Atlantic to the Urals—a population that had expanded dramatically for four consecutive centuries and that depended on farmland that had become steadily less productive for nearly as long—saw two consecutive harvests destroyed.

The actual results were terrible enough that it must have seemed that the Apocalypse was at hand. So horrified were eyewitnesses that their testimony needs to be read not as survey data but as evidence that they believed that the disaster was utterly without precedent. A chronicle of the kings of Bohemia—the *Königsaller Geschichts-Quellen*—stated that five hundred thousand people had died in the diocese of Metz over a six-month period . . . obviously an exaggeration, since the population of the city of Metz never exceeded twenty thousand during the fourteenth century. In the same vein, an "infinite number perished" in Lübeck. During 1315, a chronicler wrote that in "Germania," "a third of the people were brought low." Another famine chronicle from the Rhineland city of Trier recorded that in 1316, "the dead bodies of many paupers, infected by famine and pestilence, were found in the public streets, and in many cities, great communal pits were consecrated in the cemetery." In the Thuringian town of Erfurt, "innumerable dead bodies were seen lying in the public streets, in the cities, in the towns, and in the villages, [and] five great pits were made before the city, where innumerable cadavers were thrown in daily."

In 1341, Pope Benedict XII issued a papal bull announcing a memorial service for 8,100 named citizens of the city of Erfurt who had perished in the famine twenty-five years before.

As the "great hunger" of 1315 was succeeded, in the words of the chroniclers, by a "great mortality" in 1316, the northern parts of the Holy Roman Empire became victims of epidemic disease on the heels of the famine. One chronicler observed that, with no food to be had, "within one day the infected"—probably from typhus—"began to fade." The use of broths made from imported fish or beans caused even more distress in people with kwashiorkor, who can't digest protein-rich foods; the *Chronicle of Sigismund Rositz* recalled that people given such soups often died of strangulation or choking.

A mother could comfort her children with a nightly prayer, a priest could offer his villagers the sacraments or a bishop lead a town in a barefoot procession, all in an attempt to enlist the power of a God who had seemingly abandoned them. And when the orthodox responses failed—as they inevitably did—there was always heresy. One sect in Germany, whose doctrine included an objection to the necessity of priestly confession, was accused of worshiping the devil, practicing incest, and attacking the Virgin Mary; hundreds were condemned to burn during 1315–1318. Another sect, which followed the so-called heresy of the free spirit, were charged not only of religious crimes but, perversely enough, with what the authorities of the city of Strasbourg termed "unauthorized" begging—that is, seeking alms while dressed in clothes that could be mistaken for religious dress. They lasted long enough to earn the name Brot durch Gott ("for God's sake"), which was the phrase that preceded their cries for help.

The fourteenth century was cruel enough even before the famine years began. When starvation becomes an everyday phenomenon, year after year, it doesn't just exhaust a people's strength, it destroys their compassion as well.

The terrible years of hunger and pestilence were still in the future when the double election of 1314 ignited war in central Europe. The war had started, like preceding disputes over the imperial crown, as a relatively low-intensity affair: no more than a few thousand taking the field against one another, and often only hundreds. The impact, however, was magnified by its context: notoriously bad weather and widespread, durable famine. Out-of-the-ordinary weather and food shortages meant that even a low-intensity war between Ludwig and Friedrich could destroy a significant fraction of German armed might, and an even more significant fraction of German agriculture.

Some benefitted, as is always the case. The Cistercians of the German-speaking parts of the Holy Roman Empire dominated the salt trade, profiting hugely from the run-up in salt prices in 1315–1317. The bishop of Metz made more from salt than from rents in one year, and the nuns of Kloster Ebstorf near Lüneberg in north Germany controlled both salt production and, through connections with the Hanseatic city of Lübeck, its transport, as well.

Most of the ecclesiastical and secular lords, however, suffered. The only imperial support for any local problem was granted for reasons of tactical advantage, rather than need; the hospitals founded by Ludwig IV in 1317 (in Amberg) and 1319 (in Ingolstadt) were selected to keep their towns loyal—and resistant to the entreaties of Friedrich of Austria. The town of Haguenau was granted privileges by Friedrich in order to win its support away from Ludwig, who had done the same.

Understandably, then, German towns were prone to sell their support to one party or another. Strasbourg essentially ran an auction for its support in 1315; when Ludwig offered a series of privileges, Friedrich counteroffered. Ludwig then sweetened his bid, which prompted Friedrich to improve his—an expensive game for the imperial aspirants, and a dangerous one for the Strasbourgers, as victorious princes have a way of punishing what they tend to view as treason.

The war for the imperial throne never became as deadly as the equivalent conflicts in France because, though the German-speaking areas of northern Europe were subject to precisely the same demographic pressures and climate changes as everywhere else, they reacted to them very differently. The passions that fueled the wars between Robert Bruce and Edward of England, or between France and Flanders, did not figure as large in the struggles of the Holy Roman Empire. For historical reasons—the way the Carolingian Empire divided itself; the absence of a conqueror in the mold of Duke William of Normandy; papal strategy—nationalism was late in coming to the German-speaking world, and so, therefore, were battles for national identity.

Even so, the war between Ludwig and Friedrich featured one notable exception: a battle at a mountain pass near Lake Lucerne that gave birth to a nation.

Sometime around 1307, as Robert Bruce was reigniting his rebellion in Scotland, representatives of three forest "cantons"—Uri, Schwyz, and Unterwalden—bound themselves together with an oath: the *Rütlischwur*, named for the meadow where, in legend, at least, it was born. The oath added an emotional coda to a Letter of Alliance, signed in August 1291, that had already formed an "eternal," autonomous unit within the empire that recognized no sovereign other than the emperor himself.* Switzerland was born.

At the time of the *Rütlischwur*, the Austrian Habsburgs had been trying for more than a century to annex the territories of the cantons, particularly the Gotthard Pass, which was the shortest route between the German-speaking center of the empire and its rich provinces in northern Italy. When the double election offered the choice between a Wittelsbach and a Habsburg, the confederacy didn't have to think very hard before supporting Ludwig's claim. In early 1315, that support turned violent: the Schwyz raided a monastery that was under the protection of the Habsburgs. Duke Leopold of Habsburg, younger brother

---

*Five centuries later, the playwright Friedrich Schiller turned the *Rütlischwur* into poetry eerily reminiscent of the Declaration of Arbroath, which the Scottish nobles issued in 1319: *Wir wollen frei sein, wie die Väter waren, eher den Tod, als in der Knechtschaft leben* [We swear we will be free, as were our sires / and die rather than live in slavery].

of Friedrich, thought it a perfect time for a strategic invasion toward the Gotthard Pass and, by the way, an opportunity to destroy the obstreperous confederation.

The great twentieth-century military historian Hans Delbrück noted, picturesquely, that both the invasion specifically, and the struggle for Swiss independence generally, are "buried beneath a mass of rubble made of legends and fables" that are widely known to a dozen generations of children, not all of them Swiss. Most famous of all is the tale of William (or Wilhelm) Tell, the steadfast peasant with uncanny skill with a crossbow, who, failing to salute the cap of the Austrian governor Hermann Gessler, was forced to shoot at the legendary apple set atop his son's head. As a model for the reluctant warrior, peaceful but resolute, Tell has few equals.

The reality, as it often is, was more complicated. Tell and his confederates were wily guerrilla fighters, and their war against the Habsburgs not "a desperate revolutionary rising of a peaceful peasantry but rather a well-planned struggle of a warlike community with battle-hardened leaders." Long before their intentionally provocative attack on the Habsburg-protected monastery, Schwyz troops had set up elaborate obstacles along the only roads possible through their mountain valleys. These *letzinen*—of which nearly a hundred survive today—were intended to channel invading cavalry on to ground where the advantage shifted from armored knights to well-drilled infantry.

So when Duke Leopold, brother of Friedrich, led his two thousand knights and three thousand infantry along the east bank of Lake Aegeri, he found that the Schwyzers had built a roadblock of tree trunks and boulders along the main road, which forced the column onto the narrow Morgarten path. There, on November 15, 1315, Leopold found still more roadblocks, and, on the heights above the pass, fifteen hundred armed infantry.* Led by the semi-legendary Schwyz leader Werner Stauffacher, the Swiss sprang their trap. Smaller space meant

---

*In another part of the William Tell legend, outlaws had offered their services to the Schwyzers, been rebuffed, but determined to fight for their country, started an avalanche at Schafstetten that broke the Austrian advance.

no room for the mounted Austrians to maneuver, and the Schwyzers, along with men from Uri and Unterwalden, were able to fight downhill, armed with the *voulge* (a Swiss version of the Lochaber ax, a halberd with a spear point, with an ax on one side, and a hook for pulling knights from their horses on the other) and morningstars: spiked clubs.

It was another Stirling Bridge or Bannockburn. Or, even more accurately, another Courtrai, since the Swiss, like the Flemings, had no delusions about any chivalric brotherhood with their opponents and therefore took no prisoners. At least two thousand Austrians died, no more than a hundred Swiss. The monk Johannes of Winterthur, who wrote his own recollection of the battle twenty-five years after the fact, recalled that Duke Leopold seemed not just "greatly sad, but half-dead." His sorrow was understandable; the Swiss confederacy retained its stubborn independence, over the next century adding cities like Lucerne, Zurich, and Bern, and regularly defeating Habsburg incursions. Though the modern country of Switzerland wasn't formally founded until 1848, its independence as an autonomous nation would never be seriously in question after Morgarten.

The name of the next Holy Roman Emperor took a bit longer to decide. Over the course of the next seven years—the same seven during which "Germania" suffered through the lost harvests of 1315 and 1316; successive plagues of sheep, goats, and horses; and the horrific winters of 1318–19 and 1321–22—Ludwig and Friedrich fought one indecisive battle after another, usually, as with Morgarten, through proxies.

In September 1322, the two aspiring emperors finally met, though the exhausted "armies" they led barely deserved the name. Friedrich invaded Bavaria, hoping to lure Ludwig into defending his own duchy. He led only fourteen hundred knights, plus another five hundred or so mounted Hungarian archers. Ludwig commanded only eighteen hundred knights. Evidently Friedrich's plan had been to link up with another force led by his younger brother, Leopold, and trap Ludwig; but, in an age in which armies didn't even have reliable timepieces, much less communication, coordinating such maneuvers was a chancy proposition. When the Austrians and Hungarians met Ludwig's army at the Bavarian city of Mühldorf, on the River Inn, Leopold had not yet arrived. Even so, Friedrich decided not to wait but to force the action (in at least one dubious legend, he is said to have mused, "This war has already caused enough widows"). Even more dubiously, he did so by dividing his forces—never a good idea—sending his archers across the Inn River, where the Nuremberg knights destroyed the unprotected Hungarians. Ludwig had been given an overwhelming numerical advantage, and he used it to win a decisive battle against Friedrich, taking him, and up to one thousand of the Austrian knights, prisoner. Leopold escaped.

The victory at Mühldorf freed Leopold to turn his attention to another adversary: Pope John XXII. John, like his predecessor, Clement V, had claimed a right not merely to approve the elevation of the King of the Germans to the title of Holy Roman Emperor, but even his authority as king: a prerogative that Ludwig found more than objectionable. When Ludwig sent an army into Italy in 1323, putatively to defend the imperial city of Milan from the Kingdom of Naples, Pope John, still fighting for the principle that papal authority trumped secular power, excommunicated him. Ludwig responded by deposing him on grounds of heresy, thus proving the principle's flaw: secular powers had troops with which to enforce their commands. He then seated a friendly replacement in the chair of Saint Peter (Pietro Rainalducci, retrospectively the antipope Nicholas V), instigating what some modern historians call the "final struggle" between emperor and pope.

The political consequences of seven years of civil war and famine in German-speaking Europe were dramatic and significant: the decline of papal influence, the emergence of the Habsburgs, and the birth of what would become a federal Swiss state. But it may be that the most durable heritage of the years 1315–1322 was literary: tales based on real events have endured long after those events are forgotten.

One such tale survives to the present as a powerful folk memory in Germany, known there as the story of the Mouse Tower of Bingen. As the story goes, Bishop Hatto of the Rhineland city of Bingen was so avaricious that he denied the people of his town access to the granaries. Worse, he forced them to fill these granaries even as the famine deepened. When the bishop finally responded to his townspeople's entreaties, he did so by locking them in an empty granary and burning them alive. But a flood of mice would emerge from the embers, and, well . . .

> He beat them off by the score; he trampled them under his feet; he tore at them savagely with his hands—all to no purpose; he might just as well have tried to beat back the ocean. The rats surged against him like waves breaking on a cliff, and very soon the Bishop was overwhelmed in the horrid flood. Little was left to tell of the tragedy when his servants plucked up courage to enter the building some days later.

Even outside of Germany, any child will recognize another story of the famine years from its opening lines:

> Hard by a great forest dwelt a poor wood-cutter with his wife and his two children. The boy was called Hansel and the girl Gretel. He had little to bite and to break, and once when great dearth fell on the land, he could no longer procure even daily bread.

Stories involving cannibalism are one of famine's most reliable companions. The presence of a witch in this particular one—and, not at all coincidentally, a dark forest, evoking a deep folk memory of the great woodlands that, centuries before, had covered most of Europe and whose destruction was one of the markers of the Medieval Warm Period—offers, like all enduring stories, a way of making sense of what would otherwise be senseless: children starving for a crust of bread.

Another of the Grimms' tales dating from the Great Famine is so dark that it is regularly excluded even from collections untroubled by the harshness of the punishments visited, for example, on Cinderella's stepsisters. Generally known as the "Story of Children Living in a Time of Famine," it goes something like this:

> *Once upon a time there was a woman with two daughters, so poor that they lacked even a crust of bread. So poor were they that the mother despaired, telling her older daughter, "I shall be forced to kill you so I will have something to eat."*
>
> *To which her older daughter said, "Dear mother, please spare me, and I will find something for us to eat, without begging." And she did, returning with a piece of bread. She shared it with her mother and sister, but they were still hungry.*
>
> *So the mother said to her younger daughter, "Now, I shall be forced to kill you so I will have something to eat."*
>
> *To which her younger daughter said, "Dear mother, please spare me, and I will find something for us to eat, and no one will be the wiser." And she did, returning with two pieces of bread. She shared them with her mother and sister, but they were still hungry. So the mother said to both her daughters, "I shall be forced to kill you, or all of us will die."*
>
> *To which both daughters said, "Dear mother, please spare us, and we will lie down and sleep, and never awake until Judgment Day." And they did, sleeping so soundly that they never did awaken. And their mother left, and not a soul knows where she is.*

CHAPTER ELEVEN

"Long Years of Havoc"

1323–1328

In 1322, Robert the Bruce defeated Edward II for the last time, and Edward finally removed the threat from the earl of Lancaster. In the same year, Philip V of France died, and with him the Flemish War. The number of claimants to the throne of the Holy Roman Emperor was cut in half after Ludwig's victory over Friedrich at Mühldorf.

It was also the last year of the Great Famine.

The trials and tribulations of Edward II, however, continued. In the summer of 1323, Roger Mortimer escaped from his prison in the Tower of London. The bishop of Hereford, Adam Orleton, who was both a key ally of the queen and a longtime supporter of the Mortimers, enlisted two Londoners, Richard de Bettoyne and John de Gisors, to smuggle liquor and a rope ladder into the apartment where Mortimer was confined. The Marcher Lord extended an offer of hospitality to his jailers, and proceeded to drink them insensible; he was then escorted by another member of the conspiracy, Gerard d'Alspaye, the deputy constable of the tower, through the kitchens, where he used the ladder to descend the outside of the tower to the bank of the Thames. There, Orleton had thoughtfully arranged for a boat and supplies to be waiting, and Mortimer was halfway to France, apparently, before his guards awakened.

France meant freedom, not least because the current relationship between Edward and Charles IV, never especially congenial, was now near open warfare over Gascony. The Gascons were, by feudal custom, subjects of the English king but were nonetheless obliged by French law to air their grievances in the Parlement of Paris. By summer of

1323, dozens of those complaints were pending, and one—a dispute between two of Edward's vassals in Gascony—was resolved by the simple expedient of executing the one most defiant of Charles IV's authority. This was a violation of Edward's feudal rights, and a clear provocation. To further vex Edward, in the fall Charles built a fortified town around the priory of Saint-Sardos—technically French territory, since it was a fief of the Benedictine abbey at Sarlat, and, through the chain of hierarchy, to the king of France. However, since Saint-Sardos was part of Aquitaine, it was therefore also technically Edward's possession, and subject to the English king. In November, Sir Ralph Basset, Edward's seneschal—the English king's representative in Aquitaine—attacked the fortified town, burned it, and hanged a French soldier on a gallows decorated with the arms of the French king. Charles then called the offending seneschal to trial, and when Sir Basset failed to appear, declared that his absence forfeited Saint-Sardos to the French Crown.

Part of the French king's hostility was his resentment at the still-undelivered homage that Edward owed for his French possessions, which suggested an obvious diplomatic solution: making homage. As should by now have been clear to every crowned head of Europe, however, the king of England's personal talent for diplomacy was virtually nonexistent. Even Edward recognized his own shortcoming, which is why he deputized his most reliable proxy, the earl of Pembroke, to act in his place. However, when the earl died in Paris on June 23, 1324, the opportunity for a peaceful solution died with him. In August 1324, Charles invaded Gascony and Ponthieu.

War loomed. Edward panicked. In September 1324, he ordered all French subjects in England arrested, including twenty-seven members of Isabella's own household. Five months later, in February 1325, he tried diplomacy again, sending an embassy, consisting of two bishops plus the earl of Richmond, to Charles. They failed to move the needle on any of the outstanding issues: Edward's refusal to pay homage (or fealty) to Charles; the French troops in Gascony; even a hoped-for marriage alliance between Edward's thirteen-year-old son and a French princess.

At that point, Pope John XXII intervened, as much out of a desire to remain politically relevant as to promote peace. He suggested that the best way to resolve the tension was to send a different envoy: Isabella, Charles's sister and Edward's queen.

The brief for Edward's obliviousness doesn't have any stronger evidence than the fact that he agreed. Isabella's feud with the Despensers had been simmering ever since 1324, when, at their urging, Edward seized her lands in Cornwall under the feeble excuse that they might be used as a base for a French invasion. It boiled over when three of her children—John, Eleanor, and Joan—were given into the care of Hugh the Younger's wife, Eleanor de Clare.

In 1325, Isabella was twenty-nine years old, and far more politically sophisticated than the girl who had been Piers Gaveston's rival fifteen years before. She had learned that even a queen needed allies, and was clever enough to recognize that the Despensers' heavy-handedness had produced hundreds of potential supporters of her cause. The Despensers were not only rapidly becoming the de facto rulers of England but were advertising their status by obnoxiously building castles and mausoleums that were direct copies of their royal equivalents.* Hugh the Younger had such a high opinion of himself—partly deserved; he really was a gifted administrator, ruling entire provinces on behalf of the Crown, including the flashpoint in Franco-English relations, Gascony—that he took to using the royal pronoun in personal correspondence: "It seems to our lord the king and to us."

If the Despensers had intended to help Isabella's recruiting, they could hardly have done any better; lords both ecclesiastical and temporal flocked to Isabella's cause: Adam Orleton, the bishop of Hereford (who had arranged Mortimer's escape from the Tower of London); John Stratford, bishop of Winchester; William Airmyn, bishop of Norwich; and the earl of Kent, the earl of Richmond, and the earl of Leicester (brother to the late Lancaster). All agreed that the ultimate goal was the elimination, once and for all, of the Despensers, and that

---

*Caerphilly, the Welsh castle that Hugh the Younger had more or less stolen from the estate of the earl of Gloucester, was already the second largest castle in England (after Windsor) *before* Despenser enlarged it.

Isabella could best achieve this by distancing herself from their reach. In March 1325, she returned to her brother's court, swearing, in the words of the author of the *Vita Edwardi Secundi* (who almost certainly died in early 1326—that is, with no knowledge of any subsequent events), "She will not return until Hugh le Despenser is wholly removed from the King's side."

Isabella wasn't the only one to have learned a new strategy for opposing her enemies. Thousands of men and women at the very opposite end of the feudal continuum had learned exactly the same lesson over the preceding years, and were ready to put that knowledge into action.

The first great peasant revolt of the fourteenth century began in Flanders in 1323 and continued for five years. The Flemish uprising deserves to be remembered not as a peasant insurgency but as a revolt of the not-yet-named bourgeoisie—in the most urbanized region of northern Europe, collective action proved easier when thousands of potential recruits live within shouting distance of one another. In another way, though, it marked the beginning of peasant revolts as a regular feature of life in Europe—yet another collateral effect of the fault lines in feudal manorialism four centuries after its birth. The French king, his successors, and his rivals would face one uprising after another over the next two centuries, from the Jacquerie of 1358 to the English Peasants' Revolt of 1381 and dozens more.

The roots of the 1323 rebellion date to the succession of Louis de Nevers, grandson of Count Robert III of Flanders, as the province's feudal overlord in 1322. Two years earlier, in 1320, he had married Isabella's niece, Margaret, and allied himself with the French court. What was good news for France was very bad news indeed for Louis's subjects. The Flemings had a long suspicion of French alliances, and didn't have to wait long to be reminded why, as Louis increased their taxes, acting as the factor for the French king. After the disastrous famine years of 1315–16 and another lost harvest in 1321, with nearly constant threat of war in between, the Flemings were in a notably ungenerous mood, and ready for revolution.

Leading the revolt was a prosperous farmer named Nicolaas Zannekin, who took a rural uprising into the towns of Flanders in the fall of 1323, capturing half a dozen of them, including Nieuwport and Kortrijk. In 1325, shortly after Isabella's arrival in Paris, he captured Louis himself. For three more years, until Zannekin was defeated by a French army in support of their puppet ruler, the wealthiest province in Europe was in revolt not just against its feudal lord but the entire Catholic Church, which placed all of Flanders under interdict.

The proximate causes of the Flemish "peasant" revolt were local and immediate; its roots, the reason it could occur in the first place, were four centuries in creation. As Europe's population increased threefold between the ninth and thirteenth centuries, the Continent's demographic pyramid changed its shape. The base grew larger relative to its peak, and more distant: the gap between nobility and peasantry got bigger and bigger. Families that were noble by birth became more and more "noble" in behavior: dressing more opulently, entertaining more lavishly, and housing themselves more extravagantly, while the rural peasantry lived more or less the same as their many times great-grandparents. While Europe's villages housed families of six in two rooms, one of them shared with sheep and cattle, its manors and castles featured two-story aisles of stone pillars, fitted out with colorful paint, floral ornamentation, double-curved arches, mullioned windows, upholstered window seats; even that most expensive of luxuries, glass. Wall hangings were made of silk, wool, damask, or velvet; floors were laid with tile and strewn with herb-scented rush mats. The highest nobles of England and France came back from crusading with carpets from Turkey and farther east. Isabella's pillows were stuffed with down and feathers, and covered with the sheer silk known as dimity. From the twelfth century on, medieval custom accelerated the process separating Europe's highest classes from everyone else—*"courtesie"* in French, "courtesy" in English, revealingly the "courtly" manners expected at court.

Meanwhile, as the desire of nobles to cover feather pillows with silk dimity increased, their ability to do so was deteriorating. The income of the manorial system depended on rents that were fixed by tradition, which made them vulnerable to price inflation; even though inflation in the thirteenth century averaged only around 0.5 percent annually, a hundred years at that level turned an annual rent of £10 into a little more than £6. The only way to spend more while collecting less was to raise rents, impose abusive policies such as requiring farmers to pay more for milling their own grain, and engage in other practices unlikely to endear them to their tenants. The same practices that provoked Scottish peasants to take up arms against English kings, or Swiss burghers against the Holy Roman Emperors, made Flemish townsmen a recurring problem for the French Crown.

Which is why, when Isabella returned to her brother's court, Charles had more on his plate than his ongoing conflicts with the king of England, or maintaining his hold on the Avignon popes. Even so, by the summer of 1325, Isabella had persuaded her brother to restore Gascony and Ponthieu to English rule, subject to Edward finally offering formal homage *and* fealty. It was a notable diplomatic achievement, but one greeted in England not with acclaim but suspicion. Spies in the employ of Hugh the Younger had reported that if Edward declined the offer, Charles would attack Gascony *and* mount an invasion of England from Normandy. Worse, he would do so in alliance with Robert Bruce, who had never forgotten that Scotland was strongest whenever England was warring with France, and would simultaneously invade from the north. Edward could either give homage for Gascony, in the hope that Charles would then return it, or prepare for battle. Faced with the choice of swallowing his pride or risking a two-front war, Edward agreed to swear the oath to Charles in August 1325.

He did so reluctantly. Partly, this was due to the indecisiveness that had been such a prominent theme of his entire reign, but partly the fear that once in France, he would be completely at the mercy of Charles, even to the point of being taken hostage. It's also worth recalling that England's king decided a lot of matters of state on more emotional grounds than reasoned ones. Edward was loath to put himself in a position of inferiority to another king not out of some rational calculus of interest but simply because he saw it as a humiliation. When the king is "the state," it's hard to see much daylight between the national interest and personal self-regard.

If Edward was fearful of leaving England for France, Hugh the Younger was positively terrified. If he accompanied the king to France, he would be in far greater danger than the king; if he stayed behind without his patron, he'd be vulnerable to the ever-growing regiments of his enemies at home. The Despensers insisted that the king stay in England, and at the last minute Edward acquired a diplomatically convenient illness that precluded his departure.

Isabella then delivered her masterstroke: She proposed that her elder son do homage on his father's behalf. What this would require, though, would be his installation as duke of Aquitaine, and count of Ponthieu and Gascony. Edward was boxed in. In September, the heir to the English throne arrived in France, and on the twenty-fourth, Charles accepted his homage; he then announced that he intended to keep the Agenais, the Gascon county lying between the Dordogne and the Garonne.

When the news reached England, Edward exploded. He immediately declared that he was to be the administrator of his son's estates, at which point Charles announced that this meant that the English territories were, again, forfeit.

As diplomatic mess-making goes, Edward was nothing if not consistent. In the same declaration that allowed Charles to call his bluff, the English king also demanded the return of his wife and son. He had no leverage that would force Charles to send his sister and nephew home, but he weakened an already enfeebled hand by transmitting his demand via Walter Stapledon, the bishop of Exeter—an envoy who was so detested in France that he was apparently threatened with imprisonment and torture if he ever showed his face there.

Despite Edward's ham-handedness, Isabella could almost certainly have persuaded her brother to send her home. Instead, she supposedly replied—in public—"I felt that marriage is a union of a man and a woman, holding fast to the practice of a life together, and that someone has come between my husband and myself and is trying to break that bond; I declare that I will not return until that intruder is removed, but, discarding my marriage garment, shall put on the robes of widowhood and mourning until I am avenged of this Pharisee."

Even Edward recognized an ultimatum when he heard one. Isabella had demanded the Despensers' heads. His response was a speech given to Parliament on November 18, 1325:

> The Queen crossed to France to make peace . . . on her departure, she did not seem to anyone to be offended; but now someone has changed her attitude. Someone has primed her with inventions [and] she says that Hugh Despenser is her adversary and hostile to her . . . I firmly believe that the Queen has been led into this error at the suggestion of someone, and he is in truth wicked and hostile.

Edward was correct. By the time of the king's speech to Parliament, and probably before, Isabella was engaged in adulterous relationship with Roger Mortimer, which had become scandalously known by the end of 1325. Mortimer was irresistible to the queen: Whatever his physical charms—and they seem to have been considerable—the queen and the Marcher Lord had a classic attraction based on mutual interests: both loved Arthurian legends, luxurious living, and the destruction of the Despensers. Edward may have learned of the liaison from Bishop Stapledon upon his return from France; certainly, he knew of it by February 1326, when Isabella's servants returned carrying word of the affair, and the king accused his wife of being with Mortimer "within and without house."

Knowledge of his cuckolding didn't prevent Edward from continuing to plead, via letter and envoy, for the return of his wife and son. Isabella replied with contrived despair—longing to return, but fearing for her life should she do so—but her real attention was elsewhere. The queen of England had opened secret negotiations with Robert Bruce.

As was so frequently the case during the first decades of the fourteenth century, the communication channel ran through the one location where every sovereign in Europe maintained some diplomatic presence: the papal court at Avignon. That was where, for more than a year, Thomas Randolph, the earl of Moray, had been pleading the Scottish case to Pope John XXII. At the same time, Edward had his own envoys representing England's interests, one of which was freeing the country from the threat of interdict and excommunication. The preceding year, Edward had even invited Edward Balliol, son of the once-and-forgotten King John, to come from Picardy to England, which Randolph—and Bruce—could only have read as a provocation: an attempt to restore a more docile king to Scotland. It also, unintentionally, gave the earl of Moray and Isabella (who had evidently forgiven the earl's attempts to kidnap her years before) interests in common. Through Randolph, she promised King Robert that, if he agreed to foreswear invading England, she would recognize an independent Scotland upon her return. It was the first hard evidence that she was planning not just the fall of the Despensers, but of the king himself.

By then, however, even the pope had learned of Isabella's affair with Mortimer, and let his displeasure be known to, among others, the king of France, whose brotherly affection had already been strained by the scandal. Isabella was notified that her continued presence at the French court was no longer desired, and, in the summer of 1326, she decamped to the court of William II, the count of Hainaut, Holland, and Zeeland.

Isabella's goal was not sanctuary but victory. While she commanded no troops, and her lands remained in the control of her estranged husband, she did have one very large strategic asset: her son Edward, the duke of Aquitaine and heir to the English throne. Isabella offered to marry young Edward to the count of Hainaut's daughter Philippa in return for his support. Marrying his daughter to the future king of England seemed attractive enough that William agreed, as an advance against his daughter's dowry, to pay for an army and to provide a general to lead them: his brother, John of Hainaut, who would share command with Mortimer. By August 27, they had a deal, and on September 23, 1326, Isabella's army—a small one, probably no more than fifteen hundred, largely mercenaries from Hainaut and some German-speaking principalities of the Holy Roman Empire— sailed from Dordrecht, landing on the east coast of Suffolk the following day.

Even after nineteen years of failed wars against the Scots, a decade of rebellion by his own earls, and seven years of famine, Edward II might still have mustered a respectable defense of his own kingdom. Against the wife who had cuckolded him, allied with the most unpopular nobleman in England, he hadn't a chance. The fleet Edward and the Despensers summoned to meet Isabella's invading force was so mutinous that it never even left harbor. Of the two thousand soldiers sent to contest the landing in Suffolk, only fifty-five showed up. (Meanwhile, adding incompetent strategy to inept leadership, King Edward and Hugh the Younger led their own force, some sixteen hundred soldiers, on a raid—of Normandy, because of the king's continued fears of a nonexistent French invasion.)

With her husband on the wrong side of the English Channel, Isabella spent the night of September 24 in the castle of her ally, the earl of Norfolk. The following day, she made a pilgrimage to Bury St. Edmunds, where her supporters—or, more likely, opponents of the Despensers—appeared, first in the hundreds, then by the thousands. A year earlier, she had sworn "to put on the robes of widowhood and mourning" until she was avenged against the Despensers, and that's how she traveled, further evidence of her acquired gift for political theater. Even better (or more theatrically) her confederates spread the story that she had discovered nearly £500 while en route, and that, instead of keeping it for her own household, she was distributing it to the farmers of England as payment for the cattle and food her still-small army was in process of requisitioning. Similar stories transformed the march into a queenly triumph. Popular opinion, already hostile to the Despensers, shifted dramatically in her direction. The invaders proceeded in an arc from Ipswich through Cambridge to the west of London, growing in numbers each day. The king commanded the city burghers of Oxford to deny her entrance; on October 2, they greeted her with open arms and presented her with a silver cup.

Isabella then marched the sixty miles east to London, her pace leisurely enough that the entire city had time to declare for the queen. On the same day that Isabella was receiving the keys to the city of Oxford, Edward correctly decided that London was indefensible and departed his capital for Wales, where he hoped to raise an army to defend his throne. His retinue included the Despensers, father and son; the earls of Arundel and Surrey; several hundred men-at-arms; and the chancellor, Robert Baldock, who carried some £29,000 in gold and the Great Seal of England.

On October 14, Isabella arrived, and London welcomed her. Boisterously. Rioters took over the city's streets, looting the royal treasury along with dozens of homes and businesses of Edward's few remaining loyalists. As reward for aiding in Mortimer's escape, Richard de Bettoyne and John de Gisors, were made, respectively, Constable of the Tower and Mayor of London. Isabella's men released the most prominent prisoners from their cells in the Tower of London, including Mortimer's sons. Her supporters were less merciful with Walter Stapledon, who had carried the story of Isabella's infidelity back to the king. A mob beat him to death on the steps of St. Paul's Cathedral, and then beheaded him with a bread knife. Two days later, the head of the former bishop of Exeter was presented to the queen at Gloucester, where she and Mortimer had stopped for a brief respite before resuming their pursuit of the king and the Despensers.

Sometime between October 16 and 21, Edward crossed the River Wye to Chepstow, in Wales. His escort had melted away; only a dozen archers remained. The king of England had become a hunted fugitive, abandoned by his wife, his son, and all but three of his earls. His support in England was virtually gone, and in Wales nearly so.* Hugh the Elder, the newly made earl of Winchester, recrossed the Wye and headed south, where he had his last card left to play: Edward and Isabella's daughters, the princesses Eleanor and Joan, who had been given into his family's care by the king. The elder Despenser attempted to trade the princesses for his own safety—a desperate measure, with no chance of success. In Bristol, as in London, city sentiment turned to the invader. On October 26, he surrendered to the queen.

Edward and Hugh the Younger, meanwhile, left Chepstow and took ship for Ireland, but, abandoned even by the winds, were forced into

---

*Not completely. See the story of the Dunheveds, below.

Cardiff Harbor. On the twenty-seventh, Isabella learned that the king had left England, which gave her precisely the pretext she needed to form a new government. She formed a council composed of the nobles and bishops who had accompanied her on her headlong pursuit of the king and the Despensers, and announced that her son, in his father's absence, was the Keeper of the Realm.

On the same day that Edward, Duke of Aquitaine, was made Keeper of the Realm (with his mother as regent de jure, Mortimer de facto), the earls of Leicester, Norfolk, and Kent sentenced Hugh le Despenser the Elder, Duke of Winchester, to death as a traitor—the first of England's highest nobles to receive such a sentence since the earl of Lancaster four years before. And, unlike Lancaster, whom Edward had, mercifully, ordered beheaded, the earl of Winchester was awarded the traitor's death: "drawn for treason, hanged for robbery, beheaded for misdeeds against the Church . . . and because your deeds have dishonoured the order of chivalry, the court awards that you be hanged in a surcoat quartered with your arms, and that your arms be destroyed forever."

Destruction of the Despenser coat of arms would be lacking in practical force as long as Hugh the Younger was still flying it, and at the end of October, he was doing precisely that, at Caerphilly Castle, where he and King Edward had taken refuge. Caerphilly was by far the most formidable castle in Wales, and one of the strongest in Europe—it sprawled over nearly three acres: two concentric parallelograms surrounded by two artificial lakes, honeycombed with murder holes, with tunnels and paths for quick reinforcement, defended by towers more than thirty feet high with walls twelve feet thick—and one that was well supplied for a siege, with its own wells and granaries. Moreover, the king had the £29,000 in gold he had taken from London, enough to put a well-armed mercenary army in the field. After all, John of Hainaut's Dutch and German soldiers weren't going to stay in England forever, and as long as the king was behind Caerphilly's walls, he was next to invulnerable, and certainly able to negotiate for the best terms imaginable.

Which is why it still defies belief that, on either the second or third of November, Edward and Hugh the Younger left Caerphilly, heading for the westernmost part of Wales, leaving £13,000 behind. In the first week of November, the king arrived at the Abbey of Neath, and sent the abbot to Isabella to open negotiations for his surrender. Her response was to send a party headed by the earl of Leicester and a Welshman named Rhys ap Howel with orders to capture him. Belatedly realizing their mistake in leaving Caerphilly, the king's party galloped east, but six days later, in a torrential rainstorm, Edward, Hugh the Younger, the erstwhile chancellor Robert Baldock, and six other men—all that were left of the king's loyalists—were taken, in the open country near Llantrisant on the River Ely, in the most southerly part of Wales. It was a poetic end to the journey that had begun thirty-seven years before, when Edward, the very first prince of Wales, had been born in the province's northernmost castle, at Caernarfon.

While Isabella was careful to have her husband imprisoned in comfortable apartments in Kenilworth Castle in Warwickshire, the queen had no reason to ease the final journey of the remaining Despenser. She ordered that Hugh the Younger be tied to a horse and be forced to stumble along behind on foot, preceded by heralds playing cymbals so that everyone along the route back to England would have sufficient warning to line the road where they could curse him and pelt him with clods of dirt and rotten fruit. If her intent was to humiliate her "Pharisee," she overachieved: Despenser announced that he would starve himself to death. After only a week into his hunger strike, Isabella grew anxious and decided to have him tried at Hereford, only sixteen miles or so from the Welsh border. On November 24, the man who had been only two months before the second most powerful man in the kingdom was accused of a long list of charges, including the execution of the earl of Lancaster; of advising the king to abandon the queen at Tynemouth; of stealing the queen's dower; and of persuading the king to invade Scotland and then failing to secure a victory. At his trial, Hugh the Younger was forced to wear a tunic with the legend *quid gloriaris in malicia qui potens in iniquiate?* (from Psalm 52: Why do you glory in malice, you who are mighty in iniquity?).

The *Chronicle of Jean Froissart*, the court poet and official historian of Philippa of Hainaut (later the consort of Isabella and Edward's son), is one of the great documents of medieval history, written only thirty or so years after the trial of Hugh le Despenser the Younger. It leaves little to the imagination:

> When he had been tied up, his member and his testicles were cut off, because he was a heretic and a sodomite, even, it was said, with the King, and this was why the King had driven away the Queen on his suggestion. When his private parts had been cut off they were thrown into the fire to burn, and afterwards his heart was torn from his body and thrown into the fire, because he was a false-hearted traitor, who by his treasonable advice and promptings had led the King to bring shame and misfortune upon his kingdom and to behead the greatest lords of England, by whom the kingdom ought to have been upheld and defended; and besides that, he had so worked upon the King that he, who should have been their consort and sire, had refused to see the Queen and his eldest son, at the hazard of their lives.
>
> After Sir Hugh Despenser had been cut up in the way described, his head was struck off and sent to the city of London. His body was divided into four quarters, which were sent to the four principal cities of England after London.

Isabella had her vengeance, but she did not have the throne. Her son had assumed royal powers during the absence of the king, but once Edward II arrived in Kenilworth Castle, that particular legal argument had no weight. Instead, on November 20, Isabella sent Adam Orleton, the bishop of Hereford, to demand that the king give up the Great Seal of England and abdicate voluntarily.* Edward surrendered to the first but refused the second—irrelevantly, since Isabella then

---

*One of the strongest arguments for the widespread belief in a homosexual relationship between Edward and Hugh the Younger is that Orleton had been giving sermons accusing them of sodomy ever since Isabella's return. However, Orleton's strong affiliation with Isabella's rebellion makes him a less than disinterested party.

used the Great Seal to summon a parliament to meet at Westminster on January 7, 1327. Its purpose was to depose a king.

The January parliament was more a mass demonstration than a calm legislative assembly. Mobs rushed Westminster Hall. Bishops preached in churches and on the streets. Lords and commons gave speeches. Walter Reynolds, the archbishop of Canterbury, gave a sermon on the text *vox populi vox dei.* Sometime around January 15 the Articles of Deposition were finally read. They included charges that the king had been an incompetent administrator, a failed general, a persecutor of the clergy, and had "shown himself incorrigible, through his cruelty and weakness, and beyond all hope of amendment."

A problem, however: young Edward, the duke of Aquitaine, though hailed by Parliament as England's new king, flatly refused to accept the crown unless granted to him by his father. After three days of fruitless attempts to persuade him otherwise, on January 20 another deputation visited the king at Kenilworth, again demanding abdication. This time, they threatened Edward not only with losing his own crown but with the deposition of his son, strongly implying that Roger Mortimer would be England's next king. With this threat, the king finally surrendered. At his actual abdication ceremony, the king, dressed in mourning black, actually fainted; when he was dragged to his feet, he saw Sir Thomas Blount, the steward of the household, break his staff of office as a formal renunciation of his duties, since the king's household had now been disbanded. On February 1, 1327, Edward Plantagenet, the duke of Aquitaine, age fourteen, was crowned King Edward III of England. Edward II, no longer king of England, was now to be called "The Lord Edward, sometime King of England."

Under that title, and while in the custody of the new earl of Lancaster (brother to the king's former nemesis), the king put his poetic gifts to use, writing

> In winter woe befell me
> By cruel Fortune thwarted
> My life now lies a ruin
> Full oft have I experienced,

There's none so fair, so wise,
So courteous nor so highly famed,
But, if Fortune cease to favor,
Will be a fool proclaimed

When not writing poetry, Edward spent most of the next year composing letters entreating his wife to join him in his captivity. She always responded with feigned reluctance, claiming that she would gladly see him but Parliament forbade it.

Even if she had wanted to visit her husband, she had more pressing matters requiring her attention. In June 1327, James Douglas and the earl of Moray led another raid—an invasion, really—of England, intended to take advantage of the unsettled situation in England by, yet again, burning harvests, stealing cattle, and destroying farms. By all accounts, their intent was to force the hand of the new regents, Isabella and Mortimer, and bring them to the table where Scottish independence might finally be negotiated. With the approval of Mortimer, the new king raised an army and marched north to meet the Scottish hobelars, but the third Edward had no better luck bringing Scots to battle than either of the first two. The closest he came was at the River Wear in County Durham, where King Edward found himself on the opposite bank from James Douglas. The fourteen-year-old king did what fourteen-year-olds do, kingly or not: he dared the Black Douglas to a "fair fight." That is, either the Scots or the English would offer the other side free passage across the river, after which they could engage in combat on honorable terms. Douglas was unmoved by the offer. The old campaigner wasn't especially sporting when it came to war; this was, after all, the author of the "Douglas's Larder" massacre, whose best-remembered terror tactic was to remove either the right eye or right hand of any captured archer, aware that, as the proverb has it, "every English archer carries 24 Scottish lives in his belt." Moreover, he had already noticed that the English outnumbered his force by roughly two to one. While Douglas pretended to consider the challenge, his troops stole away through a supposedly impassable swamp by tying bunches of twigs to their feet and those of their horses. By the time the English had noticed that the only Scots remaining on the north side of the Wear were two heralds, who approached the English battle line and politely asked what they were all suited up for, Douglas and Moray had already slipped back over the border, and home.

King Robert, the earl of Moray, and James Douglas continued to ravage Northumberland through the fall of 1327, with little practical resistance from either Edward III or either of his regents, who were occupied with other matters—specifically, what to do about the "Lord Edward, sometime King of England."

The sometime King Edward wasn't completely without supporters. Two brothers with long and checkered pasts—Thomas and Stephen Dunheved, the first a onetime pirate and murderer, the other a Dominican friar, both of them loyal courtiers of Edward—attempted to engineer his escape on three separate occasions, nearly succeeding at least twice. Even worse, when they weren't planning jailbreaks, they traveled throughout England, "not only secretly but even openly, stirring up the people of the south and north to rise for the deposed and imprisoned king." Though they were eventually captured—Stephen was briefly imprisoned at Newgate, from which he almost immediately escaped; Thomas died at Pontrefact—they were a reminder of the dangers of leaving even a widely unpopular monarch alive.

The death of Edward II remains a mystery to this day. Nothing is truly known about its particulars, up to and including its precise date; the only certainty is that the official announcement of the death of the former king was issued on September 21, 1327. If there is a historical consensus about anything, it is that the final act was ordered by Mortimer after the Dunheveds' last failed rescue. As to the method of the king's execution, there is even less agreement. In 1342, Ranulf Higden, a monk of the Benedictine Abbey of St. Werburgh, Chester, wrote, in his *Polychronicon* (a history of the world) "[Edward] was ignominiously slain with a red-hot spit thrust into the anus," which was considered an appropriate punishment for the king's sodomy, and also the sort of death blow that left no obvious marks on the corpse. Shortly thereafter, the red-hot poker passed into popular legend—popular enough to make it one of the best-remembered things about Edward II, even though it's almost certainly not true.

Edward II earned some part of his place in any catalog of the worst monarchs in English history; he possessed a deadly combination of kingly arrogance and ineptitude, and his virtues, such as they were, were singularly useless for a fourteenth-century king. He had an unerring talent for finding the most destructive and ambitious men in England, and promoting them to the realm's highest positions. Moreover, he was a less-skilled wartime leader than either his father or his son, which exaggerated his weaknesses even more than they deserved.* And needless to say, kings who are deposed by their wives tend to suffer in historical memory. Four hundred years after Edward's death, Thomas Gray—the first poet to name Isabella the "She-Wolf of France"—did his best, in his poem entitled "The Curse Upon Edward," to redeem the king's reputation. It's not much of a poem, but Gray got one thing right: the enduring image of Edward's reign:

> Fell Thirst and Famine scowl
> A baleful smile upon their baffled guest.
> Heard ye the din of battle bray,
> Lance to lance, and horse to horse?
> Long years of havoc urge their destined course.

Edward II may not have been the worst king in England's history, but he has a very good claim to being the unluckiest. He had no triumphs, however fleeting, to balance either his cuckoldry by Isabella or his defeats by Robert Bruce. Most especially, nothing he could have done could have mitigated, even slightly, the seven years of rain, cold, and pestilences both animal and human that comprised the Great Famine. For a king's reputation to survive the horrors of the first two decades of the fourteenth century in northern Europe—"long years of

---

*It's less clear that either Edward I, who was just as unsuccessful in pacifying Scotland, or Edward III, who failed just as notably to defeat France, were superior in any strategic sense.

havoc," indeed—it would have to be that of someone who could legiti-
mately be called larger than life. As the last piece of Edward's almost
supernaturally bad fortune, his greatest adversary really was.

In October 1327, Robert Bruce's queen, Elizabeth de Burgh, died. She
had been his wife for twenty-five years, though they probably spent
fewer of them living together than apart, so frequently was Robert on
campaign. Elizabeth had missed, by five months, the denouement to
more than thirty years of almost constant warfare that began with
the death of Alexander III in 1296. In February 1328, Edward III of
England, holding parliament at York, finally issued a true treaty of
peace and recognition; one that

> will and concede for us and all our heirs and successors . . . that the
> kingdom of Scotland shall remain forever separate from the king-
> dom of England, in its entirety, free and in peace, without any kind
> of subjection, servitude, claim or demand, with its rightful bound-
> aries as they were held and preserved in the times of Alexander of
> good memory . . . to the magnificent prince, the lord Robert, by
> God's grace illustrious king of Scots, our ally and very dear friend,
> and to his heirs and successors.

The document that finally recognized the independence of Scotland, which had been negotiated by James Douglas, was signed by
March 17, 1328, by King Robert as the Treaty of Edinburgh, and ratified as the Treaty of Northampton by the English parliament on May 1;
evidently the old adversaries still felt obliged to disagree about its
name. The treaty also included a payment of £20,000 in war indemni-
ties from Scotland to England; King Edward's promise to intercede
with the pope to get the interdict on Scotland lifted; and the promise
of a marriage between Robert and Elizabeth's only surviving son,
David, then three years old, and Princess Joan of England, sister to
Edward III. The wedding feast held to celebrate the joining of four-
year-old David to seven-year-old Joan a year later required, among

other items, 4,360 pounds of almonds, 600 pounds of rice, 180 pounds of pepper, and 55 pounds of mace—a concrete reminder that the Great Famine was truly over.

Two years before the wedding, Robert Bruce had completed the construction of a manor—notably, not a fortified castle—in the village of Cardross, where the River Leven flows into the Firth of Clyde. There he lived comfortably, though not lavishly, hunting, keeping falcons, and, in an unconscious replay of the plebeian interests of his lifelong rival, Edward II, sailing and even shipbuilding. On June 7, 1329, he died there, after a long illness generally thought to be leprosy.

For an ordinary man, this would be the end of his story, but Robert Bruce had one more chapter to bequeath to his biographers. For years, if not decades, King Robert had regularly announced his desire to serve in a Crusade: to join the supranational effort to do battle against the enemies, not of Scotland, but of Christendom. As a practical matter, this meant that his last will and testament requested that, when his body was interred at Dunfermline, the traditional resting place for Scotland's kings, his heart should be removed from his body, embalmed, and carried into battle against the heathen.

There was little question, among the Scottish magnates hovering at King Robert's deathbed, about the right man to discharge this duty; to be Little John one last time to his Robin Hood. Since, in 1329, there was no way to enlist in a traditional crusade—the only Crusader states still in existence were in Rhodes and Cyprus—James Douglas placed Robert Bruce's heart in a carved casket of silver and sailed to Flanders, and from there to Spain, arriving in Seville sometime in June. He carried a safe-conduct from King Edward III, and letters to King Alfonso XI of Castile, then embroiled in a war with Muhammad IV, the sultan of Granada. The Reconquista that had, by then, been under way for centuries, had nothing to do with liberating the Holy Land, but it was a conflict between Christians and Muslims, and was the next best thing.

On August 25, 1330, James Douglas rode into battle at the head of a division of Alfonso's army besieging the Andalusian town of Teba, in the modern province of Malaga. Cut off, and apparently unfamiliar with the classic Moorish tactic of feigning a cavalry retreat only to turn and attack, Douglas was killed; a later legend has him throwing Bruce's embalmed heart at his enemies, saying that he would, as always, follow. Douglas's bones, and the casket containing Bruce's heart, were recovered from the battlefield, and carried back to Scotland for burial, the latter in the parish church of Douglas, the former at Melrose Abbey.

It was a suitable ending for the onetime tournament knight who became one of the greatest irregular warriors of all time; the Anglo-Norman who founded a Scottish nation in a Celtic country. The last act of Bruce's overlarge life recapitulates in miniature the way in which his era pulled the loyalties and affections of its people in opposite directions: on the one hand, toward a nation made up of countrymen sharing a common history, language, and affection for a particular piece of territory; on the other, to a creed uniting all nations under the banner of Christendom. One direction pointed to the past, the other to the future. Robert Bruce's dying wish was in conflict with his life, and his heart remains in Scotland to this day.

The Delicate Balance

Nonfiction narratives generally end with a contrivance—an attempt to polish off the rough edges and give a neat resolution to the lives of real people and the course of real events. But the ends of most histories, and definitely one about the first decades of the fourteenth century, are inherently arbitrary. We choose the threads to follow closely, and which not: England, rather than Spain; farmers more than priests. And we choose where to cut those threads off. Scotland, for example, did not enjoy its independence very long after the Treaty of Edinburgh/Northampton. In 1332, Thomas Randolph, who had been named regent for David Bruce, the five-year-old son of King Robert and Queen Elizabeth, died. With the Bruce, the Black Douglas, and the earl of Moray all dead, Edward Balliol—the one invited by Edward II to return to England from his exile in Picardy—struck for the throne, and ruled Scotland as a vassal of Edward III until 1336, when the Scots threw him out and restored King David to the throne.

David was the last of the Bruces. When he died without a son, Robert, the son of Walter Stewart and Marjorie Bruce, took the throne as Scotland's first Stewart king.* Stewarts, or their regents, would rule Scotland for the next two and a half centuries, regularly intermarrying with Europe's other royal families. So it was that, when Elizabeth I died in 1603, another Stewart, James VI of Scotland, a direct descendant of the man who first took up arms against England as part of the Wallace rebellion, became James I of England, ruling both nations. A little less than a century (and several civil wars, the execution of one English king, and the rise and fall of the Commonwealth in England

---

*Or Stuart. The change in spelling probably occurred during the twelve years that James's mother, Mary, Queen of Scots, spent in France.

and Scotland under the Lord Protector, Oliver Cromwell) later, Mary, the daughter of the last of the Stewart / Stuart kings, returned to Britain with her husband, William of Orange. And eighteen years after *that*, the two nations were united in the 1707 Acts of Union.

In the end, geography trumped patria. An island the size of Britain would eventually be consolidated under a single sovereign, and both Scotland and England can argue which nation eventually "conquered" the other. Nor is that the end of the story; as of this writing, referenda on Scottish independence (and "devolution," the reestablishment of a separate Scottish Parliament, which was approved in 1998, and seated the following year) have been debated and voted on half a dozen times, and seem certain to reappear. The third verse of Robert Burns's "March to Bannockburn" calls on "Who, for Scotland's King and Law / Freedom's sword will strongly draw." The passions that drew men to William Wallace and Robert Bruce continue to burn north of the Firth of Forth.

As for England, Edward III overthrew his onetime guardian and regent in October 1330, arresting Roger Mortimer in Northampton Castle and trying him in London, where he was, in a repeat of the grim justice of the day, given a traitor's death. Isabella was banished from court to a country manor in Norfolk and given an allowance of £3,000 a year, on which she kept what must have seemed to her an unnaturally modest court until her death in 1358. She had lived long enough to be the daughter of one king of France, the sister of three more—Louis X, Philip V, and Charles IV, the latter of whom died a year to the day after his nephew had been crowned Edward III of England—wife to one king, and mother to another. She also lived long enough to see her son claim the throne of her father.

When Charles IV died, he was survived by one living daughter and one pregnant wife; when she delivered yet another daughter, the Capetian dynasty, which had ruled France for four hundred years, ended. The reason was the Lex Salica, or Salic Law, a sixth-century judicial artifact that, in addition to promoting trial by combat, prohibited inheritance by a woman. But while this meant neither of Charles's daughters could inherit his throne, Salic Law was ambiguous on whether inheritance could pass *through* a woman. This, indeed, was Edward III's reading of the thing: that as the grandson of Philip IV, he was the rightful king of France.

The result was the Hundred Years' War, a series of wars between 1337 and 1453 that succeeded in accelerating the progress of European nationalism in its two great birthplaces—England and France—while continuing to undermine the military basis of feudalism. After the French disasters at Crécy (1346) and Agincourt (1415), where English longbowmen turned the flower of French chivalry into pincushions, no one could doubt that the age of the mounted knight was at an end. Manorialism was not far behind.

The Hundred Years' War was a disaster by any measure, with estimates of its butcher's bill as high as three million European lives. That number is more controversial than usual, however, because the years of the war overlapped with another disaster, even more terrifying: the Black Death.

The "great mortality" that likely first appeared in the Black Sea port of Caffa in the spring of 1347 killed as many as 100 million people across Europe and the Mediterranean by the year 1400 and recurred steadily through the eighteenth century. The Black Death, which was triggered by a profoundly unlucky alignment of the density of rat populations, the susceptibility of fleas, and the bacterium known as *Yersinia pestis*, was the world's second encounter with pandemic bubonic plague, and is such an overwhelming event in human history that the Great Famine that preceded it is frequently lost in its shadow.* As a case in point, for centuries, historians have believed that the fresco in the Camposanto of Pisa known as the *Trionfo della Morte* or *Triumph of Death* had been painted in 1350—three years after the arrival of the plague. Barbara Tuchman, in her classic history of the fourteenth century, *A Distant Mirror*, even calls it "a strange personification of Death [that] emerged from the plague years." The fresco, however, is now known to have been painted in 1338—eight years *be-*

---

*The first, the Justinianic Plague that originated in the sixth century CE, was nearly as destructive: 25 million dead in a population that was only a third as large.

fore the plague. Its subject is not disease, but hunger: a memory of the Great Famine.

Those memories were still fresh in European minds in 1338. Though the famine had ended by 1322, the summer of 1335 was nearly as rainy as that of 1316. In 1338, major floods destroyed dozens of towns and villages in central Europe, to be followed by a swarm of locusts that devoured crops from Hungary to Austria to Bohemia, after which an early snowfall destroyed fruit trees and vineyards. In England, the autumn harvest of 1341 was so poor that the Crown granted relief from taxation. And in 1342, flooding was so widespread as to destroy some of the most important bridges in Europe: across the Danube at Regensburg, across the Main at Bamberg and Frankfurt, and across the Elbe at Dresden. A year later, Lake Constance burst its banks and flooded surrounding towns.

Whatever the connections between famine, climate change, plague, and a century of war, they together added up to a demographic shock that upended the arithmetic of feudal manorialism. A population crash in a region that had spent hundreds of years increasing its farm acreage meant that, for the first time in centuries, labor was more valuable than land. For the survivors, at least, this represented a dramatic though temporary improvement in the lives of the rural peasantry as their labor became relatively more valuable. The long-term consequences of the end of the Medieval Warm Period, from the decline in the power of the papacy to the rise of national armies to the replacement of feudal manorialism by mercantilism—the doctrine that made control of foreign trade the most important economic responsibility of national governments—to even, in some readings, the Renaissance, were profound indeed.

Inevitably, a disaster story about the resonant forces set off by unexpected climate volatility multiplied by nations acting in what they saw as their own short-term interests resonates today, even without reference to the massive increase in atmospheric CO_2 that followed humanity's discovery of fossil fuels. With or without climate change, famines would be with us still, even more harmful in absolute terms than the Great Famine of the fourteenth century. Greater population densities (plus, to put it kindly, political volatility) in nineteenth-century Ireland or twentieth-century China resulted in the deaths of tens of millions. Malnutrition remains a daily fact of life for *billions*. And cereal monoculture—today maize rather than wheat—is even more fraught in the first decades of the twenty-first century than it was in the first decades of the fourteenth.

The temptation to extract useful lessons from the history of the Great Famine, or the Scottish Wars of Independence, or the machinations of a French princess turned English queen, or even the Viking raids, is next to irresistible. The first decades of the fourteenth century have lessons to teach about economics, power politics, and, of course, the potent energies released during the complex dance between atmosphere and ocean.

But the Great Famine was the product of a mechanism even more complex than climate. Famines occur because of a sudden disruption in the food supply, which is almost by definition a short-run proposition. Weather, if it's bad enough, can disrupt harvests all by itself, but even the low-productivity farms of medieval Europe were generally robust enough that weather alone rarely caused widespread shortages. Real food crises, in the fourteenth century or the twenty-first, require human action—usually the sort of action taken with weapons in hand. When the two combine—drought plus rebellion; floods plus invasion— the mixture results in famine just as surely as combining yellow and blue produces green.

Still, two years of bad weather didn't kill a quarter of the city of Ypres, and neither did the knights of Philip IV. The conditions that destroyed millions of lives during the seven years of the Great Famine appeared during the four centuries of the Medieval Warm Period. From 900 to 1300, as ten million mouths grew to thirty million—and as the least productive acres in Europe were cultivated to feed them—the balance between producing food and consuming it grew more fragile every year. By the time the North Atlantic Oscillation shifted, and the weather started to change, that balance could be destroyed by a strong wind.

At the Château d'Angers in France's Loire Valley is the modern home of one of the greatest of all medieval artworks: the Apocalypse Tapestry, commissioned by the duke of Anjou fifty years after the Great Famine. In its original form, six huge weavings—each an incredible seventy-eight feet wide and twenty feet high—contained ninety different scenes from the last book of the New Testament, the Revelation of Saint John the Divine. Only seventy-one survive, depicting the fever-dream visions from the book—the seven seals, the destruction of Babylon, the archangels fighting the dragon, the Great Whore riding on the Scarlet Beast with seven heads and ten horns, and, of course, the Four Horsemen of the Apocalypse.

In the popular iconography of the day, the Third Horseman, riding the black horse, carries a set of scales, an admission that famine is really a measure of dearth: the cost of food. But it is also a reminder that famine is a matter of equilibrium: of the delicate balance between life and death. The seven years of the Great Famine, and the evil times that accompanied them, are powerful evidence of how sensitive the scales had become, after four centuries of growth, to a sudden shift in the weather.

ACKNOWLEDGMENTS

At the time of the events described in *The Third Horseman*, the root of the word that would enter the English language as "acknowledgment" two centuries later still had overtones of "confession": an admission of sin. Expiation follows.

Matthew "Sweetness and Light" Arnold described culture as the "pursuit . . . of the best that has been thought and said in the world." Books like *The Third Horseman*, works of synthesis, would be impossible without the institutions whose duty it is to collect "the best." I am, as always, forever grateful to Lara Moore and Margaret Sherry at Princeton University's Firestone Library and to Leslie Burger and her staff at Princeton Public Library. Even if I never had a manuscript to show for it, I'd be thankful for the hundreds of hours I have been able to spend in the company of other, better, books.

The authors of those books—and papers, journal articles, blog posts, and lectures—are owed thanks as well. I am indebted to hundreds of scholars, living and dead, whose works appear in the bibliography of *The Third Horseman*, but a few deserve special mention: A. A. M. Duncan, both for his translation of John Barbour and his works on Bannockburn and King Robert Bruce; Caroline Bingham and Seymour Phillips each wrote an indispensable biography of Edward II, as did Alison Weir for Queen Isabella. Brian Fagan's works on historic climate change are extraordinary, and Robert Fogel's calculation of food production and consumption provided a frightening insight into the fragile food economy of medieval Europe. I seem forever to be thanking Gregory Clark for his careful research into English economic history and the late Lynn White for helping me to understand medieval technological innovation. Most especially, I am grateful to William Chester Jordan of Princeton, who not only produced the most, and the best, scholarship on the Great Famine, but introduced me to Andrew Collings, who provided me with the best sort of research support:

Finding and correcting a huge number of errors, but also proposing a dozen different lines of exploration. Any mistakes that remain in *The Third Horseman* were introduced by gremlins after he signed off on it.

Though I have been observing the process for more than thirty years, the transformation of a manuscript into a book still awes me. As a onetime editor and publisher, I am more aware than most authors of the importance of the team that gets recruited for this exercise, and far more critical of its quality. So when I say how thankful I am to the people at Viking, I hope it carries the weight I intend. Thanks to Rick Kot, who first suggested the idea that became *The Third Horseman*; likewise thanks to Clare Ferraro and to Wendy Wolf, who invested in both the idea and in me. Most especially, I am grateful to Melanie Tortoroli, whose extraordinary editorial skills have left me gap-jawed in amazement. It is one thing to provide more than seven hundred (I counted) editorial comments, every one of them erudite and helpful; another to do so on a brutally tight schedule. To do both while never losing either enthusiasm or good humor is very special indeed. I envy every other author who is lucky enough to be placed in her hands.

My envy doesn't stop there: Carla Bolte designed the book's interior, and recruited the amazing David Lindroth to provide the book's maps and illustrations. Jaya Miceli, who designed the cover, marries an elegant sense of design to a ghoulish sensibility—clearly an asset to authors who write about famines and plagues for a living. Jennifer Tait shepherded the book through the production process with extraordinary skill and Rachelle Mandik is an extraordinary copyeditor who is talented enough to save me from a hundred different embarrassing errors, and kind enough to do so without ever giving offense.

And, last but far from least, I thank the good luck that provided me with an extremely forgiving family, for reading such a macabre book in its earliest stages and putting up with my enthusiasm for sharing the most grotesque discoveries without—much—groaning. Thanks to Gary Rosen and Holly Goldberg Sloan, Quillan Rosen, Alex Rosen, and Emma Rosen. And, most of all, thanks to Jeanine, who challenged me to write my first book and has supported me uncomplainingly, and lovingly, through every one since.

NOTES

✎

Chapter One: "The Fury of the Northmen" • 793–1066

7   **Closer to home, in Ireland Or not.** There's a large and respectable minority opinion that the term *Finngaill*—along with *Dubgaill*, usually translated as "dark foreigner," doesn't refer to skin or hair color at all, but rather is best translated as "old" and "new" foreigners. (Downham 2009)

7   **"rapine and slaughter"** (Jones 1984), quoting *The Anglo-Saxon Chronicle*

7   **"to become their mistresses"** (Sorensen 2012)

8   **"the torpid courage of their barbarous natives"** (Gibbon 1994)

9   **quicker to respond to change** In the words of climatologist George Philander, one partner, the atmosphere, is "quick and agile, and responds nimbly to hints from the . . . ponderous and cumbersome ocean." (Philander 2000)

9n   **Which is not to say that the Norse were just lucky** (Ferguson 2009)

10   **sixteen hundred times that of the atmosphere** (Brown 2001)

11   **Lower solar activity, more Carbon-14** (Hughes 1994)

11   **the early Iron Age from about 200 BCE** (Hughes 1994)

13   **altitudes of more than a thousand feet** (Fagan 2000)

13   **vineyards started appearing** (Bailey 1981)

16   **were able to produce barley** (Fagan 2008)

16   **and "a few other men"** (Thorvaldsson 1906)

16   **any time in the last one hundred twenty-five thousand years** (Fagan 2000)

16   **"people would be attracted to go there"** (Thorvaldsson 1906)

16   **more than four *hundred* times the volume** (Brown 2001)

16–17   **at least one hundred kilometers away from Iceland** (Fagan 2008)

17   **Germany and Poland nearly tripled** (Findlay 2006), citing McEvedy and Jones's *Atlas of World Population History*

18   **at least 100 *million* acres were deforested** (Williams 2006) The total land area of western and central Europe is approximately 1 million square miles, or 640 million acres.

18   **to reclaim the tree-rich sanctuaries of pagan worship** (White 1966)

18   **saved by the "prayer book and the ax"** (Williams 2006)

18–19   **southeast of England, Brittany, and Normandy** (Gies 1990)

19   **the Silva Carbonnaria, or charcoal-burners forest** (Williams 2006)

19   **frequently as few as three** Modern calculations of fourteenth-century agricultural yields are wildly variable. The low numbers are taken from (Jordan 1996); the higher from (Allen 2005) who documents net yields of 8.8 for wheat, and up to 13.4 for barley. However, these calculations are taken from lands planted for the exclusive use of feudal lords—their *demesne* lands—which were, presumably, the best land available.

20   a bribe to go away In 876, Charles the Bald paid off a one-hundred-ship raiding party with 5,000 *livres*. (Ferguson 2009)

20   the bishops of Noyon, Beauvais, Bayeux, and Avranches (Ferguson 2009)

26   by contract, rather than blood (Fukuyama 2011) Fukuyama is largely citing the work of the twentieth-century French historian Marc Bloch.

27   fifteen times as much as a cow (DeVries 2007)

27   "the destructive progress of the Normans" (Gibbon 1994)

Chapter Two: "Henceforth Be Earls"   •   *1066–1298*

32   "only a few homesteads had yet to be carved" (Rimas 2010), quoting from Miller and Hatcher, *Medieval England*

32   might rule fifty or more villages (Gies 1990)

33   "by the year from the shire" (Tennant 2011)

34n   true slavery had virtually disappeared (McGarry 1976)

36   "nor do I hold it of any but God" (Scott 1996)

37   a monk named Thomas of Otterbourne (Phillips 2010)

37   "often accompanied by a single follower" (Maxwell 1913)

39   The first six Guardians (Barrow 2005)

40   "one of the most able and ably advised" (Scott 1996)

40   "whatever he likes he says is lawful" (Scott 1996), quoting *The Song of Lewes,* an anonymous chronicle

40   virtually ruled both Aberdeen and Berwick (Scott 1996)

42   "riches were the sea, and the water its walls" (Scott 1996), quoting *The Chronicle of Lanercost*

42   and only a few dozen today (Pinker 2011)

42–43   "saving the rights of the King of England" (Scott 1996)

43   "that I am *not* the rightful Suzerain" (Barrow 2005), quoting *The Chronicle of William Rishanger*

44   "the realms of England and Scotland are joined together" (Barrow 2005)

47   that all died at their posts (Scott 1996)

48   "If he won't come to us, we'll go to him" (Scott 1996)

48   what was left of Scottish resistance (Barrow 2005)

48   "Have we nothing to do but win kingdoms for you?" (Barrow 2005)

51   "or return to your homes" (Barrow 2005)

53   "to defend ourselves and liberate our kingdom" (Scott 1996), quoting *The Chronicle of Walter Guisborough*

54   "baldrick for his sword" (Maxwell 1913)

54   plunder back to Scotland (Scott 1996)

54   open to trade with the Hanseatic cities (Scott 1996)

54   "by consent of the community of the realm" (Barrow 2005)

55   "William Wallace, Knight" (Barrow 2005)

55   journeys were the opposite of easy (Barrow 2005)

56   "other free men of the kingdom" (Bingham 1973)

56   flayed prisoners, killed babies, and raped nuns (Scott 1996)

56   more than two thousand Welsh bowmen (Prestwich 1988) Citing English payroll documents, Prestwich gives somewhat higher numbers: 3,000 cavalry, 10,900 Welsh infantry, and 14,800 English foot.

56–57   "instead of rebuking you I shall praise you" (Barrow 2005)
58   "Lochaber ax" . . . well-designed for pulling a man from his horse (Barrow 2005)

Chapter Three: "Penalty for Their Betters" • *1298–1307*

59   "Know that we have divided" Shakespeare, *King Lear*, I, 1, 37
59   "I love your majesty" Shakespeare, *King Lear*, I, I, 94
61   "leapt at the Earl of Carrick and seized him by the throat" (Scott 1996), quoting the report of an English spy, now preserved at London's Public Record Office
62   with the throne of Saint Peter as the prize (Orlandis 1985)
65   "that he has to expedite" (National Archives 1981) While the letter from Philip to Boniface is undoubtedly authentic, no one has been able to document whether Wallace actually made it to Rome.
65   for all disputes in Christendom One of Boniface's papal bulls, *Unam Sanctam*, is a categorical statement of papal authority over, well, everyone: "It is necessary to salvation that every human creature be subject to the Roman pontiff." (Tuchman 1978)
65   "for the love of Mount Zion and Jerusalem" (Scott 1996), quoting *The Chronicle of William Rishanger*
65   "nor silence for Jerusalem" (Scott 1996)
66   "through evil counsel" (Scott 1996), quoting Stone, *Anglo-Scottish Relations*
66   "promises Robert assistance and counsel as before" (Barrow 2005)
67   25 percent more than England's (Maddison 2006) Note that the statistics from Maddison's enormous work attempt to provide longitudinal data, which means country data frequently refers to nations that did not yet exist. The data for Flanders, in this case, appears as "Belgium."
68   directly over Flanders (Brown 2001)
69   Guy of Namur and Willem van Gulik . . . were named to command (DeVries 2011)
70   the Battle of the Golden Spurs (DeVries 2011)
71   "than any other single event" (Barrow 2005)
72   "forced them to brew and bake" (Phillips 2010)
72   some £3,795 annually from the royal household accounts (Phillips 2010)
73   "driving carts, rowing [and] swimming" (Weir 2005)
73   another eight thousand armed and horsed troops As always, different sources give different numbers. (Prestwich 1988) lists the peak number of foot soldiers at 7,500.
73   three bridges prefabricated At the fairly economical cost of £938, according to (Prestwich 1988).
73   besiege Stirling Castle from the north (Pollington et al. 2011)
74   "to whoever shall capture Wallace" (Barrow 2005)
74   in the tavern where he was taken (Scott 1996) Another story has Wallace captured in the house of Robert Rae, a servant of Sir John Menteith.
75   a warning to anyone who might be tempted to rebellion (Barrow 1965)
76   "time ever made such progress" (Scott 1996)
76   "no success whatever" (Scott 1996)
76   "and try to obviate it" (Barrow 2005)

77   returned to the church to do just that (Barbour 1997)

79   official companions of Edward Caernarfon (Bingham 1973) The nature of the companionship he offered is still debated by the sort of historians who demand the sort of proof required in a criminal prosecution. And, it's true that there are reasonable doubts about whether the relationship between Edward and Gaveston was sexual.

79   "before all other mortals" (Bingham 1973)

79   "and so Piers was accounted a sorcerer" (Childs 2005)

79   "too much given to sodomy" (Bingham 1973)

79   "desire for sinful, forbidden sex" (Weir 2005)

80   "how would I sink into your embraces" (Berkowitz 2012)

80   in the same category as incest and sorcery (Berkowitz 2012) By this time, the Latin Empire that, confusingly, had placed Duke Baldwin of Flanders on the throne of Constantine. After his defeat in 1205, Constantinople was restored to eastern rule.

81   almost immediately headed north (Scott 1996)

81   "that you could find in any country" (Barbour 1997)

81   "as the rich had taken to flight" (Phillips 2010), quoting *The Chronicle of William of Rishanger*

82   only one in ten had more than six hundred (Gies 1990), citing Hilton, *A Medieval Society*

84   subject to rape or murder without consequence (Scott 1996), citing *Liber Pluscardiesis*, a chronicle from the Plusarden Priory in Elgin, Scotland

84   where each one was imprisoned (Bingham 1973)

85   "had not his match in his time, in any clime" (Fordun 1872)

86   "Of Good King Robert's Testament" (Scott 1996)

87   "at the point of the sword" (Phillips 2010)

Chapter Four: "Douglas's Larder" • 1307–1312

88   "you should never enjoy your inheritance" (Bingham 1973)

88   providing £66 annually for his living (Phillips 2010)

89   "strengthen Piers, and surround him with friends" (Childs 2005)

89   "younger and harder knights of the kingdom" (Childs 2005)

89   "the most beautiful woman in the kingdom and the Empire" (Phillips 2010)

89   "one of the fairest ladies in the world" (Weir 2005)

89–90   sixty seamstresses alone (Phillips 2010)

90   they used up thirty pounds of candles (Weir 2005)

91   constructed to house Scotland's Stone of Destiny (Phillips 2010)

92   "that the community of the realm should determine" (Bingham 1973)

93   "and followed the advice of the young" (Childs 2005)

94   "a traitor to his liege lord and his realm" (Phillips 2010)

94   were still in force (Phillips 2010) The Charter of the Forest, or *Carta de Foresta*, was drafted as a complement to the Magna Carta; as its name implies, it was largely concerned with changes to the traditional laws of the forest and, as such, actually provided more protections for commoners than its better-known predecessor: Eliminating the death penalty for hunting venison, for example, in the royal forests.

95   "or keep up your household, except by extortions" (Locke 1919)

95   to whom he owed some £22,000 (Phillips 2010)

95   "an open enemy of the king" (Phillips 2010)

95   "for all time and without hope of return" (Weir 2005)

96   the two earls would guarantee his personal safety (Bingham 1973)

96   "I think you know me" (Weir 2005)

96   the body lay there until found by four shoemakers (Weir 2005)

96   "and brought it to the king" (Locke 1919)

96   "and grain is so meager" (Dean 1996)

97   The knightly orders of Calatrava (Moeller 1908) Calatrava and Alcantara were affiliated with the Cistercian monastic order; the Order of Santiago, with the Augustinians.

97   "settled by German peasants from the west" (Lewis 1958)

98   "hacked down and divided into assarts" (Lewis 1958)

98   rents increased, substantially (Findlay 2006), citing Lewis

99   planting peas and legumes does the same thing (Clark 2006) Pasture is even better at converting airborne nitrogen to ammonia—the same stuff used by modern industrial fertilizers—than legumes. Legumes fix approximately 65 pounds of nitrogen per acre; pasture grass fixes nearly 100 pounds per acre, while clover fixes 150 pounds per acre. What this means, in practice, is that taking an arable field—able to fix enough nitrogen to produce only six to eight bushels of wheat annually—and alternating it with a pasture that fixes enough to produce seventeen bushels per acre is actually far more productive over any period of time than just using land for wheat every year.

100   the unsustainable use of arable land (Clark 1992)

101   "obtaining the original figure by dividing by x" (Angell 1913)

101   more than the entire value of the country (Allen 2005), One of the most endur-ing constants of agricultural history is that, in every society, in every era that can be documented, the market price of a piece of farmland over time is approximately four times its annual productivity. In 1300, the aggregate value of *all* the arable land of England, which was producing rents for its feu-dal landlords of between 10 and 12 shillings per acre was therefore approxi-mately £2.6 million in the currency of the day: roughly fourteen million acres, at a selling price of four shillings an acre. Scotland, with its lower rents—Gregory Clark estimates .77 shillings per acre in 1300—and less than two million acres under cultivation, was therefore "worth" less than £300,000 (Clark 2006).

101   was sent to France for his own safety (Davis 1974)

101   they even recorded the horse's name (Davis 1974)

102   "gladly and well rewarded his service" (Barbour 1997)

102   "there was not one among them there . . . more than James Douglas" (Barbour 1997)

104   the true and nearest heir to Alexander III (Barrow 2005)

104   "did them all the injury that he could" (Scott 1996) The original source is the still-mysterious "Monk of Malmesbury," the anonymous author of a manuscript in the British Museum said to chronicle English history up to the year 1129.

105   "no food for their horses" (Scott 1996), quoting *The Chronicle of Lanercost*

105   "all levied and foolishly spent" (Locke 1919)
106   what amounted to a national English property tax (Barrow 2005)
106   "a great number of cattle" (Scott 1996), quoting the *Vita*
106   armor and weapons from Flanders and the Hanse (Bingham 1973)

Chapter Five: "Scots, Wha Hae" • *1313–1315*

107   the earls of Pembroke and Surrey aligned with the king (Phillips 2010)
108   more heavily on England's peasantry than its aristocracy (Phillips 2010)
108   who had taken over for Frescobaldi (Phillips 2010) Philip IV loaned his son-in-law £33,000, and remitted all penalties incurred by Edward's subjects in Gascony. The pope was tapped for another £25,000, and other sources were good for more than £40,000.
109   made vows to join each other on crusade (Phillips 2010) It seems likely that neither one gave much thought to the rural peasants whose productivity paid for all the pomp; a single banquet—there were six—required 94 oxen, 189 pigs, 380 rams, 200 pike, 160 carp, and 80 barrels of wine.
109   nothing more than light scaling ladders (Davis 1974) The ladders were supposedly invented by Sim of Ledhouse, one of the soldiers under the command of James Douglas.
109   "through which the two ropes could be passed" (Scott 1996), quoting *The Chronicle of Lanercost*
110   he immediately ordered the mustering of his army (Duncan 2010)
111   "to traverse all Scotland" (Davis 1974)
111   "third best knight of his day" (Barbour 1997)
111   "That was unwisely done, indeed" (Scott 1996)
111   a few hundred mounted skirmishers (Barrow 2005) The Scots were seriously understrength in not just cavalry but missile artillery. King Robert had well understood, ever since Falkirk, the importance of archers, and especially Scotland's deficiency in them relative to England. Almost from the time he became king, he regularly converted the traditional feudal obligation of knight service—essentially cavalry, either armed-and-armored heavy cavalry for the richest or light cavalry for their men-at-arms—to archer service. In 1309, for example, he rewrote the grant to the baron of Tweeddale from a single knight's fee to ten archers; the same for the barony of Cessford—that is, five archers. He notably granted hereditary pensions, essentially fiefs-for-money in return for archer service.
112–13   10 percent of them more than £40 (Ayton 1999)
113   one of Edward II's horses cost him more than £70 (Phillips 2010)
113   only raise their swords on behalf of virtue (Tuchman 1978)
113   "the adventure of life in death" (Tuchman 1978)
113   and thereby make it more tolerable (Sjøgren 2011)
113   turned them into scavenger meat at Courtrai (Moyer 2011)
114   "the gradations of wealth were less steep" (Scott 1996)
114   from blowing his horn too vigorously (Aberth 2010)
114   "rather than an army on the march" (Bingham 1973), quoting the *Vita*
115   "to bunch at a single well-guarded spot" (Barrow 2005)
117   "myssit the nobile king" (Barbour 1997)

117 was, somehow, ignoble (Keegan 1961)
118 "as to keep your honour" (Scott 1996), quoting various extracts from (Barbour 1997)
118 "These men will win all or die" (Barbour 1997)
119 the Great Seal of England and the Royal Shield (Duncan 2010)
119 "fell before the Flemings at Courtrai" (Bingham 1973)
120 "England would have prospered well" (Locke 1919)
120 "and other improper occupations" (Phillips 2010)
120 "With a rumbelow" (Locke 1919)
120 "Scots, wha hae . . ." (Burns 1994)
121 "Successful Expeditions and Shortened Wars" (Aberth 2010)
121*n* how to poison wells; and so on (Stathakopoulos 2004)

Chapter Six: "The Floodgates of the Heavens" • 1315–1316

122 "or store it safely in the barn" (Childs 2005)
123 records their start in the middle of April (Lucas 1930) Friar Guillaume actually died in 1300, but his chronicle was continued until 1368.
123 it rained for 155 days in a row (Jordan 2010)
123 the four worst winters in four centuries (Alexandre 1901), quoted in (Jordan 1996)
123–24 "the whole world was troubled" (Jordan 1996)
124 were washed away (Aberth 2010) and (Field 2012)
124 the loess can be hundreds of feet deep (Brown 2001)
125 from forests, swamps, and pasture (Findlay 2006)
126 virtually all production on Europe's manors (Bois 2009)
127 even had vassals of their own (Jordan 1996), citing Arnold, *German Knighthood*. This "caste" of German knights, which Arnold anglicized as "ministerials" were high status, but not legally free, even to wed, or inherit. Ministerialis major had vassals; ministerialis minor did not.
127 higher status in most villages than a poorer freeman (Gies 1990)
128 nearly ten inches (Brown 2001), citing Boardman and Mortlock, *"Climate Change and Soil Erosion"*
128 or dictate to a defeated one (Bingham 1973) From the *Vita*: "The earls said that the Ordinances had not been observed and therefore events had turned out badly for the king . . . The King granted their execution; he denied the earls nothing."
128 a successful revalidation of the Ordinances (Aberth 2010)
128 a parliament meeting in Westminster in the spring of 1315 (Bingham 1973)
128 on the increase in England since 1305 (Mate 1991)
128 another price increase in sheep, and therefore wool (Jordan 1996)
128 costing nearly £8,000 a year (Phillips 2010), citing (Maddicott 1975)
129 "floodgates of the heavens" Genesis 7:11, NIV
129 "in pride, in craft, and in perjury" (Childs 2005)
129 the relatively untouched farms of the Mediterranean (Brown 2001) Tree-ring data from lower latitudes (45° N, 10° E; Italy's Po Valley) actually shows the decade of weather beginning in 1310, which brought such distress to Britain, France, Flanders, Poland, and Germany, was by any measure, mild.

130   "like wild oxen" (Ó Gráda 2009)

130   "a countless multitude entered the city" (Ó Gráda 2009)

130   "the flesh of a son was preferred to his love" (Brown 2001)

131   "eight of Shantung's twelve rivers" (Ó Gráda 2009), citing MacFarquhar *The Origins of the Cultural Revolution*

131n   *maxima, permaxima,* and even *intollerabilis* (Jordan 1996)

132   the eruption of the Vanuatuan volcano Kuwae in 1452 (Ó Gráda 2009)

132   corresponding droughts in Brazil and southern Africa (Ó Gráda 2009)

132   "the most costly natural disaster in the history of the western hemisphere" (Ó Gráda 2009), citing Mike Davis, *Late Victorian Holocausts*

132   fewer of them in antiquity (Braudel 1981) *Almost* everyone. Fernand Braudel, the single most important historian of medieval peasant life, found ten famines in tenth-century France, twenty-six in the twelfth, thirteen in the sixteenth, eleven in the seventeenth, and sixteen more in the eighteenth.

133   The excess mortality during the seven years of the Great Famine (Ó Gráda 2009)

133   turns a modest problem into a cascade (Arnold 1991)

134   even six times the normal rainfall (Aberth 2010) Dendrochronology (the calculation of climate by the measurement of the size and nature of tree rings) bears this out: Ireland's oaks—a tree whose growth is very sensitive to rainfall—grew 7 percent more than normal in 1315 and 10 percent more in 1316, and 8 percent more in 1318.

134   a once-every-two-hundred-years event (Ó Gráda 2011)

134   starvation for at least some people (Fischer 1996)

134   at least three times normal (Aberth 2010)

134   lawlessness, already rife in medieval Europe Crime during later famines is even better documented. In Ireland during the famines of the 1840s, incidents of burglary and robbery increased fivefold . . . while rapes plummeted, probably due to a loss of interest in sex because of hunger, which has been documented in famines for centuries. Also, prisoners convicted of crimes committed during nineteenth-century famines tended to be taller, better educated, and younger than those convicted of crimes committed during non-famine years, which suggests that crimes were being committed by a better class of people, those who hadn't been criminals before. Tellingly, though, crime increased mostly during the early stages of famine. Once true starvation starts to occur, energy levels dropped so low that even crime declined, as with Ireland in 1840 compared with 1848. (Ó Gráda 2009)

134   a third of all thefts (Kershaw 1973)

135   blackmailed a parson for a ransom of £40 (Waugh 1977)

135   to sell them for food (Russell 2005), citing Key Ray Chong, *Cannibalism in China*

135   the mothers were fed the children (Lucas 1930)

135   "women ate their children out of hunger" (Aberth 2010)

135   "jailed thieves . . . devoured themselves" (Aberth 2010)

136   *"pauperes enim pueros"* (Marvin 1998)

136   hanging from gibbets (Aberth 2010)

136   this phenomenon replicates itself in long-term climate change (Bodri 1994).
        Bodri found fractal dimensions in temperature over time scales as small as ten
        years, and as large as a million.

136   ice caps in Arctic Canada and Iceland (Miller 2012)

137   "many thousands perished" (Riley 1863)

137   things reverted to normal (Campbell 2000)

137   dogs could hunt rabbits (Fagan 2000)

137   largely confined to Europe (Brown 2001)

137   variations in solar radiation (Brown 2001) Analysis of an isotope of Beryllium
        (Be-10, which is cosmogenic—that is, produced by solar radiation) in core
        samples taken at the South Pole shows it peaking in 1075, dropping by more
        than a third by 1130, and peaking again in 1450, suggesting low solar activity,
        and therefore higher cosmic rays. The Wolf Sunspot Minimum, occurring be-
        tween 1280 and 1330, parallels this.

137   a minimum not seen since the third century BCE (Thompson 2010)

138   a heavy, and unprofitable, discount (Lucas 1930)

139   "there is nothing to be had" (Aberth 2010)

139   returning with enormous herds of cattle (Lomas 1996)

139   *"The Black Douglas/Shall not get ye"* (Davis 1974)

139   "deserted by men and wild and domestic beasts" (Aberth 2010)

139   "the houses where they had been able to take refuge" (Aberth 2010), quoting
        The Lanercost Chronicle

139   The value of a typical fishery (Jordan 1996)

140   "it could neither be mown or gathered" (Childs 2005)

140   "that made men more agaste" (Jordan 1996)

140   "unsurpassed in the last 2,000 years" (Bailey 1981)

141   eight villages in Sussex alone were submerged (Bailey 1981)

141   by the newly unstable sea (Bailey 1981)

141   "an unheard-of barrenness" (Jordan 1996)

141   "hitherto unheard-of in the realm" (Jordan 1996)

Chapter Seven: "A Dearness of Wheat" • 1316–1317

142   "scarcely any bread could even be bought" (Lucas 1930) In the original, *"unde
        terra tanta penuria premebatur . . . vix poterat panis venalis pro suae specialis
        familiae sustentatione, inveniri."*

143   huge quantities of protein (Woolgar 2010)

143   whether the earl's family was in residence or not (Tannahill 1988)

144   a miraculous knack (Fernandez-Armesto 2002)

144   heavy consumption of rye (Fernandez-Armesto 2002)

144   strong preference for six-rowed barley (Pearson 1997)

144   an eighth of the protein consumed in the modern world (Fernandez-Armesto
        2002)

145   "kneader of the dough" (Tannahill 1988)

145   "Wheat's unpardonable fault" (Braudel 1981)

146   "join together to do mischief" (Henley 1890)

146   struggling to feed 5 million (Fagan 2008) These estimates should be taken with
        at least a tablespoon of salt. Gregory Clark, in "Interpreting English Economic

History," calculates that the acreage under cultivation in 1300 was even greater: 14.6 million acres. Others put the number at 12 million acres, with another 2 million for pasture and meadow, leaving perhaps 20 million unimproved common pasture. Bruce Campbell, in *English Seigniorial Agriculture, 1250–1450* calculated that the maximum population that could be fed by England's agricultural output in 1300 was 4.25 million; other estimates get as high as 6.5 million. Clark's own estimate is about 5.7–5.9 million.

147   the amount needed to support a family (Gies 1990)

147   "and a sixteenth of a rood" (Gies 1990) They mistranslate the rood as a rod, which is a length measure.

149   to define the borders of the village (Gies 1990)

149   the single biggest driver of growth in landlord income (Bois 2009)

149   "till that building be thrown down" (Fischer 1996)

149   "war of wind and water against human muscle" (Bloch 1985)

149   surveyed in the Domesday Book of 1086 (Williams 2006)

150   still only nine bushels an acre of wheat (Mate 1991)

150   seed corn for the next harvest (Fagan 2008)

150   for at least another five years (Slavin 2010)

151   the priory closed (Aberth 2010)

151   in 1316 it had quadrupled (Kershaw 1973)

151   promoted the eating of all sorts of fish (Fagan 2008)

152   brokered into ports on the North Sea (Fagan 2008)

152   fish prices were the highest in a century (Jordan 1996), citing Rogers, *A History of Agriculture and Prices in England*

152   "and devoid of charity" (Aberth 2010)

152   "no wine in the whole kingdom of France" (Jordan 1996)

152   "a trifling quantity" (Fagan 2000)

153   yields dropped as much as 80 percent by 1317 (Jordan 1996)

153   a Benedictine nunnery in Essex (Woolgar 2010)

153   flans and cheese tarts on Rogation (Woolgar 2010)

154   more prosperous peasants (Dyer 1998) This evidence is extracted from agreements in manorial court rolls that allowed peasants to draw something like a pension once they had grown too old to work. Even when they didn't own it outright, the most valuable asset for most peasants was the right to work a particular piece of land—a right that could be sold, bequeathed, and inherited. In one case, a five-acre holding was transferred from one peasant to another, in return for access to a "curtilage" (or kitchen garden) plus two bushels of wheat and two of rye, four bushels of barley, and four bushels of peas annually (each distributed at harvest times, or holidays like Michaelmas or Christmas).

154   and possibly some fish (Dyer 1998)

154   Ale was also very cheap (Gies 1990)

154n   twice as much grain as a typical peasant brew (Bennett 1996)

155   the monks at St. Paul's in London (Rimas 2010)

155   an average of around four thousand calories (Singman 1999)

155   more than nine thousand calories a day (Pearson 1997)

155   Rouche's stratospheric number (Pearson 1997)

155   doubling the amount of land under cultivation throughout Europe (Pearson 1997) Grain yields, on a per-hectare basis, range from 400 to 666 kilograms of edible grain per hectare; legumes about the same. Five hundred grams of whole-grain bread demands 390 grams of flour, while "white bread" needs 487.5 grams. Beer requires around 72 grams of grain per liter; pottage or gruel is made in a ratio of around 5:1.

155   a gallon of milk to produce a pound of cheese (Pearson 1997) More precisely, 4.18 liters of milk for 500 grams of cheese, and between 18.9 and 35 liters of milk for a kilogram of butter.

156   to a single boar and six sows (Jordan 1996) For the same reason, virtually all the flocks of domesticated fowl in Europe—especially geese, which, while slower to reproduce than chickens, are much easier to feed, scratching for insects and the like, even able to actually survive temporarily in the wild—were decimated as replacement food. As, indeed, were Europe's great pigeon flocks; in Burgundy, almost every farmhouse had a dovecote, and some northern French manors had cells for as many as 4,500 birds.

156   8 to 10 million wool-producing sheep (Campbell 2000)

156   neither of which were raised for food (Allen 2005)

157   required to perform substantial manual labor (Pearson 1997), citing Jan Peter Pals, "Observations on the Economy of the Settlement," in *Farm Life in a Carolingian Village*. Pals is far more precise in his actual calculations, coming up with an estimate of between 1,986 and 2,138 calories daily.

157   the fungi that contaminate stored grain (Pearson 1997)

158   minerals like calcium, magnesium, and zinc (Mollat 1986)

158   "poor and beggars were starving" (Phillips 2010)

158   "that men could hardly bury them" (Kershaw 1973)

159   "grazed like cows on the growing grasses of the field" (Jordan 1996), quoting Curschmann, *Hungersnöte*

159   "so much dearth and famine to have prevailed in the past" (Russell 1966)

160   a simple rhinovirus . . . can become a killer (Rivers 1981)

160   not all infections are affected by malnutrition (Livi-Bacci 1983)

160   to keep it away from a pathogen (Carmichael 1983)

160   virtually independent of nutrition (Livi-Bacci 1983)

161   neither was likely at birth (Livi-Bacci 1983), citing Hollingsworth, "Mortality in the British Peerage Families since 1600," and Wrigley, *The Population History of England, 1541–1871*

161   nine years ignoring the treaty's terms (Lucas 1930)

162   "from day to day the price increased" (Jordan 1996)

162   more than 300 percent in five months (Lucas 1930)

162   "because they had no more" (Jordan 1996), quoting Curschmann, *Hungersnöte*

162   "great complaint, swollen with hunger" (Jordan 1996)

162   "fetid with the stench" (Jordan 1996)

163   two new cemeteries were created (Jordan 1996)

163   The thirty-week total was nearly 3,000 (Lucas 1930) Note that the weekly total is missing five weeks out of the total and that the total is for those buried at town expense—that is, those who had no family, church, or guild to bury them.

163　to create a *"parc à gibier"* (Jordan 1996) The original law was specific for the creation of parks for the cultivation of wild rabbits.

164　"avaricious cupidity" (Jordan 1996)

Chapter Eight: "She-Wolf of France" • 1313–1320

165　he would support Gaveston's enemies (Weir 2005)

166　To manage the household stable's (Weir 2005)

166　so lavish that it cost the treasury £140,000 (Weir 2005) This is pretty clearly nonsense; the cost of five hundred pears purchased at Rochester while en route was only 18 pence, and the offering made at the shrine of Saint Thomas—a gold nugget—cost less than £5.

169　Thirty-six died under torture (Tuchman 1978)

170　to the thirteenth generation (Weir 2005) This particular story didn't appear anywhere before the king and pope actually did die, which suggests that it was a later embellishment, though one that was widely believed true.

172　displayed for all to see (Weir 2005)

173　or sometimes all three (Maddicott 1975)

173　the population least able to cope with them (Pollington et al. 2011)

173　the pound lost more than half its value (Kershaw 1973)

174　"daily dying from famine and starvation" (Aberth 2010)

174　"having grain and refusing to sell it" (Jordan 1996)

174　"of taxes and tribulation" (Jordan 1996), quoting the fifteenth-century chronicle of the historian and theologian Ericus Olai who is better known for popularizing the theory that the Goths originated in Sweden.

174　England's only likely sources of grain (Jordan 1996) For decades, historians have debated the source of imported grain into northern Europe, and seem unlikely to resolve it anytime soon. As with France, the best guess is that the grain Edward imported may have arrived on Italian ships but was grown in southern France and northern Spain, from which England certainly imported other, less mundane, food items like figs and walnuts.

175　the smuggling and piracy that fueled their economies (Heebøll-Holm 2011)

175　"a cruel pirate" (Barrow 2005)

175　a kind of legal self-help (Heebøll-Holm 2011)

175　not the pirate himself (Heebøll-Holm 2011)

175　ships burned, and warehouses ransacked (Jordan 1996)

175　"coming to this realm with victuals" (Lucas 1930)

176　an unsubtle public-relations stunt (Smith 1993)

176　"outside the circle of his sycophants and clients" (Jordan 1996)

177　prevented by the ever-prudent earl of Pembroke (Phillips 2010)

178　"his chief counselor against the earls and barons" (Bingham 1973)

178　one of the strongest fortresses in Britain (Phillips 2010)

178–79　"would obtain the whole earldom" (Childs 2005)

179　"by every possible means" (Childs 2005)

179　"they plundered for themselves" (Aberth 2010), quoting Walsingham, *Historia Anglicana*

179　they were destroyed as a fighting force (Phillips 2010) In January 1316, they declined a battle at Ardscull that would almost certainly have been not just a victory (they significantly outnumbered their opponents) but a decisive one, since it would have left Dublin unprotected.

179   "many of them died of hunger" (Aberth 2010)

180   "men ate each other in Ireland" (Aberth 2010)

180   Bolton Priory counted three thousand sheep in its herd in 1316 (Kershaw 1973)

181   even the cities of the eastern Baltic (Jordan 1996), citing Bain, *Calendar of Documents Relating to Scotland*

181   within sight of the Scottish coast (Jordan 1996)

181   English soldiers were forced to eat their own horses (Phillips 2010)

181   welcomed Bruce's soldiers into their town (Davis 1974)

181   William, had surrendered it to the English twenty-two years before (Phillips 2010)

182   apologize to his closest advisers for his gullibility (Phillips 2010)

182   "to prove by combat with him" (Maxwell 1913)

183   would germinate for the next nine years (Johnstone 1936) Not everyone believes that Isabella's decisive moment came with the Powderham scandal; one notable biographer, Alison Weir, for example, is unconvinced.

183   its composition more or less evenly divided (Bingham 1973) The treaty, which was executed on August 9, 1318, provided for a standing council of eight bishops; four earls, including Pembroke, Hereford, and Arundel; and four barons. According to the terms, two of the bishops, one baron, one earl, and Lancaster's representative—Roger Mortimer, the Marcher Lord who was Hugh the Younger's most hostile antagonist—would serve for three months at a time.

183   to be held in May 1319 (Phillips 2010)

184   "they melted with disease" (Virgil 1916)

184   "cattle died of a plague all over Europe" (Spinage 2003)

185   That first outbreak lasted for at least three years (Spinage 2003)

185   Unlike its close cousin, measles (Furuse 2010) Both rinderpest and measles are morbilliviruses, and a lot of textbooks claim that they are both about as old as the domestication of cattle; that measles has been around as a distinct disease since prehistoric times. However, recent research actually shows that the two diseases diverged only around the time of the eleventh or twelfth centuries.

186   Only after the immune system is rendered irrelevant (Anderson et al 1986)

186   multiplied the load horses could pull nearly fivefold (Findlay 2006)

187   frequently harnessed together (Gies 1990) Sometimes four horses and four oxen; in the village of Elton, the popular assortment was two horses and six oxen.

187   cattle, sheep, and goats (Slavin 2010)

187   annually to 45 gallons (Slavin 2010)

187   to control of royal castles (Phillips 2010)

188   140 knights and 350 men-at-arms from the earl of Lancaster (Phillips 2010)

189   "if the Queen had at that time been captured" (Childs 2005)

189   "laughed his intelligence to scorn" Weir (2005) citing Strickland, *Lives of the Queens of England*

190   died trying to swim across the Swale (Battlefields Trust 2003)

190   "and ransomed at a heavy price" (Maxwell 1913)

190   killed virtually all the oxen (Spinage 2003)

190   "seized great numbers of men" (Childs 2005)
190   "with a very large spoil of men and cattle" (Davis 1974), citing *The Chronicle of Lanercost*
191   "are carried on more prosperously" (Barrow 1965)
191   "which no good man gives up except with his life" (Phillips 2010)

Chapter Nine: "The Dearest Beef I've Ever Seen" • 1320–1322

193   "we are certain that we should not swear it" (Phillips 2010)
194   unwilling to sign anything but another truce (Phillips 2010)
194   "a bribe was usually necessary" (Phillips 2010)
195   "on her knees, for the people's sakes" (Weir 2005), citing the *Annales Paulini*, supposedly written by a canon of St. Paul's Cathedral, between 1307 and 1341
195   "that love another more than himself" (Bingham 1973), citing the *Vita*
196   suffered a worse failure in 1321 (Kershaw 1973)
197   frozen for at least a month (Pfister 1996)
197   travel on the frozen sea all the way to Sweden (Pfister 1996)
197   a three-century peak in the decade 1310–1320 (Jordan 1996)
198   capable of producing only inferior coats (Power 1955)
198   from the uplands of northern Spain to the plains of Andalusia (Power 1955)
198   "carrying wool to England" (Power 1955)
198   thicker-than-female fleeces (Gies 1990), citing Trow-Smith, *History of British Livestock Husbandry*
198   almost entirely devoted to livestock by 1300 (Brown 2001), citing Campbell and Power, "Mapping the Agricultural Geography of Medieval England"
199   "a fifth part of the value of the whole land" (Power 1955, emphasis added)
199   a net reduction of population of close to 15 percent (Jordan 1996)
199   at least 25 percent greater than normal (Russell 1966)
200   it regularly reached 50/1,000 (Harvey 1991)
200   between fifty-six and seventy-nine towns and cities with populations greater than ten thousand (Jordan 1996), quoting Contadine, *Economie Medievale*
200   no more than four hundred people per square mile (Campbell 2000)
201   more than twenty-three hundred square miles (Jordan 1996) Jordan spends some time explaining alternate methods for calculating the area in question, since it's not as if it appears on any contemporaneous maps. Some use topography, looking for natural barriers to trade in agricultural products like mountains or unnavigable rivers, or the reach of a particular monopoly regulation, on the production and sale of wine, for example. Another way is examining parish records for the locales from which immigrants made their way to the towns; a map of the most frequent places of origin tends to reflect the catchment for the town. Yet another (and one that tends to expand the reach of the city by as much as 100 percent) is to identify the hinterland with the areas where the coinage of a particular town dominated.
201   a quarter of England's stock of arable land (Fagan 2008) The word "hinterland" originally meant the catchment area behind a port town, later to include the rural area surrounding any town or city.
202   that is, not being worked (Jordan 1996)

202   died from either pestilence or hunger (Jordan 1996)

203   municipal properties pledged as guaranty (Jordan 1996) In 1316, Dominican monks of the town of Würzburg actually pawned their illustrated and annotated Bible to their own vicar . . . and, when the vicar needed cash, he sold it to the Cistercians in 1317.

203   "saints and other relics to be adored" (Lucas 1930). This is a quotation from Guillaume of Nangis, a monk at the Abbey of St. Denis.

204   selling the grain at cost to the city-licensed bakeries (Jordan 1996)

204   "Then they were exiled from France" (Lucas 1930)

205   "evil and outrageous" (Jordan 1996)

205   by his code name, "King Arthur" (Phillips 2010)

205   "How will a man who cannot keep faith with his own lord keep faith with me?" (Phillips 2010), quoting *The Chronicle of Lanercost*

207   Lancaster's men were executed, exiled, or imprisoned (Weir 2005)

207   his head mounted on the city gate (Phillips 2010)

207   one estimate calculates a knight's fee (Harvey 1970)

207   she did get to marry her longtime lover (Bingham 1973)

207   "as has been hitherto accustomed" (Phillips 2010)

208   at far below market price (Kershaw 1973)

208   with remarkable specificity, he demanded repayment (Waugh 1977)

208   flooded half the lands in Gloucestershire (Waugh 1977)

208   people were crushed at the gate of the Preaching Friars (Hanawalt 1995)

208   The army that Edward led north (Phillips 2010) Estimates put the numbers at 20,000 infantry, 2,100 light cavalry, and 1,250 heavy cavalry.   •

209   "it cost a thousand pounds or more" (Barbour 1997)

209   "they were obliged of necessity to disband" (Grey 1836)

209   the respiratory disease known as glanders (Woolgar 2010)

210   "compelled to go through the countryside, begging" (Aberth 2010)

210   reducing the income available to pay for them (Aberth 2010) In 1317, more than two dozen parishes in Yorkshire had been reduced to half their taxable value by Bruce's raids; in 1318, seventy-seven. In 1319, King Edward's agents in Yorkshire were forced to waive the entire annual tax for forty-nine villages in the North Riding and forty-six in the West Riding, entirely because of Scottish raids. In 1322, fifty-five parishes in the East Riding of Yorkshire were worth less than half their pre-raid value. The village of Easingold, a fief of the earl of Lancaster, was completely unable to pay their annual rent: at least thirty-one of the earl's tenants had been killed, seventeen had their homes and lands destroyed, and seven had been driven into exile.

211   "chicken-hearted and luckless in war" (Davis 1974)

211   agree to pay England a war indemnity (Phillips 2010)

Chapter Ten: "The Mouse Tower of Bingen"   •   800–1323

217   identical to that of the French-speaking areas to their west (Jordan 1996), quoting Curschmann

217   "All are one in Christ" (Soll 2012)

218   "some of the overtones of patriotism" (Elliott 1992), citing (Strayer 1970)

219   the "mercenary knight" of Edward I of England (Heer 1968)
220   a different majority of electors (Heer 1968) In the first vote, the archbishop of Cologne; King Henry of Bohemia; the count palatine of the Rhine; and Duke Rudolf of Saxe-Wittenberg cast their votes for Duke Friedrich. The archbishop of Mainz, the archbishop of Trier, and Margrave Waldemar of Brandenburg voted for Ludwig. In the second vote, Friederich retained his four supporters, but because of confusion over the legitimate voters, Ludwig added his own King of Bohemia, *and* his own Duke of Saxony. To make matters even more complicated, the coronation of King of the Germans was traditionally performed at the Cathedral of Aachen (not at all coincidentally Charlemagne's capital) by the archbishop of Cologne. Ludwig was, indeed, crowned at Aachen, but by Peter Aspelt, the archbishop of Mainz. Friedrich, meanwhile, was *also* crowned—by the correct archbishop (Heinrich von Vimeburg, of Cologne) but at the wrong place: the Minster of Bonn.
221   thousands of tons of salted fish (Jordan 1996)
223   formed the Hansa (Jordan 1996)
224   "the year of penury and the severest hunger" (Jordan 1996)
224   lifted off its foundations and swept away (Lucas 1930)
224   remained solid enough for travel (Lucas 1930)
224   the population of the city of Metz never exceeded twenty thousand (Lucas 1930)
224   "infinite number perished" (Jordan 1996), quoting Curschmann
224   "a third of the people were brought low" (Jordan 1996), quoting Curschmann
225   "cadavers were thrown in daily" (Aberth 2010)
225   who had perished in the famine twenty-five years before (Lucas 1930)
225   "began to fade" (Jordan 1996), quoting Curschmann
225   often died of strangulation or choking (Jordan 1996), quoting Curschmann
225   Brot durch Gott (Jordan 1996)
226   the nuns of Kloster Ebstorf near Lüneberg (Jordan 1996)
226   Ludwig then sweetened his bid (Jordan 1996)
227n   "and die rather than live in slavery" (Schiller, 1909–1914)
228   "a mass of rubble made of legends and fables" (Delbrück 1990)
228   "a warlike community with battle-hardened leaders" (Delbrück 1990)
229   "greatly sad, but half-dead" (Delbrück 1990)
229   He led only fourteen hundred knights (Colish 1983)
230   "This war has already caused enough widows" (Colish 1983)
230   the "final struggle" between emperor and pope (Offler 1954)
231   "He beat them off by the score" (Gask 1910)
231   "Hard by a great forest" (Grimm 1972)
232   "Story of Children Living in a Time of Famine" (Tatar 2010) and others. This is my own paraphrase of the story.

Chapter Eleven: "Long Years of Havoc" • *1323–1328*

233   before his guards awakened (Bingham 1973)
234   a clear provocation (Phillips 2010)
234   hanged a French soldier (Bingham 1973)
234   including twenty-seven members of Isabella's own household (Phillips 2010)
235   given into the care of Hugh the Younger's wife (Phillips 2010)

235   "It seems to our lord the king and to us" (Phillips 2010) The letter in question was from April 1325.

236   "until Hugh le Despenser is wholly removed from the King's side" (Childs 2005)

236   The French king, his successors, and his rivals would face one uprising after another (Winks 2005) None were even close to successful, with the exception of the so-called Remença uprising in 1462 Catalonia, which was finally settled in favor of the *"pagesos de remença"* (the Catalan term for serfdom) by King Ferdinand of Aragon in 1486.

237   Isabella's pillows were stuffed with down and feathers (Weir 2005)

237   the "courtly" manners expected at court (Elias 2000) Among the rules of etiquette documented by Elias: "A number of people gnaw a bone and then put it back in the dish—this is a serious offence." "A man who clears his throat when he eats and one who blows his nose in the tablecloth are both ill-bred, I assure you." "If a man wipes his nose on his hand at table because he knows no better, then he is a fool, believe me."

238   a hundred years at that level (Clark 2007) The causes of the so-called medieval price revolution continue to be a matter for debate, but the best argument is the population explosion that is such a general aspect of the Medieval Warm Period, with the rate of increase really picking up after 1170 and continuing for at least the next three generations (Fischer 1996).

238   unlikely to endear them to their tenants (Turchin 2011) points out that in agrarian societies, "population growth in excess of the productivity gains of the land . . . leads to persistent price inflation, falling real wages, rural misery, urban migration, and *increased frequency of food riots and wage protests.*" (emphasis added)

239   "until I am avenged of this Pharisee" (Phillips 2010) and (Childs 2005)

240   "he is in truth wicked and hostile" (Bingham 1973)

240   "within and without house" (Phillips 2010) Historians continue to debate the precise beginnings of the Mortimer/Isabella affair, with some arguing it started as early as 1321.

241   she would recognize an independent Scotland (Weir 2005)

241   some German-speaking principalities of the Holy Roman Empire (Phillips 2010)

242   Of the two thousand soldiers (Phillips 2010)

242   fears of a nonexistent French invasion (Phillips 2010)

242   presented her with a silver cup (Weir 2005)

243   some £29,000 in gold (Weir 2005)

244   "and that your arms be destroyed forever" (Weir 2005), quoting the *Annales Paulini*

245   in the open country near Llantrisant (Weir 2005)

245   "Why do you glory in malice" (Phillips 2010) For those who know this psalm as number 51, you are correct . . . but so are those who know it as number 52, because Psalms 9 and 10 (in the original Hebrew) are combined into Psalm 9 in Greek and Latin translations.

246   "His body was divided into four quarters" (Froissart 1978)

247   Its purpose was to depose a king (Bingham 1973)

247   "beyond all hope of amendment" (Weir 2005)

247–48   "Will be a fool proclaimed" (Bingham 1973) The French original reads, *"En temps de iver me survynt damage / Fortune trop m'ad traverse / Eure m'est faili tut mon age / Bient sovent la ay esprové / En mond n'ad sib el ne si sage, / Ne si curtois en si preysé / Si eur ne lui court de avantage / Que il ne serra pur fol clamé."*

248   "every English archer carries 24 Scottish lives in his belt" (Davis 1974)

249   to rise for the deposed and imprisoned king (Maxwell 1913)

249   "was ignominiously slain" (Phillips 2010)

250   "Fell Thirst and Famine scowl" (Gray 1966)

251   "and to his heirs and successors" (Barrow 2005)

251   The wedding feast held to celebrate the joining (Davis 1974)

253   carried back to Scotland for burial (Barrow 2005)

Epilogue: The Delicate Balance

255   "Freedom's sword will strongly draw" (Burns 1994)

256   That number is more controversial No one can truly give a reliable figure, and the most careful historians don't come anywhere near agreeing with one another. The population of France, for example, declined from between 17 and 20 million at the beginning of the war to either 11 million (Maddison 2006), 9 million (Pregill 1999), or 10 million (Baumgartner 1995). However, if the Black Death is responsible for death rates of between 25 and 30 percent, the war deaths are only the remainder. (Thanks to the invaluable Matthew White, the world's most assiduous collector of disaster statistics.)

256   "a strange personification of Death" (Tuchman 1978)

257   Its subject is not disease, but hunger (Behringer 2009)

257   Lake Constance burst its banks (Behringer 2009)

BIBLIOGRAPHY

Aberth, John. *From the Brink of the Apocalypse: Confronting Famine, War, Plague, and Death in the Later Middle Ages.* Oxford: Routledge, 2010.

Alexandre, Pierre. *Le climat en Europe au moyen age* [The climate of Europe in the Middle Ages]. Paris: Ecole des hautes etudes en sciences sociales, 1901.

Allen, Robert C. *English and Welsh Agriculture, 1300–1850: Outputs, Inputs, and Income.* A paper delivered at the International Economic History Conference at Helsinki, Finland, Aug 21–25, 2006.

Anderson, J., T. Barrett, and G. R. Scott. *Manual on the Diagnosis of Rinderpest.* New York: Food and Agriculture Organization of the United Nations, 1986.

Anonymous. "The Vision of Viands, from the Irish of Anair MacConglinne." In *A Treasury of Irish Songs and Lyrics, Volume 2*, edited by Charles Welsh. Ann Arbor, MI: University of Michigan Library, 2009.

Arnold, Benjamin. *German Knighthood, 1050–1300*, New York, Oxford University Press, 1985.

Arnold, David. *Famine: Social Crisis and Historical Change.* London: Wiley-Blackwell, 1991.

Bailey, Mark. "Per impetum maris: Natural Disaster and Economic Decline in Eastern England, 1275–1350." In *Before the Black Death: Studies in the "Crisis" of the Early Fourteenth Century*, edited by Bruce Campbell. Manchester, UK: Manchester University Press, 1981.

Bain, Joseph (ed.). *Calendar of Documents Relating to Scotland Preserved in Her Majesty's Public Record Office, Vol. II.* Edinburgh: Public Records Office, 1884.

Barbour, John. *The Bruce.* Translated by A.A.M. Duncan. Edinburgh: Canongate Books, 1997.

Barnes, Patricia M., and G.S.W. Barrow. "The Movements of Robert Bruce between September 1307 and May 1308." *The Scottish Historical Review* (Edinburgh University Press) 49, no. 147 (April 1970): 46–59.

Barrow, G.W.S. *Robert Bruce and the Community of the Realm of Scotland.* Edinburgh: University of Edinburgh Press, 2005.

Battlefields Trust. *Myton Battle and Campaign.* St. Albans: Battlefield Text, 2003.

Baumgartner, Frederic J. *France in the 16th Century.* New York: Palgrave Macmillan, 1995.

Behringer, Wolfgang. *A Cultural History of Climate.* Malden, MA: Polity Press, 2009.

Bennett, Judith M. *Ale, Beer, and Brewsters in England: Woman's Work in a Changing World.* Oxford: Oxford University Press, 1996.

Berkowitz, Eric. *Sex and Punishment.* New York: Counterpoint, 2012.

Bingham, Caroline. *The Life and Times of Edward II.* London: Weidenfeld and Nicolson, 1973.

Boardman, J., and D. T. Favis-Mortlock. "Climate Change and Soil Erosion in Britain." *The Geographical Journal* 159, no.2 (1993): 179–183.

Bodri, I. "Fractal Analysis of Climatic Data: Mean Annual Temperature Records in Hungary." *Theoretical and Applied Climatology* (Springer-Verlag) 49, no. 1 (1994): 53–57.

Boffa, Sergio, and Kelly DeVries. "Low Countries." In *The Oxford Encyclopedia of Medieval Warfare and Military Technology*, edited by Clifford J. Rogers. Oxford: Oxford University Press, 2010.

Bois, Guy. *Crisis of Feudalism*. Cambridge: Cambridge University Press, 2009.

Braudel, Fernand. *The Structures of Everyday Life: The Limits of the Possible*. New York: Harper & Row, 1981.

Brown, Neville. *History and Climate Change: A Eurocentric Perspective*. London: Routledge, 2001.

Burns, Robert. *Selected Poems*. Edited by Carol McGuirk. New York: Penguin, 1994.

Campbell, Bruce. "Britain, 1300." *History Today* 50, no. 6 (June 2000).

———. *English Seigniorial Agriculture, 1250–1450*. Cambridge: Cambridge University Press, 2000.

Campbell, Bruce, and John, Power. "Mapping the Agricultural Geography of Medieval England." *Journal of Historical Geography* 15, no. 1 (Jan 1989): 24–39.

Carmichael, Ann G. "Infection, Hidden Hunger, and History." In *Hunger and History*, edited by Robert I. Rotberg and Theodore Rabb. Cambridge: Cambridge University Press, 1983.

Chavas, Jean-Paul, and Daniel W. Bromley. "Modelling Population and Resource Scarcity in Fourteenth-century England." *Journal of Agricultural Economics* 56, no. 2 (2005): 217–37.

Chibnill, Marjorie, trans. *The Ecclesiastical History of Orderic Vitalis*. Oxford: Oxford University Press, 1978.

Childs, Wendy R., ed., trans. *Vita Edwardi Secundi: The Life of Edward II*. New York: Oxford University Press, 2005.

Chong, Key Ray. *Cannibalism in China*. Wakefield, NH: Longwood, 1990.

Christiansen, B., and F. D. Ljungqvist. "The Extra-Tropical Northern Hemisphere Temperature in the Last Two Millennia: Reconstructions of Low-Frequency Variability." *Climate of the Past* 8 (2012): 765–86.

Clark, Gregory. "The Economics of Exhaustion, the Postan Thesis, and the Agricultural Revolution." *The Journal of Economic History* (Economic History Association/Cambridge University Press) 52, no. 1 (March 1992): 61–84.

———. "Interpreting English Economic History 1200–1800: Malthusian Stasis or Early Dynamism?" *XIV International Economic History Congress*. Helsinki, May 30, 2006.

———. *A Farewell to Alms: A Brief Economic History of the World*. Princeton: Princeton University Press, 2007.

Coale, A., and P. Demeny. *Regional Model Life Tables and Stable Populations*. New York: Academic Press, 1983.

Colish, Marcia L. *The Mirror of Language: A Study of the Medieval Theory of Language*. Lincoln, NE: University of Nebraska Press, 1983.

Curschmann, Fritz. *Hungersnöte im Mittelalter*. Leipzig: B.G. Teubner, 1900.

Davies, Mike, and Jonathan Kissock. "The Feet of Fines, the Land Market, and the English Agricultural Crisis of 1315 to 1322." *Journal of Historical Geography* (Elsevier) 30 (2004): 215–30.

Davis, Mike. *Late Victorian Holocausts: El Niño Famines and the Making of the Third World*. New York: Verso, 2002.

Dean, James M., ed. "The Simonie: Symonye and Covetise, or On the Evil Times of Edward II." In *Medieval English Political Writings*. Kalamazoo, MI: Medieval Institute Publications, 1996.

Delbrück, Hans. *Medieval Warfare: History of the Art of War, Volume III*. Translated by Walter J. Renfroe. Jr. Lincoln, NE: University of Nebraska Press, 1990.

DeVries, Kelly. "Courtrai, Battle and Siege of." In *Oxford Encyclopedia of Medieval Warfare and Military Technology*, edited by Clifford J. Rogers. Oxford: Oxford University Press, 2011.

DeVries, Kelly, and Robert Smith. *Medieval Weapons: An Illustrated History of Their Impact*. Santa Barbara, CA: ABC-CLIO, 2007.

Dodd, Gwylim, and Anthony Musson. *The Reign of Edward II: New Perspectives*. York: York Medieval Press, 2006.

Downham, Claire. " 'Hiberno-Norwegians' and 'Anglo-Danes': Anachronistic Chronicles in Viking-Age England." *Medieval Scandinavia* 19 (2009): 139–69.

Duncan, A.A.M. "Bannockburn, Battle of." In *The Oxford Encyclopedia of Medieval Warfare and Military Technology*, edited by Clifford J. Rogers. Oxford: Oxford University Press, 2010.

———. "Robert I (the Bruce)." In *The Oxford Encyclopedia of Medieval Warfare and Military Technology*, edited by Clifford J. Rogers. Oxford: Oxford University Press, 2010.

Dyer, Christopher. "Did the Peasants Really Starve in Medieval England?" In *Food and Eating in Medieval Europe*, edited by Martha Carlin and Joel T. Rosenthal. London: The Hambledon Press, 1998.

Einhard, and Notker the Stammerer. *Two Lives of Charlemagne*. Translated by Lewis Thorpe. Harmondsworth: Penguin, 1969.

Elias, Norbert. *The Civilizing Process: Sociogenetic and Psychogenetic Investigations*, 2nd Edition. New York: Wiley-Blackwell, 2000.

Elliott, J. H. "A Europe of Composite Monarchies." *Past & Present* (OUP) 137 (1992): 48–71.

Fagan, Brian M. *The Great Warming: Climate Change and the Rise and Fall of Civilizations*. New York: Bloomsbury USA, 2008.

———. *The Little Ice Age: How Climate Made History 1300–1850*. New York: Basic Books, 2000.

Ferguson, Robert. *The Vikings: A History*. New York: Viking, 2009.

Fernandez-Armesto, Felipe. *Near a Thousand Tables*. New York: Free Press, 2002.

Field, Christopher, Vicente Barros, Dahe Qin, and Thomas Stocker. *Managing the Risks of Extreme Events and Disasters to Advance Climate Change Adaptation*. Geneva: IPCC, 2012.

Findlay, Ronald, and Mats Lundahl. "Demographic Shocks and the Factor Proportions Model: From the Plague of Justinian to the Black Death." In *Eli Heckscher, International Trade and Economic History*, edited by Ronald Findlay, Rolf Henriksson, Håkan Lindgren, and Mats Lundahl. Cambridge, MA: MIT Press, 2006.

Fischer, David Hackett. *The Great Wave*. Oxford: Oxford University Press, 1996.

Florence of Winchester. *Chronicle of Florence of Winchester*. London: H. G. Bohn, 1854.

Fogel, Robert W. *The Escape from Hunger and Premature Death, 1700–2100.* Cambridge: Cambridge University Press, 2004.

Fordun, John. *John of Fordun's Chronicle of the Scottish Nation.* Edited by W. F. Skene. Edinburgh: Edmonston and Douglas, 1872.

Forsyth, Katherine. "Scotland to 1100." In *Scotland: A History,* edited by Jenny Wormald, 1–39. Oxford: Oxford University Press, 2005.

Frank, R. W. "The 'Hungry Gap,' Crop Failure, and Famine: The Fourteenth Century Agricultural Crisis and Piers Plowman." *Yearbook of Langland Studies* 4 (1990): 87–104.

Fukuyama, Francis. *The Origins of Political Order.* New York: Farrar, Straus & Giroux, 2011.

Furuse, Y., A. Suzuki, and H. Oshitani. "Origin of Measles Virus: Divergence from Rinderpest Virus Between the 11th and 12th Centuries." *Journal of Virology* 4, no. 7:52 (March 2010).

Gibbon, Edward. *The Decline and Fall of the Roman Empire.* Edited by J. H. Bury. New York: Everyman's Library, 1994.

Gies, Frances, and Joseph Gies. *Life in a Medieval Village.* New York: Harper & Row, 1990.

Gray, Thomas. *The Complete Poems of Thomas Gray: English, Latin, and Greek (Oxford English Texts).* Edited by H. W. Starr and J. R. Hendrickson. Oxford: Oxford University Press, 1966.

Gregory of Tours. *The History of the Franks.* Translated and with an introduction by Lewis Thorpe. New York: Penguin, 1974.

Grey, Sir Thomas. *Scalacronica: A Chronicle of England and Scotland from AD MLXVI to AD MCCCLXI.* Edinburgh: The Maitland Club, 1836.

Grimm, Jacob, and Wilhelm Grimm. *The Complete Grimm's Fairy Tales.* New York: Pantheon, 1972.

Hanawalt, Barbara. *Growing Up in Medieval London.* Oxford: Oxford University Press, 1995.

Harvey, Barbara F. "Introduction: The 'Crisis' of the Early Fourteenth Century." In *Before the Black Death: Studies in the "Crisis" of the Early Fourteenth Century,* edited by Bruce Campbell, 1–24. Manchester: Manchester University Press, 1991.

Heebøll-Holm, Thomas. *Ports, Piracy, and Maritime War: Piracy in the English Channel and the Atlantic, 1280–1330.* Copenhagen: University of Copenhagen, 2011.

Heer, Friedrich. *The Holy Roman Empire.* London: Weidenfeld & Nicolson, 1968.

Henley, Walter de. *Walter of Henley's Husbandry.* Translated by Elizabeth Lamond. London: Longman and Green, 1890.

Her Majesty's Stationery Office. *Calendar of Patent Rolls, 1315–1317.* London: HMSO, 1971.

Hilton, R. H. *A Medieval Society: The West Midlands at the End of the Thirteenth Century.* Cambridge: Cambridge University Press, 2008.

Hollingsworth, T. H. "Mortality in the British Peerage Families since 1600." *Population,* 32nd Année (September 1977): 323–52.

Hughes, Malcolm K., and Henry F. Diaz. *The Medieval Warm Period.* New York: Springer, 1994.

Hummel, S. et al. "Detection of the CCR5–Δ32 HIV Resistance Gene in Bronze Age Skeletons." *Genes & Immunity* (Nature Publishing Group) 6 (April 2005): 371–74.

Johnstone, Hilda. "Isabella: The She-Wolf of France." *History* 21, no. 83 (1936): 208–18.

Jones, Gwyn. *A History of the Vikings*, 2nd Edition. Oxford: Oxford University Press, 1984.

Jordan, William Chester. *The Great Famine: Northern Europe in the Early Fourteenth Century*. Princeton, NJ: Princeton University Press, 1996.

———. "The Great Famine: 1315–1322 Revisited". In *Ecologies and Economies in Medieval and Early Modern Europe*, edited by Scott G. Bruce, 45 ff. Boston, MA: Brill, 2010.

Keegan, John D. "On the Principles of War."*Military Review* XLE, no. 11 (Dec 1961): 61–72.

Kershaw, Ian. "Great Famine and Agrarian Crisis in England 1315–1322." *Past & Present* (Oxford University Press) 59 (May 1973): 3–50.

Keys, Ancel, et al. *The Biology of Human Starvation*. Minneapolis, MN: University of Minnesota Press, 1950.

Lewis, Archibald R. "The Closing of the Medieval Frontier, 1250–1350." *Speculum* (Medieval Society of America) 33, no. 4 (October 1958): 475–83.

Lewis, M.J.T. "The Origins of the Wheelbarrow." *Technology and Culture* 35, no. 3 (July 1994): 453–75.

Livi-Bacci, M. "The Nutrition-Mortality Link in Past Times: A Comment." *Journal of Interdisciplinary History* 14, no. 2 (1983): 293–98.

Locke, Amy Audrey. *War and Misrule: 1307–1399*. London: G. Bell and Sons, Ltd., 1919.

Lomas, Richard. "The Impact of Border Warfare." *Scottish Historical Review* LXXV, no. 2 (October 1996): 143–67.

Lucas, Henry S. "The Great European Famine of 1315, 1316, and 1317." *Speculum* (Medieval Academy of America) 5, no. 4 (October 1930): 343–77.

MacFarquhar, Roderick *The Origins of the Cultural Revolution*, Volume 2. New York: Columbia University Press, 1983.

Maddicott, J. R. *The English Peasantry and the Demands of the Crown, 1294–1341*. Oxford: Past & Present Society, 1975.

Maddison, Angus. *The World Economy*. Paris: Development Centre of the Organisation for Economic Cooperation and Development, 2006.

Mann, Charles C. "How the Potato Changed the World." *Smithsonian*, November 2011.

Marvin, Julia. "Cannibalism as an Aspect of Famine in Two English Chronicles." In *Food and Eating in Medieval Europe*, edited by Martha Carlin, and Joel T. Rosenthal, 73–86. London: The Hambledon Press, 1998.

Mate, Mavis. "The Agrarian Economy of Southeast England Before the Black Death: Depressed or Buoyant?" In *Before the Black Death: Studies in the "Crisis" of the Early Fourteenth Century*, edited by Bruce Campbell. Manchester: Manchester University Press, 1991.

Maxwell, Sir Herbert, trans. *The Chronicle of Lanercost*. Glasgow: J. MacLehone, 1913.

McEvedy, Colin, and Richard M. Jones. *Atlas of World Population History*. London: Penguin 1978.

McGarry, Daniel. *Medieval History and Civilization*. New York: Macmillan, 1976.

McNamee, Colm. "Hobelars." In *The Oxford Encyclopedia of Medieval Warfare and Military Technology*, edited by Clifford J. Rogers. Oxford: Oxford University Press, 2010.

Melvin, Thomas M., Hakan Grudd, and Keith Briffa. "Potential Bias in 'Updating' Tree-Ring Chronologies Using Regional Curve Standardisation: Re-Processing 1500 Years of Tornetrask Density and Ring-Width Data." *The Holocene* (Sage Publications) 23, no. 3 (2013): 364–73.

Miller, Edward, and John Hatcher. *Medieval England: Rural Society and Economic Change, 1086–1348*. London: Addison-Wesley Longman, 1978.

Miller, Gifford H. et al. "Abrupt Onset of the Little Ice Age Triggered by Volcanism and Sustained by Sea-Ice/Ocean Feedbacks." *Geophysical Research Letters* 39, no. 2 (January 2012).

Moeller, C. "Military Order of Calatrava." In *The Catholic Encyclopedia*, edited by Charles Herbermann et al. New York: Robert Appleton Company, 1908.

Mollat, Michel. *The Poor in the Middle Ages: An Essay in Social History*. Translated by Arthur Goldhammer. New Haven, CT: Yale University Press, 1986.

Moore, Jason W. "Ecological Crises in the Making of the Modern World 1300–1600." Paper presented at the Annual Meeting of the American Sociological Association, Philadlephia, August 12, 2005, 1–27.

Moyer, Michael. "The Trouble with Armor." *Scientific American*, October 2011.

Munro, John H. "Industrial Transformation in the Northwest European Textile Trades, c. 1290–1340: Economic Progress or Economic Crisis." In *Before the Black Death: Studies in the "Crisis" of the Early Fourteenth Century*, edited by Bruce Campbell. Manchester: Manchester University Press, 1991.

National Archives, Kew. *Letters Concerning William Wallace*. January 30, 1981, http://www.nationalarchives.gov.uk/documentsonline/williamwallace.asp (accessed January 29, 2012).

Ó Gráda, Cormac. *Famine: A Short History*. Princeton: Princeton University Press, 2009.

———. "Population and Living Standards in England During the 'Little Ice Age.'" Working Paper, Economics, University College Dublin, Dublin: University College Dublin, 2011, 1–52.

Oestereich, Thomas. *Pope Boniface VIII*. Vol. 2. of *The Catholic Encyclopedia*, edited by Charles Herbermann et al. New York: Robert Appleton Company, 1907.

Orlandis, Jose. *A Short History of the Catholic Church*. Dublin: Four Courts Press, 1985.

Ormrod, W. M. "The Crown and the English Economy, 1290–1348." In *Before the Black Death: Studies in the "Crisis" of the Early Fourteenth Century*, edited by Bruce Campbell. Manchester: Manchester University Press, 1991.

Pals, Jan Peter, "Observations on the Economy of the Settlement," in Groenman van-Waatering et al., *Farm Life in a Carolingian Village: A Model Based on Botanical and Zoological Data from an Excavated Site*. Assen, Netherlands: Van Gorcum, 1987.

Pearson, Kathy L. "Nutrition and the Early-Medieval Diet." *Speculum* (Medieval Academy of America) 72, no. 1 (Jan 1997): 1–32.

Pfister, C. et al. "Winter Severity in Europe: the Fourteenth Century." *Climatic Change* (Kluwer Academic Publishers) 34 (1996): 91–108.

Phillips, Seymour. *Edward II.* New Haven, CT: Yale University Press, 2010.

Pinker, Stephen. *The Better Angels of Our Nature.* New York: Viking, 2011.

Pollington, Stephen, Steven Isaac, Clifford J. Rogers, and Colm McNamee. "Britain." In *The Oxford Encyclopedia of Medieval Warfare and Military Technology,* edited by Clifford J. Rogers. Oxford: Oxford University Press, 2011.

Power, Eileen. *The Wool Trade in English Medieval History.* Oxford: Oxford University Press, 1955.

Pregill, Philip, and Nancy Volkman. *Landscapes in History,* 2nd ed. New York: John Wiley & Sons, 1999.

Prestwich, Michael. *Edward I.* Berkeley, CA: University of California Press, 1988.

Riley, H. T., ed. *Chronicles of the Mayors and Sheriffs of London, 1188–1274.* London: Centre for Metropolitan History, 1863.

Rimas, Andrew, and Evan Fraser. *Empires of Food: Feasts, Famine, and the Rise and Fall of Civilizations.* New York: Free Press, 2010.

Rivers, J.P.W. "The Nutritional Biology of Famine." In *Famine,* edited by G. A. Harrison, 57–100. Oxford: Oxford University Press, 1981.

Rogers, Thorold. *A History of Agriculture and Prices in England, from the Year after the Oxford Parliament (1259) to the Continental War (1793) Vol. II.* Oxford: Clarendon Press, 1866.

Russell, J. C. *British Medieval Population.* Albuquerque, NM: University of New Mexico Press, 1948.

———. "Effects of Pestilence and Plague, 1315–1385." *Comparative Studies in Society and History* (Cambridge University Press) 8, no. 4 (July 1966): 464–73.

Russell, Sharman Apt. *Hunger: An Unnatural History.* New York: Basic Books, 2005.

Schiller, Friedrich von. *Wilhelm Tell.* Translated by Sir Theodore Martin. Vol. 26 of *The Harvard Classics.* New York: P. F. Collier, 1909–1914.

Scott, Ronald Macnair. *Robert the Bruce: King of Scots.* New York: Carroll & Graf, 1996.

Sen, Amartya. *Poverty and Famines.* Oxford: Oxford University Press, 1981.

Siebert, Charles. "Food Ark." *National Geographic,* July 2011.

Simon, Julian. "The Effects of Population on Nutrition and Economic Well-Being." *Journal of Interdisciplinary History* (MIT Press) 14, no. 2 (Autumn 1983): 413–37.

Sjøgren, Kristian. "Violent Knights Feared Posttraumatic Stress." *ScienceNordic,* December 2, 2011.

Slavin, Philip. "The Crisis of the Fourteenth Century Reassessed: Between Ecology and Institutions—Evidence from England (1310–1350)." Paper given at Meeting of the Economic History Association (2010), www.eh.net/eha/system/files/Slavin.pdf (accessed October 5, 2013).

Smith, Adam. *The Wealth of Nations.* New York: Everyman's Library, 1991.

Smith, Kathryn A. "History, Typology, and Homily: The Joseph Cycle and the Queen Mary Psalter." *Gesta* (International Center for Medieval Art) 32, no. 2 (1993).

Soll, Jacob. "History as Fantasy: A Review of Vanished Kingdoms by Norman Davies." *The New Republic*, April 19, 2012.

Sorensen, Irene Berg. "What Vikings Really Looked Like." *ScienceNordic*, July 29, 2012.

Spinage, C. A. *Cattle Plague: A History*. New York: Springer, 2003.

Starr, Paul. *Freedom's Power*. New York: Basic Books, 2007.

Stathakopoulos, Dionysios. *Famine and Pestilence in the Late Roman and Early Byzantine Empire: A Systematic Survey of Subsistence Crises and Epidemics*. Farnham Surrey: Ashgate Publishing, 2004.

Stewart, W. K., and Laura Fleming. "Features of a Successful Therapeutic Fast of 382 Days' Duration." *Postgraduate Medical Education* 49 (1973): 203–09.

Stone, Edward Lionel Gregory. *Anglo-Scottish Relations, 1174–1328*. Oxford: Clarendon Press, 1978.

Strayer, Joseph R. *On the Medieval Origins of the Modern State*. Princeton: Princeton University Press, 1970.

Strickland, Agnes. *Lives of the Queens of England, from the Norman Conquest*. London: Taggart and Thompson, 1864.

Stringer, Keith. "Emergence of a Nation-State." In *Scotland: A History*, edited by Jenny Wormald, 39–77. Oxford: Oxford University Press, 2005.

Swanton, Michael J., ed. *The Anglo-Saxon Chronicle*. London: Routledge, 1998.

Tannahill, Reay. *Food in History*. New York: Three Rivers Press, 1988.

Tatar, Maria, and A. S. Byatt. *The Grimm Reader: Classic Tales of the Brothers Grimm*. New York: W. W. Norton, 2010.

Tennant, Roy. *The Anglo-Saxon Chronicle: Part 6, A.D. 1070–1101*. The Online Medieval and Classical Library, Release 17. http://omacl.org/Anglo/part6.html (accessed January 10, 2011).

Thompson, William R. "Synthesizing Secular, Demographic-Structural, Climate, and Leadership Long Cycles." *Cliodynamics: The Journal of Theoretical and Mathematical History* (The Institute for Research on World Systems) 1, no. 1 (2010): 26–57.

Thorvaldsson, Erik. "The Saga of Erik the Red." In *The Voyages of the Northmen*, edited by Julius E. Bourne and Edward G. Bourne, 14–44. New York: Charles Scribner's Sons, 1906.

Trow-Smith, Robert. *A History of British Livestock Husbandry, 1700–1900*. London: Routledge, 2005.

Tuchman, Barbara. *A Distant Mirror: The Calamitous Fourteenth Century*. New York: Alfred A. Knopf, 1978.

Turchin, Peter. "Social Tipping Points and Trend Reversals: A Historical Approach." Tipping Points Workshop, May 2011.

Virgil. *The Georgics*. Translated by H. R. Fairclouth. Cambridge, MA: Loeb Classical Library/Harvard University Press, 1916.

Walsngham, Thomas. *Historia Anglicana*, edited by H. T. Riley. London: Longman Green, 1864.

Wang, L. et al. "A 1000-yr Record of Environmental Change in Northeast China Indicated by Diatom Assemblages from Maar Lake Erlongwan." *Quaternary Research* 78 (2012): 24–34.

Waugh, S. L. "The Profits of Violence: The Minor Gentry in the Rebellion of 1322 in Gloucestershire." *Speculum* (Medieval Society of America) 52, no. 4 (1977): 843–69.

Weir, Alison. *Queen Isabella.* New York: Ballantine Books, 2005.

White Jr., Lynn. *Medieval Technology and Social Change.* Oxford: Oxford University Press, 1966.

Williams, Michael. *Deforesting the Earth: From Prehistory to Global Crisis. An Abridgement.* Chicago: University of Chicago Press, 2006.

Winks, Robin W., and Teofilo Ruiz. *Medieval Europe and the World: From Late Antiquity to Modernity 1400–1500.* Oxford: Oxford University Press, 2005.

Woolgar, C. M. "Food and the Middle Ages." *Journal of Medieval History* (Elsevier) 36 No.1 (December 2010): 1–19.

Wrigley, Tony. *The Population History of England, 1541–1871.* Cambridge, MA: Harvard University Press, 1981.

INDEX